RELATIONAL

RESPONSIBILITY

RELATIONAL

RESPONSIBILITY

Resources
for
Sustainable
Dialogue

Sheila McNamee
Kenneth J. Gergen

with
Harlene Anderson
Ian Burkitt
David L. Cooperrider
Robert Cottor
Sharon Cotter
Stanley Deetz
Steve Duck
Walter Eggers
Marilyn Frankfurt
Mary Gergen

Arlene M. Katz
John W. Lannamann
Michael J. Mazanec
Maurizio Marzari
Peggy Penn
Eero Riikonen
Sallyann Roth
John Shotter
Karl Tomm
William J. White
Diana Whitney

SAGE Publications
International Educational and Professional Publisher
Thousand Oaks London New Delhi

For information:

SAGE Publications, Inc.
2455 Teller Road
Thousand Oaks, California 91320
E-mail: order@sagepub.com

SAGE Publications Ltd.
6 Bonhill Street
London EC2A 4PU
United Kingdom

SAGE Publications India Pvt. Ltd.
M-32 Market
Greater Kailash I
New Delhi 110048 India

Printed in the United States of America

Library of Congress Cataloging-in-Publication Data

Main entry under title:

Relational responsibility: resources for sustainable dialogue/
edited by Sheila McNamee and Kenneth J. Gergen.
    p. cm.
  Includes bibliographical references and index.
  ISBN 0-7619-1093-X (cloth: acid-free paper)
  ISBN 0-7619-1094-8 (pbk.: acid-free paper)
  1. Social psychology. 2. Responsibility. 3. Social ethics. 4.
Social Values. I. McNamee, Sheila. II. Gergen, Kenneth J.
  HM251.R444 1998
  302—dc21   98-25453

00 01 02 03 04 8 7 6 5 4 3 2

Acquiring Editor:	Margaret Seawell
Editorial Assistant:	Renée Piernot
Production Editor:	Sanford Robinson
Editorial Assistant:	Nevair Kabakian
Designer/Typesetter:	Danielle Dillahunt
Cover Designer:	Candice Harman

Contents

From Antagonism to Appreciation

Preface

Situating the Conversation

There is much talk percolating through the intellectual world these days on "the end of theory." Much of this concern is spurred by social constructionist arguments bearing on the relationship between word and world. For centuries, we have viewed theory as the crowning achievement of scholarly and scientific activity. It is one thing to document specific cases, to note this fact and describe that event. However, it is through theory, we have believed, that we collate, integrate, synthesize, and emerge with an understanding of the whole. And it is through theoretical understanding that we can generate ever more accurate understanding and prediction. In terms of Kurt Lewin's famous dictum, "There is nothing so practical as a good theory." However, times have changed; the dialogue has moved on. If, as social constructionists now propose, there is no ultimately privileged relationship between "what there is" and our accounts of it—if there are myriad possible descriptions and explanations for any condition and no means outside community standards to chose among them—then what is the function of theory? Theory does not reflect the nature of the world; rather, it serves as a linguistic forestructure from which we presume the world to be what it is. Theory does not provide us worthy marching orders for a fructuous future, for theory in itself tells us nothing about how and when it is applicable. Theory loses its special privilege.

Yet unlike some of our colleagues, we do not wish to abandon theory on this account. If words gain their meaning through their use within relationships, an idea to which we shall return shortly, then there remain many significant functions for theory. Theoretical language can, for example, draw disparate communities together, give intelligibility to the world, and furnish a sense of moral direction. For those who participate in the language game of any particular theory, there is a sense of a common relational network. At the same time, this use-based view of language also reminds the social researcher that he or she is also a practitioner. Whether in the university or on the streets, languages constitute social practices. We do things together with words—for good or ill. It is this latter phrase that is most important to us in the present volume. We have been less than satisfied with the limits of social science inquiry to cross the borders into the practices of the culture. We are all too skilled at documenting and theorizing the world for our own colleagues, using words to carry out professional relationships (e.g., gaining us tenure, promotion, merit increases, awards, fellowships, grants, and so forth). The present attempt is to cross the borders more directly and ultimately, to illuminate a range of conversational practices that may be pressed directly into social life. To be sure, we will "do our traditional thing" and furnish a theoretical context for our work; as indicated, we do feel there is a need for theory in lending intelligibility and worth to the endeavor. However, it is not specifically the theory we wish to "give away" in this instance but rather, a range of linguistic practices. Theory may stimulate the imagination and help it to take wing. However, in the end, the question is whether one comes away enriched in practice.

There is a second dialogue to which this volume attempts to speak. It is a dialogue concerning the place of moral and political commitment within scholarly work and more specifically, it is the common charge of moral relativism frequently directed at constructionist scholars. On the one hand, because social constructionists argue for the intelligibility of any form of morality within its particular community of origin, constructionists themselves seem to take no moral stand. Furthermore, because constructionists hold that there is no privileged relationship between word and world, then the ontological foundations are removed from any group that wishes to rebuke and reject "real" injustice, oppression, or intolerance. Constructionists not only seem to stand nowhere but pull the rug out from any other moral or political standing. Such criticisms are partially lodged in misunderstandings. There is no attempt in constructionism to establish a universal ethic or politics; this may be true enough. But who would wish their ethics and politics to be annunciated elsewhere? Would a constructionist ethic not constitute another form of imperialism? Furthermore, there is nothing in constructionism that argues against taking moral stands and criticizing injustice. All that is removed is an ultimate foundation, a grounds from which all other voices may be silenced and dialogue may be displaced by monologue. However, these constructionist rejoinders are ultimately insufficient. They blunt critique but offer no alternatives, no openings, no departures. The present exploration of relational responsibility moves toward answering this challenge.

The concept of relational responsibility derives from what might be viewed as a first premise of social constructionism: Meaningful language is generated within processes of relationship. In effect, all that we propose to be real and good (ontology and morality) is born of human interchange. From this perspective, there can be no moral beliefs, no sense of right and wrong, no vision of a society worth struggling for without some basis in relational process. As we shall propose in what follows, the tradition of individual responsibility—in which single individuals are held blameworthy for untoward events—has a chilling effect on relationships. It typically isolates and alienates and ultimately invites the eradication of the other—a step toward nonmeaning. In what follows, we thus shift the focus to relational responsibility, that is, toward means of valuing, sustaining, and creating forms of relationship out of which common meanings—and thus moralities—can take wing. By using the term *responsibility,* we are not sounding the trumpet for the individual's responsibility to relationship; as we shall propose, individuals are such only by virtue of their creation in relationship. Rather, we use the term responsibility here not as a moralistic wedge but as a conversational resource; it is a term that may enter conversations in ways that might sustain and support the process of constructing meaning as opposed to terminating it. The term does indeed draw moral force from our longstanding tradition of individualist morality; in the present case, we simply hope to enlist such force to render more urgent the invitation. Relational responsibility, then, lies within the shared attempt to sustain the conditions in which we can join in the construction of meaning and morality.

A final moment of context setting: If words are forms of social practice, what kind of relationships do we foster in the way we write? For example, do our words generate implicit hierarchies of knower versus the ignorant, active versus passive, leader versus follower; do they place distance between author and reader or function to reduce alienation? Such questions are doubly significant in light of our earlier credos: This is a book devoted to practice, specifically the practice of mental health, organizational development, politics, judicial systems, and education, but also the practice of everyday living as it concerns relational responsibility.

To that end, we have attempted to create and structure a volume that, itself, might serve as an illustration of relational responsibility in action. Our argument centers on the relational construction of meaning. How, then, might we write about relational responsibility and simultaneously realize the very different modes of relating to others that it invites? Relational responsibility, as we propose here, is not solely about blame and credit but is moreover about entirely different ways of engaging with others and thus of creating our worlds. Our own attempt to engage differently as scholars interested in practice as well as theory has taken an unusual form in this volume.

After writing an initial two chapters on relational responsibility, we invited a variety of other voices into conversation with us. Consistent with our thesis, we imagined that these responses would shape, extend, and amplify or redirect our proposal for relational responsibility. We asked both practitioners and theorists to read our chapters and to respond to us in a way that they imagined would keep the conversation going. We encouraged each to break from academic tradition in their replies.

In response to many of their comments, we have added in this volume a presentation of what we consider a difficult case (Chapter 3). It is within this context—the context of the painful issue of child sexual abuse—that we have attempted to further illustrate relational responsibility in action. The inclusion of this case in Chapter 3 is directly responsive to our commentators' requests.

Their entries into conversation with us follow this case. We have grouped their comments into three genres of response: (a) those that resonate with our initial essay (Resonance and Refiguration), (b) those that employ critique as the dominant mode of expression (From Antagonism to Appreciation), and (c) those that offer tangential but expansive commentary (Bringing Parallels to Play). Our groupings provide us with a more focused way of responding to varying voices that, although unique, share particular rhetorical styles and specific points of contact with our original essay. We end the volume with a rejoinder to our colleagues. Here, we attempt to draw from them in ways that might themselves give further insight into relational responsibility. As we shall find, the initial thesis does grow in dimension and self-reflection as a result of this discussion. In this sense, we see the final chapter not as the final word but as a point of departure.

PART I

Relational Responsibility

1

An Invitation to Relational Responsibility

In the beginning is the relation.
—*Martin Buber*

To live life at all is to confront conditions that are nettlesome, disappointing, irritating, and downright devastating. The problem then is not that we confront the problematic but, rather, how we respond. Perhaps the chief riposte is to seek restoration: We strive to ascertain cause and with cause in place, gain rationale for action. With responsibility assigned, we sense possibilities for admonishment, correction, coercion, punishment, and so on. In this work, we turn critical attention toward our traditional practices of assigning responsibility, of locating in the course of human affairs who is responsible for a given condition or outcome. The major discourse of responsibility is one in which the single individual serves as the critical terminus. It is to individuals that blame and credit are largely assigned and to whom we apply devices of correction and restoration. As we shall propose, the discourse of individual responsibility (and its outcomes in action) is severely limited—intellectually, ideologically, and pragmatically. Our central hope in this work is to expand the domain of discourse and related practice. We are proposing, then, a process of relational responsibility to augment the existing tradition.

We proceed humbly and in the end fail to complete our task. We recognize in the first instance that there is no means by which a fixed collection of words, sewn between inert covers, can encompass the issues in all their complexities and travel with vigor and value into practical contexts. Our more modest hope is that we can move toward rupturing—even if slightly—the existing forms of

3

discursive exchange and with these ruptures set in motion new modes of dialogue. And should these dialogues move outward toward realization in action, there is a space—be it ever so small—for altering the landscape of cultural life. Our failure to offer a completed project is not accompanied by disappointment. On the contrary, it is the very nature of the process we are proposing that militates against closure. If we succeed in generating a consequential conception of relational responsibility, the dialogue must forever remain open.

To appreciate the particular shape of this effort, it is useful to locate its roots in the writings of Ludwig Wittgenstein. One of the most significant contributions of Wittgenstein's (1953) work to contemporary scholarship is its replacement of the picture metaphor of language with a use-embedded account. We are accustomed, both in the scholarly world and in daily life, to treat language as if it pictures a world independent of itself, to hold that such words as trees, flowers, hope, and injustice can be derived from assaying the world as it is and that this same comparison of words to world will reveal the absence of fairies, magical powers, and spiritual force. Yet as Wittgenstein proposes,

> The word "meaning" is being used illicitly if it is used to signify the thing that "corresponds" to the word. That is to confound the meaning of a name with the bearer of the name. When Mr. N.N. dies one says that the bearer of the name dies, not that the meaning dies. And it would be nonsensical to say that, for if the name ceased to have meaning it would make no sense to say "Mr. N.N. is dead." . . . The meaning of a word is its use in the language. (p. 20e)

In effect, we may profitably regard words as by-products of social interchange and their meaning secured by participating in specific games of language. Yes, such words as trees and flowers may operate like guides to the world, but their capacity to function in this way is grounded in specific forms of cultural life—games of reference, instruction, presentation, admiration, and the like.

This shift to a use-governed account of language changes dramatically the status of theory in the human sciences—and thus the way in which we approach the present undertaking. Traditionally, theoretical work has been treated as subject to verification or falsification—potentially true or false—with its utility in society depending on its veracity. It is from accurate theory, it is held, that we can derive effective forms of action: improved relationships, better therapy, more efficacious public policy, and so on. Yet if theory is neither true nor false save through social interchange and there is no application save through the processes of negotiating meaning, then the traditional view that accurate theory may guide action is disqualified.

Rather, we are invited to think of theory in terms of its potential uses—how the assemblage of metaphors, narratives, and other tropes may be interpolated into the ongoing conversations of the culture and with what effects. We are encouraged to develop theory as a potential resource in the life forms of the culture, much as rational arguments, apologies, handshakes, and embraces now serve as welcomed and efficacious actions under many conditions. To us, theory is not a prescription for social life that is derived from more knowledgeable and objective sources. A theory is simply a language resource that permits particular forms of action and suppresses others. Perhaps, the central issue, then, is what kinds of social worlds do different theories make possible? It is in this spirit that the present undertaking is conducted. We make no validity claims for what we offer here as assumptions, argument, descriptions, and advice. However, it is our hope that this particular way of putting things may expand the possible ways of going on together.

There is more to the Wittgensteinian legacy: If the meaning of our words relies on their placement within forms of human interaction, then we as authors cannot, in the end, control the meaning—and thus the repercussions—of what we do. What it is we mean and how these meanings are subsequently used depends on some form of supplement (Gergen, 1994), an act of reading and responding by another, which serves further to shape the use and thus the meaning of our words. In this sense, the meaning of the text "is only partially specified and thus open to further specification, is given further specification linguistically . . . in a way that promotes . . . the coordination of diverse action" (Shotter, 1993a, p. 100). It is in this sense that we view the present essay as fundamentally open—not an expression of mind that the reader must extricate from the depths of our subjectivities but an invitation to supplementation. We have rendered the invitation concrete in this case by inviting the remaining participants in the project to "dance with us." And we, in turn, will use the final chapter of the volume to extend their meanings in ways that further elaborate the present essay.

With this précis in place, let us lay out the terrain we hope to traverse. As we shall propose, the long-standing tradition in which the individual is deemed responsible for his or her actions is deeply flawed. It is this array of problems that must initially be addressed. In light of these shortcomings, we shall then open discussion on the possibility of relational responsibility. We discuss relational responsibility as a dialogic process with two transformative functions: first, in transforming the interlocutors' understanding of the action in question (the fault, failing, crime, etc.) and second, in altering the relations among the interlocutors themselves. As actions are constructed in terms of a relational matrix, so does the relationship among the dialogic partners change. After laying out various rudiments of relational responsibility, we shall elaborate a set of orienting assumptions designed to infuse it with conceptual life. Having developed a conceptual imagery, in Chapter 2, we turn to forms of congenial practice. What forms of action are invited by this way of putting things? Then, in Chapter 3, we illustrate how these forms of practice might unfold in a difficult situation, such as sexual abuse.

THE PROBLEMATICS OF
INDIVIDUAL RESPONSIBILITY

> We must die as egos and be born again in the swarm, not separate and self-hypnotized, but individual and related.
>
> —Henry Miller

Our concepts of the person are significantly limited to our actions—both informal and institutional. Specifically, deriving from our roots in various related traditions—Hebrew, Greek, Christian, Enlightenment, Romantic—we in Western culture share a belief in the self as an originary source. More specifically, we honor a state of individual, "subjective agency," that is, a capacity for internal deliberation and control of one's actions. It is in this sphere of private consciousness, we hold, that the individual registers or experiences events or conditions in the external world and in which rational deliberation takes place—understanding, problem solving, planning, and intending. In many respects, we hold subjective agency as the essence of being human, as the basis for both our identity and our distinct value.[1] And it is precisely because of this capacity for subjective agency that we can intelligibly educate individual minds, reward and punish individuals at work, conduct psychotherapy, and hold individuals responsible for their actions—both in daily affairs and courts of law. The existence of good and evil in society, by common standards, is primarily individual in its origins.

The present work grows most immediately from widespread discontent with this individualist heritage and the institutions it serves to rationalize. There are two major forms of antipathy. The first is the increasing intellectual burden placed on those who defend the individual basis of action. Philosophers have long been discontent with the dualist metaphysics on which the belief in individual subjectivity is premised. Not only are we saddled with a problematic distinction between a material world and a psychological world (the mind-body problem), but centuries of effort devoted to the problem of how mind can reflect nature or can originate action have failed to yield solution. As Richard Rorty (1979) proposes, a history of philosophical debate shows us that the concept of an interior mind reflecting an exterior world is not a simple fact of human existence but a historically situated convention. We are not required to solve these intractable problems. They are cultural inventions and may be suspended.

Rorty's (1979) conclusion in philosophy is also fortified by burgeoning historical and anthropological studies that fully relativize the presumption of subjective agency. As historical work makes clear, the Western conception of the mental world has undergone continuous change. Many long-standing beliefs about mental states are losing credibility (e.g., soul, hysteria), and others have been almost entirely lost from cultural consciousness (e.g., Acadia, melancholy, *mal de siècle*). In addition, new mental realities are continuously entering the cultural ledger (e.g., depression, attention deficit disorder, psychological burn-out).[2] In a similar vein, anthropological study yields an array of widely contrasting ethnopsychologies or beliefs about mental life and its character.[3] In the Buddhist tradition, to define the self in terms of an independent, originary mind is to obscure the true condition of selfhood—which cannot be differentiated from an inarticulable unity. Social psychologists add an important dimension to these inquiries by demonstrating, first, the principled impossibility of locating the internal origin for an action[4] and second, elucidating the social processes by which praise and blame are allocated within groups.[5] In effect, to trace the evils of society to the minds of independent individuals may be viewed as a Western penchant, subject to critical assessment and possible abandonment.

To this converging discontent must be added important developments in literary theory. For the greater part of the century, theories of literary interpretation were essentially derivative of the individualist premise. The task of the reader was largely that of locating the "author behind the text," the "true" meaning that the writer was attempting to convey. This long-standing conception of finding the writer's meaning behind the words is now moribund. Largely inspired by continental semiotic theory, scholars have become increasingly concerned with writing as a manifestation not of the author's mentality but of systems of language, genres, or traditions of writing itself. The author's accounts of the world and self are not in this case guided by the nature of the world or the author's psyche but culturally and historically contingent practices of language use. The author is not free to express the self, but must inevitably employ forms of intelligibility that are already established within the culture.[6] To read successfully, then, is not to fathom the depth of the author's mind but to participate in culturally embedded practices of interpretation.[7] Yes, individual authors may forge new orders of words, but they do so only as participants within a domain of cultural practice.

The implications of these various critiques also carry over to political theory. Liberal philosophies of justice (from Kant to Rawls) are based in a conception of an individual self, capable of rational deliberation independent of the surrounding context of values, personal relationships, or community influences. However, as Sandel (1982) argues, a self that is prior to values, relationships, and community is essentially empty. One cannot constitute meaning alone nor engage in a rational choice among competing goods without having absorbed the intelligibilities of a community. Free choice is not free but no choice at all.

These intellectual efforts, as damaging as they are to the foundations of traditional individualism, are coupled with increasing dissatisfaction with the societal ramifications of such a commitment. In this case, critics are specifically concerned with ways in which the assumption of individual agents as the fundamental atoms of society—and thus, of moral responsibility—affects cultural life. At the outset, holding the self as the origin of action lends itself to a prioritizing of self in daily affairs. Legitimated is a preeminent concern with one's own subjectivity, beginning with one's state of well-being and proceeding through the related issues of one's own goals, needs, wants, and rights. Buttressed by Darwinian theory of species survival, the primary question we often ask of any project is, How am I affected; how do I gain or lose? To be sure, others should be considered but primarily as their actions may affect one's own well-being. Sampson (1993) refers to this as the construction of "serviceable others." Thus, altruism may be favored by the enlightened individual but only insofar as there is a positive payoff for oneself. Christopher Lasch's (1979) *The Culture of Narcissism* contains perhaps the most condemning statement of the "me-first" attitude engendered by the individualist impulse. For Lasch, the individualist orientation reduces to trivia emotional relationships and sexual intimacy (carried out to "make me feel good,"), scholarly research (conducted to "help my career"), and political discourse (chosen to "help me win.").

Closely related, the ideology of individualism also generates a sense of fundamental independence or isolation. For the individualist, persons are bounded entities—leading separate lives, on independent trajectories. We can never be certain that anyone else understands us and thus, that another can care for us deeply. By the same token, the self-contained individual can never be certain that he or she understands the mind (thoughts, needs, feelings) of others and is thereby restrained from investing too heavily in their lives. And why should such investments be pursued when they may curtail one's individual freedom? Robert Bellah et al. (1985), along with psychologists Sarnoff and Sarnoff (1989), have come to see institutions such as community and marriage deeply threatened by the individualist perspective. If one believes the central unit in society is the individual self, then relationships are by definition artificial contrivances, unnatural and alien. By implication, they must be constructed, nurtured, or "worked at." And if such effort proves arduous or disagreeable, then one is invited to abandon them and return to the native state of private agency, "my way."

Critics are also concerned with the negative effects of individualist ideology on collective well-being. Classic is Garrett Hardin's (1968) analysis of the hidden costs of individual rationality. If each individual acts so as to maximize gains and minimize his or her own costs, Hardin demonstrates, the overall consequences to society may be disastrous. Current environmental crises provide a convenient illustration: the outcome of each person seeking individual gains is the depletion of forests, lakes, and fish, and the contamination of the atmosphere. Richard Sennett's (1977) *The Fall of Public Man* describes the decline of civic life over the centuries. He argues that our individualist preoccupation, and concomitant fear of sincerity and self-revelation, militate against the kind of public life in which people mingle freely on the streets, in parks, or at public gatherings and speak with civil constraint, without embarrassment, and with a sense of the common good. As he sees it, public life has given way to privatized, claustrophobic, and defensive modes of living. Others point to the systematic inattention to broad social configurations favored by an individualist world view (Sampson, 1977, 1981). There is little attention in higher education to cooperative modes of learning; business training emphasizes individual as opposed to group performance; courts of law allocate individual blame while remaining blind to the broader social processes in which crime is embedded.[8]

Last, we must ask whether an individualist ideology may guide us safely into the future. As Alisdair MacIntyre (1984) argues, there is no reason why one who is committed to individualism should pay heed to the so-called good reasons of others. If the individual should chose what he or she believes is good and right—as the individualist perspective favors—then any opposing views constitute frustrations or interferences. To pay heed to "the opposition" is to relinquish one's integrity. Furthermore, others' attempts to hold one responsible for the ill effects of one's actions may seem unjustified, self-promoting, and hostile. For prolife activists to blame prochoice advocates for the murder of babies scarcely invokes guilt in the latter. Rather, the effect is a fusillade of counterattacks. In effect, individualism promotes interminable conflict among incommensurable moral or ideological commitments. Today, the cultures of the world are thrown into ever increasing contact with each other, problems of international coopera- tion are ever expanding, and the tools for massive destruction are increasingly effective. In such a world, the individualist mentality—each against each—may harbor disaster.

INTELLIGIBILITIES OF RELATIONSHIP

> What would happen to a novelist . . . whose forte has been the hero's forging of the autonomous self, if that novelist suddenly lost his belief in any such thing as "the autonomous self"?
>
> —*Gail Godwin*

The preceding logic places us in the following position: We confront in daily life myriad instances of agonizing action, cases of failure, stupidity, hostility, dishonesty, injustice, brutality, and so on. We inherit from the past a strong tendency to locate the source of such failings within individual minds, acting either individually or collectively. Yet we find not only that we are without the conceptual resources to justify such a tradition but that the presumption of individual responsibility also lends support to a variety of destructive practices. What alternatives now confront us? We are scarcely proposing the full abandon- ment of the individualist tradition. Nor would we wish to develop yet another rationale for policing language. Rather, if our discourse both sustains and constitutes cultural life, the favored move is that of developing new forms of intelligibility. Specifically, we may labor toward the development of intelligi- bilities that invite, encourage, or suggest alternative forms of action. We do not thus abandon the tradition but enrich it.[9]

It is our view that located within the preceding body of anti-individualist critique lies the conceptual foreground for at least one significant alternative to the individualist intelligibility. Specifically, much of this criticism is derived from a keen appreciation of the significance of relationships—intimacies, friend- ships, groups, communities, institutions, and cultures. As it is variously reasoned, it is out of relationships that we develop meaning, rationalities, the sense of value, moral interest, motivation, and so on. From such arguments we might succeed in developing discursive resources that shift attention away from individual sources of action to the sphere of relationship. Descriptions and explanations of individual functioning are everywhere in use; the discourse of the self indeed functions as a literal language in the culture at large. In contrast, relationships seem artificial contrivances born out of individual efforts. The challenge, then, is to lend to the language of relationship a palpability that grants to it the same rhetorical and pragmatic power as the intelligibility of individual minds.

How are we to proceed? It would be a mistake, in our view, to struggle toward the elaboration of a virgin syllabary of relatedness. A totally new language would not only be cumbersome but devoid of the kind of meaning-in-use required for efficacy in daily affairs. Rather, the optimal course is that of extending and amplifying existing modes of discourse. Can we locate traditions of intelligibility in which relatedness (as opposed to individuality[10]) holds a central place? Although such languages are not culturally dominant, they can be located. Within the recesses of our tradition are indeed multiple modes of realizing relationship as a unit or process. Although it would be possible to settle on one single discourse and to expand its scope and potential, our strategy is otherwise. Our hope is to set in motion a dialogic process in which all such discourses might be energized. That is, rather than fixing a specific language of relatedness, let us move toward *conversational processes in which multiple discourses of relatedness are employed.* In our view, it is within conversational processes that explore the dimensions of relatedness that transformation of the participants' relationship occurs. Let us consider four potent forms of relational intelligibility as they have emerged in the scholarly world: internal others, conjoint relations, relations among groups, and systemic process.

Internal Others

> Consciousness is never self sufficient; it always finds itself in an
> intense relationship with another consciousness.
>
> —*Mikhail Bakhtin*

In contrast to the pervasive penchant for treating individuals as independent, autonomous agents, several important lines of inquiry significantly challenge the boundary between self and other. These are chiefly forms of intelligibility that view the individual as embodying aspects of others. Or, to press the implications, there are no independent selves; we are each constituted by others (who are themselves similarly constituted). We are always already related by virtue of shared constitutions of the self. There are a variety of theoretical departures that tend—in varying degree and with varying emphases—toward such a conclusion. For symbolic interactionists, such as Cooley (1922) and Mead (1934), the self comes into being through incorporating the other. For Cooley, incorporation of the other is through the process of social imitation and for Mead, through role taking. Similarly, a broad range of scholarship (see for example, Bruner, 1990; Harré, 1979; Wertsch, 1985) has now been stimulated by Vygotsky's (1978) view of individual thought as the reflection of social process. If all that can be thought is first present within social interchange, the concept of an autonomous individual is nullified.

Resonant with Vygotsky's explorations are the works of the Russian literary theorist, Bakhtin (1981). As Bakhtin reasoned, because we are each exposed to multiple domains of language use and because language itself is a composite of multiple influences, we are "multivoiced." Furthermore, because language is essentially a vehicle for communication, its use is always relationally dependent. This is so in two ways: The collation of voices used by an individual at any point (a) always gains its bearing from preceding conversation and (b) is always fashioned according to the relationship into which one is speaking. Bakhtinian writings have also stimulated more recent inquiries into multiple selves (Penn & Frankfurt, 1994), the dialogic self (Hermans & Kempen, 1993) and "social ghosts" (M. Gergen, in press).[11]

These various forms of intelligibility have substantial implications for carrying relationally responsible dialogue. Collectively, they suggest that what we typically index as another's autonomous action is grossly misleading. The individual's actions—words, gestures, performances, and so forth—are scarcely his or hers alone but bear the mark of myriad others. It is not he or she alone who is speaking or acting but a mother, father, sister, brother, friend, teacher, fictional character, and so on. Furthermore, these same words and deeds are related to those to whom they are directed. When the other speaks to us, we are in some sense included in the utterance. These views also subvert the conventional rituals of blame and punishment. Traditionally, if the other attacks, we are inclined to defend; if the other is mistaken, we are moved to correct; if the other is rude, we desire to punish. However, if the other's actions are not the manifestation of an autonomous and unified self but the remnants of myriad relations, then defense, correction, and punishment are denatured. Our understanding of the others within invites us to break the taken-for-granted flow of interchange and to explore the myriad identities at play and rest. We may variously inquire,

Who is speaking and acting here, Who is listening, What voices are not being heard, What selves within are suffering, Why is this voice dominant and not some other, and How can we help these suppressed potentials into being? We can understand that the conflict, the anguish, the retribution, and so on are being played out by fractional impulses acquired from others and because, in Walt Whitman's terms, "we contain multitudes," we are invited to expand the retinue of guests at the table of responsibility.

Conjoint Relations

It takes two to tango.

In considering others within, we remained within the traditional internal-external binary, with the individual psychological world separated from an external physical world. Let us consider a mode of understanding that makes no foundational reference to a private, psychological world but rather, focuses on the domain of public interchange. More specifically, attention is drawn to patterned interaction among two or more persons. Here, we are not speaking of causal patterns in which A causes B to respond (and so on) but rather, A-B patterns in which each of the constituent actions depends for its intelligibility on the other. Rather than action and reaction, we have what Shotter (1980) has termed *joint-action*. Sexual intercourse is an apt example: Intercourse as an identifiable phenomenon cannot be carried out alone nor can it be reduced to the mere summation of individual actions. Rather, the phenomenon requires the coordinated actions of both participants.

Again, broad-ranging inquiry bears on the intelligibility of conjoint realities. Garfinkel's (1967) work on ethnomethodology, or the collaborative practices by which persons achieve a sense of reason and reality, forms a landmark contribution. Subsequent inquiry into turn taking (Schegloff & Sacks, 1973), conversational endings (Albert, 1985), and rituals of relationship (Marsh, Rosser, & Harré, 1978) emphasize the patterned character of interaction and thus the incapacity of any action to stand alone. Communication theorists Pearce and Cronen (1980) have demonstrated the power of such patternings to persist—even when undesired by participants. Therapists have been drawn to the importance of family rituals of relationship in sustaining various forms of suffering (Caplow, 1968; Reiss, 1981).

A central concern of much recent work has been on the way in which meanings are generated, sustained, and disrupted in relationships. As it is reasoned, actions in themselves have no meaning; they acquire meaning only as they are supplemented by the actions of others (Gergen, 1994). Thus, meaning is a by-product of relatedness. Congenial with this premise are inquiries into the way in which persons together construct the world, whether they be scientists in a laboratory (Latour & Woolgar, 1979), students and teachers in a classroom (Edwards & Mercer, 1987), or families determining what shall be counted as a proper memory (Middleton & Edwards, 1990).

Again, we find the intelligibility of conjoint relations opens a variety of options in ongoing interaction. One major implication is that there is no means of extricating self from other. That is, one's actions are never independent but acquire their very intelligibility as actions by virtue of others with whom one is (or has been) engaged. In the same way that a joke is not funny save through the laughter of another, a hostile action is not hostility until another treats it as such. An apology is only apparent when the other acknowledges it as genuine.

The intelligibility of conjoint relations must ultimately be expanded outward to a broader community. So far, we have opted for replacing the presumption of individual, interacting selves with conceptions of *we*. It is we who generate the hostile remark, the sense of injury, the cruel retort. At the same time, no conjoint relationship is self-contained. As we form meanings, rituals, and realities together, we are always grappling with an aggregation of alterior relationships in which each of us is (or has been) engaged. Thus, every conflict within a relationship bears the contribution of still other relations in which the interlocutors are (or have been) enmeshed. Broadly speaking, the actions of participants within a relationship are all sanctioned by some standard exterior to the relationship itself. Although an action may be scorned by one participant in a relationship—branded as stupid, calloused, or inhumane— this action is honored by at least one other interlocutor (and typically more) with whom the errant actor is (or has been) engaged. Persons do not commit evil actions if such actions are evil to them only. Required for their perpetration is at least one domain of intelligibility in which they are approved. Thus, for any action that is blameworthy in a given relationship, there are silent interlocutors who look on approvingly. We must be prepared to ask, In what other relationships is this action an honorable move? How does it make its way into the present relationship? If we do not recognize this action as sanctioned within some other relationship—if we punish or obliterate it—what other relationships (of which we are a part) will be injured as a result?

Relations Among Groups

The invention of Them creates Us, and We may need to reinvent Them to reinvent Ourselves.

—R. D. Laing

A third form of relational intelligibility is more prominent in the public sphere. This is a hybrid discourse, drawing its currency primarily from the individualist tradition. Here, we find that the language for rendering individuals intelligible can readily be employed in describing or explaining collective units. We find it fully convenient to characterize organizations in individual psychological terms: We say, "the government decided . . . ," "the Supreme Court reasoned that . . . ," "the company believes . . . ," "the team was demoralized . . . ," or "the family feels . . ." With such intelligibilities in place, we also can account for the relations between aggregated units. We speak of America's relationship to France, the beliefs of the business community about government, management's perceptions of employees, and the Smith family's anger at the Joneses. These common idioms are also reflected in various academic writings, particularly in history, political science, and sociology. Here, it is common to speak of the way in which nations struggle or compete, the interaction between parties and the voters, and the ambitions of various social movements. As Larry May (1987) discusses, there are also instances in which we hold collectivities legally responsible in the same way we do individuals. We are justified, argues Peter French (1984), in treating the corporation or any other organization, as a moral person.

These languages of group interaction are also valuable resources in moving from rituals of individual blame into the relational sphere. Rather than sharpening the focus on individual malfeasance, they enable us to speak of individuals' actions (and our reactions) as manifestations of larger aggregates. In this respect, we may explore a husband's unprovoked hostility as a manifestation of workplace competition; theft, for example, as an outcome of economic class relations; rape as resulting from male gender identity; and so on. It is not the individual who is acting here: He or she is a manifestation of a collectivity; it is not I, myself, who am the target of this action but I as an exemplar of a particular group. Furthermore, we may be prepared to understand our construction of another's actions in terms of the larger institutions by which we are constituted. We may, for example, see that the very act that we term *theft* is so by virtue of our privileged place in the class structure and that within the framework of those engaged in the action, its definition is otherwise (e.g., heroism, self preservation).[12] Although some may argue that these discursive maneuvers simply have the effect of replacing individual blame with group blame, they do so only temporarily. For the process of relational responsibility, as we envision it, is never, in principle, terminated.

Systemic Process

> Indra's net [is] the cosmic web of inter-relatedness extending infinitely in all directions of the universe. Every intersection of intertwining web is set with a glistening jewel, in which all parts of the whole are reflected. . . . Indra's net captures the web, network, pattern, tapestry, textured imagery of our time.
>
> —*Linda E. Olds*

Our resources finally include a melange of less fully developed discourses—drawn from such diverse domains as mysticism, ecology, physics, and mechanical engineering—that give rise to images of full relatedness, all to all. Often, they envision a universe in which there are no isolated units per se nor any relationships between units that themselves are autonomous. One of the most fully elaborated of these orientations is general systems theory, as variously pioneered by Bateson (1979), von Bertalanffy (1968), and Laszlo (1973). Although such theorists scarcely speak with one voice, one of the more common agreements is captured in Laszlo's (1973) view of a system as "an ordered whole in relation to its environment" (p. 38). Typically, the *ordered whole* is characterized as dynamic, with subsystems operating in synergistic fashion—producing outcomes greater than the sum of the individual subparts. It is interesting, however, that for most theorists, there is no principled statement regarding the boundaries of a system. Once an interaction between any two units has been identified, it can now be conceptualized as a system. Thus, we may view systems as fields within fields, and any identification of a system is but a temporary index to be abandoned as one grasps the higher order system of which it is a part.[13] The recent eruption of chaos theory metaphors has fortified these holistic conjectures with numerous examples from nature. The butterfly in China may contribute to the hurricane in Florida. Family therapists (see, for example, Andersen, 1991; Anderson & Goolishian, 1988; Boscolo, Cecchin, Hoffman, & Penn, 1987; Hoffman, 1981; among others) have explored and enriched the systemic orientation in numerous ways.

Holistic intelligibilities emerge in many other social science locales. Drawing from physical field theory, the group dynamics movement (Cartwright & Zander, 1964) made an early contribution to the inseparability of individual actions from group process. From early semiotic theory (Saussure, 1983) to more recent theories of literary deconstruction (Derrida, 1976) and language-power relations (Foucault, 1978), much inquiry has centered on language as a dynamic system. It is the systemic process that shapes specific instances of speech just as the specific acts potentially reverberate throughout and potentially redefine the whole. Recent social studies of science have featured actor network constellations (Callon, 1986). Although previous study had centered on social actors alone and the way in which they construct scientific knowledge, actor network theory extends the range of actants to include physical objects (such as scientific instruments, computers, fax machines), documents, laboratory facilities, and so forth. A *network* (including persons) is constituted by the interdependent relations among the participating elements, and from this standpoint, it is the operation of the network as a whole that yields what we take to be legitimate scientific knowledge.

These systemic accounts of relatedness augment the dialogues of responsibility in profound degree. This is so both generally and specifically. More broadly, we are drawn to the possibility that there are no untoward events (crimes, injustices, inhumanity) to which we have not all made a contribution, whether by our language, actions, or physical existence. If we are all constituted by and within a so-called systemic soup, then there are no events that escape the flavoring of our being (and conversely). We must at every turn be sensitive to the possibility that if we had been otherwise, so would those actions we hold subject to censure. More specifically, we are also invited by systemic accounts to multiply the discourses of exploration. If any recognizable entity, organizational unit, or form of relationship can be related to any other, then the landscape of possibilities for understanding any untoward action is without horizon. How are our problems as a couple, for example, related to the strong bonds between our parents, to the harmonious relationships among our offspring, the state of the economy, the increasing crime rate, the depletion in the ozone layer, or the conditions in Bosnia? We may further inquire into the circulation of metaphors, images, technologies, and other cultural artifacts and the ways in which they too contribute to oppressive and exploitive acts. As these connections are explored, so is the impetus to blame the errant individual mitigated, and alternative actions become plausible.

To us, these four domains of intelligibility—others within, conjoint relations, relations among groups, and systemic process—all stand as alternatives to

individualist accounts of responsibility. They provide multiple means of understanding human action as deeply and inextricably embedded within forms of
cultural (and environmental) life. It remains now to consider the process by
which these understandings are energized.

A PROCESS OF RELATIONAL RESPONSIBILITY

> We are formed in webs of interlocution.
> —*Charles Taylor*

Let us take nourishment from these disparate traditions and extend the horizons
of conversation. We are first prompted to abandon the traditional concept of an
originary point of action—a locus in space or time, an agentive impulse, or an
instigatory moment in a conversation—from which subsequent action ensues.
As each of the previously discussed intelligibilities demonstrates, there is no
means of extricating a particulate action from the whole of what there is; any
action is both a manifestation of and a constituent part of the array. There is,
then, no fixed and identifiable locus of origin for what is the case. Rather than
systematically seeking an originary source, we propose a continuous and open-
ended process of exploration, a conversation that itself takes place in relationships and concerns itself with relationship. This process of inquiry is directed
toward multiple loci of concern or points of practical leverage. Each individual
locus may be rendered intelligible and thus subject to deliberation and action—
but only temporarily. Because the conversation is inherently open-ended, each
moment of insight can give way to further exploration; each clear and compelling understanding can be treated as but a single atom in a field without
boundaries. As the exploration continues, not only is each conversational object
transformed through an array of understandings, but the relationship of those
engaged in the pursuit may thereby be altered.[14] In effect, we begin with a
tradition that invites us to hold individuals responsible and replace its practices
of sanction (degradation, removal of privileges, incarceration, execution) with
an ongoing process of relational responsibility.

We hold relationally responsible actions to be those that sustain
and enhance forms of interchange out of which meaningful action
itself is made possible. If human meaning is generated through
relationship, then to be responsible to relational processes is to

favor the possibility of intelligibility itself—of possessing selves, values, and the sense of worth. Isolation represents the negation of humanity.[15]

The practice of relational responsibility may proceed with a set of latticed concerns, questions, deliberations, and other actions moving outward from the individual to embrace the ever expanding domain of relatedness. Each of these conversational moves, in turn, may broaden and deepen our forms of discourse and enrich the range of reasonable actions in such a way that cultural participants are more fully (or less lethally) coordinated.

Can we chart a set of practices that we would consider relationally responsible? Although we are skeptical about a single and sovereign answer to this question, there is a rich range of practices that, to us, seem highly promising. For simplicity, let us consider these practices in two separate registers: orienting and performative. By *orienting practices,* we mean a set of theoretical intelligibilities that may help us position conversational participants so as to generate alternative ways of indexing actions, open new domains of curiosity, and provoke catalytic questions. These are theoretical resources that may help participants to frame the process of relational responsibility, to step out of the taken for granted, and to deliberate on promising alternatives. We do not view these theoretical suppositions as foundational so much as catalytic. After considering these orienting practices, we will turn to concrete performances of relational responsibility.

Orienting Resources for Relational Responsibility

Relationships serve as the major source of what we take to be "the real" and "the good."

As Wittgenstein proposed, words gain their meaning within ongoing social interchange. As words function within relationships to name, direct, approve, correct, and so on, so do they acquire ontological and moral dimension. Local vocabularies come to represent a world of objects, individuals, actions, rights, duties, values, and so on. In effect, language generates the sense of what is real and what is good. The manner in which participants supplement and counter-supplement each other's actions gives shape to intelligibility itself.

The implications of this view for relational responsibility are substantial. At the outset, we are confronted with the painful realization that all our common-sense presumptions—all that we take to be sensible, reliable, honest, and just—are parochial, particularistic configurations. This suggests that anything we might do or say can be viewed with suspicion, hostility, or even shocking disbelief from other standpoints. And simultaneously, those actions we view as most mistaken, misconceived, immoral, or detestable are intelligible, accept-able, and even worshipped within other configurations. Any belief or value can acquire credibility and vitality as people coordinate their activities with each other.

It also follows that there is no particular account of reality or the good that can lay claim to transcendent foundations or justifications. Any rationality employed for purposes of justifying a given ontology or ethic is itself a move in an ongoing language game. It is a rationality born of a particular tradition of discourse and practice. And when such pronouncements are placed in motion, when they become indefensible statements about what is or must be, they operate to the detriment of alternative ways of life. Thus, attempts to adjudicate conflicts in terms of principles or foundational goods are fraught with danger. Arguments regarding who is ultimately right cannot be solved so long as the interlocutors remain within separated domains of intelligibility.

It also follows that all beliefs about the world and self, about worthy and unworthy actions, are culturally and historically contingent. They are sustained only so long as communities continue to speak in certain ways. Any discourse purporting to map the terrain of the real or the good is precariously perched in juxtaposition to all that is not. Thus, an effort is required to sustain valued traditions—from the grand level of political and moral institutions to the common traditions of marriage or friendship. At the same time, to arrogate these local traditions to the level of fundamental necessities is not only to threaten all others but is ultimately to threaten self-annihilation. What we are suggesting instead is an appreciation of the contingent, indeterminate, historical, and relational aspects of our modes of constructing reality.[16] In the attempt to assign responsibility, then, there is no "getting it right." Certitude walks hand in hand with eradication of the other.

Personal identity (motive, character, intention, action) is a by-product of negotiations within relationships.

Building on the argument that meaning arises in the emergent flow of actions and supplements, we find that any way of identifying or describing the self is also dependent on relationship. Thus, any language purporting to describe the mental world of the individual—the language of perception, memory, emotion, desire and so forth—is a by-product of culturally and historically located traditions. The self—both in terms of public identification and private surmise—is born of relationship. One important implication for present purposes is that the ways in which we portray our feelings of love, sorrow, or anger; how we explain our good or bad intentions; or our justifications of our actions are moves in a relationship. Rather than viewing such talk as a reflection of mental states within the person, we are drawn to the function of such language in the relationship. If there is no locating what the individual truly intends, really desires, or actually feels, then we are drawn to consider the relational repercussions of portraying one's feelings, for example, in terms of being saddened or disappointed as opposed to irritated or outraged. In the same way, we might ask what social functions are served by attributing intentions or agency to self and others? To be relationally responsible is to place a strong emphasis on the negotiability of mental states and conditions.

This view of the constructed self also draws attention to the ways in which conversational practices can place limits over identity. A circumscribed vocabulary of the self (or the other) operates as a constraint on being within a relationship. This point gains additional significance in light of the previous argument concerning the tendency of relationships to generate an obdurate sense of the real and the good. Thus, there is a common tendency toward crystallization of the participants' identities and sanctions developed for violating these presumptions. Patterns of blame and punishment may thus reflect and sustain traditions of long-standing relational scenarios—scenes created, rehearsed, and performed over time. However, each tradition may function as a blinder for alternatives of potentially greater promise.

In the same way that personal identity is realized within relationships, so can forms of relatedness themselves be constructed.

Just as identity is constructed in relationships, the reality of relationships is also created in the ongoing practices of dialogue. Relationships, like personal identities, are not things in themselves. They are by-products of particular forms of talk. To participate in a friendship, a family, a marriage, a team, or an organization requires conversational work: an effort to create a reality that is different from or not reducible to individual selves. In saying this, our hope is not to replace individuals with relationships but, rather, to de-essentialize any notion of either persons or relationships as "things" (i.e., objects) to be examined or as originary sources of action. Thus, we find that each conception of relationship described earlier—selves within, conjoint relations, relations among relations, and macrosocial formations—represents a form of intelligibility with a history and a situated applicability. We are invited to see each concept as a potential move in a conversation, one that may generate a new sense of reality and thus of possible actions. Most important, as the reality of relationship is realized, so is the tendency to blame the individual reduced.

As we also find, with each new form of constructing relations, there may be a concomitant transformation in the way we construct the individual participants. Construction of selves and relationships are interdependent. Of special relevance to relational responsibility, we can now consider that as we construct the reality of relationships, so do we reduce the sense of separation and alienation. If there is a problem and we attempt to locate which of us is at fault, then we enter the doors of "the blame game." We each try to locate ways in which we are not responsible and the other has erred. Yet if it is *our* problem, something *we* have done, then the quality of our conversation changes. We work as compatriots or allies in searching for a solution. The introduction of "we" is more than word play. It is to fashion what we are to each other.

Persons represent the intersection of multiple relationships.

Let us here distinguish *selves* from *persons*, viewing the former as constructions of relations and the latter as individual bodies. This will allow us to speak of relations as constituted by individual bodies without treating these bodies as self-contained individuals in the traditional sense. Given this distinction, we can treat persons as the intersection of multiple relationships, local and immediate manifestations of relational histories. Normal life history will bring one into relationship with countless others. In each of these relationships, a particularized construction of the world will develop, one that may often appear seamless and coherent. Yet the reality developed in one relationship will seldom be identical with any other. At times, there may be substantial discrepancies in the world views of which any individual is a part.[17] Any person who moves among relations with family members, friends, lovers, colleagues, teachers, and so on will become an expression of these different modes of being, and these modes may conflict in many ways.

When any two persons enter into a new relationship, they must necessarily draw on the vast and multiple resources born of these relational histories. The participants will not be drawing on identical histories of relatedness. Thus, any discursive interchange will carry multiple senses of the good or the real. Within the matrix of the relationship, multiple vocabularies are interfused. The meaning generated within the relationship will represent a unique coordination of multiple communities. Yet within this relationship, many possible voices will also be silent, those that are available to the participants but that are inessential to getting on in the local circumstance. These silent interlocutors stand ready at any moment to enter the arena of interaction. They may derogate or detest, they may applaud or inspire; they are always close at hand, readied for entry into the interchange.

In a broad sense, this is to say that any given relationship is, itself, constituted by those relational engagements with which it is interlaced. Thus, when persons join in conversation, they are creating the possibility for a broad array of relational forms to merge into ever new configurations. We do not, then, consider the character of ongoing relationship simply as an effect generated by a series of external causes—for example, the economy, housing conditions, education, or politics. Rather, we would like to suggest that relationships are usefully described as processes within which many of these local and broader relational engagements intermingle, are recreated and transformed. This emphasis on processes of relating rather than on objects in interaction underscores the complex crisscrossing of multiple and extended networks of relations in any interactive moment.

Of specific relevance to relational responsibility, this line of reasoning again emphasizes the limitations of person blame, holding individuals responsible for so-called character flaws or evil intentions. Blaming another person for his or her wrong-doing is only one possible conversational move. Attention is invited here to the process of relating within which the fact of wrong-doing comes into existence. This is not to shift blame to those processes (yet another "evil actor") but rather to raise questions about how certain actions become viable and intelligible within particular relational forms. The by-product of such inquiry may be the opening of new lines of action, new ways of framing events, and a new way of relating.

Conflict and disharmony are a natural and inevitable outcome of
social existence; likewise, all that is good and valuable within a
relationship is dependent on others.

From the present perspective, disruptions, annoyances, and even wrenching
upheavals within any relationship should not be considered unusual or deeply
problematic deviations from the normal; they are the very warp and woof of
cultural life. Given the person's existence in a multitude of relationships, each
itself is a pastiche of sundry traditions, and given the presence of these varied
and incoherent vocabularies within any particular interchange, complete harmony is bought at the price of vast suppression. Although all action is intelligible
and warranted within some form of relationship, local idioms do not always leap
their boundaries with ease. Felicitous in their local context, they may elsewhere
constitute egregious breaches. Furthermore, because we bring to bear on any
action multiple voices of evaluation (many ways of visioning the true and the
good), there is virtually no behavior that cannot be faulted by at least one
available standard. At any point in an otherwise harmonious relationship, any
participant may halt the proceedings to locate fault in the other. Thus, to despair
of a relationship because of failures in understanding, in achieving mutual
agreement, or running smoothly is, to a degree, unwarranted. Such glitches are
the normal order of things. From the present standpoint, so-called good understandings are always partial, mutual agreement is precariously situated, and
smooth interchange is often just the result of habit. Not every fault demands a
culprit.

But let us explore the positive potentials of inherent conflict. In a sense,
conflict within a relationship is emblematic of the broader linkages of the
antagonists, a manifestation of their meaningful connection to a broader world
and to a cultural history. As we have argued, each participant in a relationship
is constituted by those relational processes of which he or she is a part. Thus,
the ability to act intelligibly in the present relationship, the capacity to create
happiness of any kind (for example, to participate in scenarios of love, support,
mirth, curiosity, adventure, sexuality, intellectual exchange, or giving life a sense
of meaning) are all derived from others. More broadly speaking, whatever is
vital and valuable in any relationship owes a debt to the surrounding network of
connection, past and present, actual and vicarious.

We are thus left with the irony that the very sources of conflict in a relationship
are also the wellsprings of its strength. To hold the individual responsible for his

or her ill doing is not only to blind oneself to the broader processes in which a relationship is embedded but is tantamount to relational solipsism (e.g., "There is nothing but you and me."). At the same time, to hold others responsible for the problems within a relationship ("If it weren't for your mother . . . ," "It's this crummy neighborhood . . . ," "If you were only paid a decent wage . . . ,") is to deny the positive contribution made by the surrounding connections to whatever is valuable in the relationship. This does not mean that we must settle disgruntledly for an ironic status quo. Rather, it is to invite protagonists into a process of relational responsibility, an exploration of what has happened and why that is potentially without end, within each iteration a possible opening to new insights and potential moves in interaction. It is to invite ambient voices into the dialogue but without drowning the essential identities necessary for the relationship. It is to explore the multiple voices inherent in the individual without denying the potential to be treated as a unified self. It is to take account of the broader systems that impinge on local realities without presuming the inevitable outcome of these impingements. Last, it is to counsel against the easy solution of simply leaving the field—abandoning the conflictual relationship in favor of so-called personal freedom. There is no moment of free action, because the very intelligibility of action itself is always already freighted with otherness. We do not move out of relationships but simply traverse the terrain of connection.

Each determination of the real and the good is simultaneously a deconstruction.

The story we are crafting has persons bringing into relations a repertoire of intelligible actions born of other relations. Thus, the words we offer as candidates for meaning within a relationship are necessarily borrowed, ripped from other contexts and thrust into the immediate interchange. As the novel vocabulary is imported into a relationship, it takes on new and different meanings. As it loses its previous anchorage in words and actions and is incorporated into the immediate interchange, three transformations occur. First, there is a loss in originary meaning: That is, there is a loss of the precise implications of these words and phrases within their original setting. The word *democracy* does not mean the same thing in a high school civics class as it does in a Boston ward or a Detroit ghetto. Second, and most important for the present analysis, there is a proactive transformation in meaning within the relationship, an often subtle shift in the use of various utterances and their implications. For the teenage civic student to suggest at dinner that he feels his family is democratic is to introduce a metaphor with myriad implications— for both ensuing conversation and practice. A new vision of democracy is now available, and for it to be negated by a parent is to redefine the very meaning of the negation. What had been *authority* is now *authoritarian*. Last, there is a preactive transformation, in which the words or phrases introduced into the new context act back on the structure of meaning in the preceding setting. As the term "democracy" is used at home for talking about patterns of speaking at dinner, the implications of the term are thereafter altered as the teenage student returns to class. As language slips its boundaries, so does it gain revolutionary potential.

The implications of this condition are many. Consider first, there are no permanent solutions to problems besetting a relationship, no arrangement of words or shifts in practice that will provide the final key to harmony and good will. Problems are seldom resolved "once and for all"; resolutions are often temporary, drawing from vocabularies brought to fore at a given interactive moment. By the same token, problems are not fixed in stone; today's unbearable action may ultimately be seen, for example, as a developmental phase or even a sign of strength as the process of infinite resignification proceeds. There is strong reason, then, for pursuing a process of relational responsibility. Not only is such a process designed to disturb the patterns giving rise to present anguish—to oil the wheels of resignification—but if effective, such a process ramifies throughout a broad spectrum.

Last, we must consider the idealistic undertext. As meanings are transported across boundaries of use, so do they bring with them relational remnants, fragments of meaning and accompanying implications. As they enter other arenas, they add and they modify. The local mosaic of meaning never thereafter carries the same configuration. And as the borrowings are conveyed again into their earlier setting, so do they change the configuration of that setting. With sufficient time and bidirectional ripplings, the different relational spheres gain increased capacity for coordination. No, they are not necessarily homogenized. However, what was distant becomes intelligible—possibly real and possibly right. In this sense, relational responsibility may work toward a coordination of coordinations.

To engage in multivocal inquiry is to transform the relationship among interlocutors.

This last entry serves at once to summarize much of the preceding discussion and to reflect more directly on the outcomes of relational responsibility. As we are suggesting, relational responsibility does not function simply to locate a source of the problem outside the individual. Rather, its chief outcome should be a change in the relationship of those engaging in the process. Thus far, we have emphasized the possibility of multiple constructions of self and of relationships, we have drawn attention to the many voices on which a person can draw, and we have focused on the tendency of individual relationships to stabilize the real and the good. Yet as relational inquiry takes place and each of the interlocutors takes on different voices and entertains alternative intelligibilities, so is their relationship subtly transformed. This change is not simply an addition of new forms of discourse, as just discussed. More important, it is a change in the actions of the interlocutors toward one another.[18] To talk with a new voice is to invite the other to treat one in a different way; to define oneself differently also defines the other in a new way. Alternative dances of relationship are thus invited. For example, to move from the position of authority to questioner, from the assured to the ambivalent, or from the angry to the sympathetic invites an alternative identity from the other. To become the questioner invites the other's authority; to be ambivalent opens the way for the other's ambivalence, and to replace anger with sympathy enables defensiveness to be replaced by good will. If effectively pursued, relationally responsible inquiry has transformative potential for the participants.

NOTES

1. For a more formal account of Western ethnopsychology, see D'Andrade (1987).
2. See, for example, Harré (1979) and Graumann and Gergen (1996).
3. See, for example, Lutz and Abu-Lughod (1990), Heelas and Lock (1981), and Shweder, 1991.
4. See Gergen, Hepburn, and Comer (1986).
5. See, for example, Antaki (1981); Harvey, Orbuch, & Weber (1992).
6. See, for example, Derrida (1976).
7. See Fish (1980).
8. Several authors have attempted to move beyond the individualist account in education (Giroux, 1993), in organizations (Reed & Hughes, 1992; Weick, 1995), and in the area of legal studies (Altman, 1990; Sarat & Kearns, 1996; Unger, 1986). These treatments represent a growing move toward relational forms of practice.
9. The present arguments are essentially for an expansion in the communicative resources available within the culture. Resonant with Stone's (1987) arguments for a moral pluralism in the

service of a viable ecology, the present attempt is to increase the available intelligibilities of responsibility.

10. It is important to realize here that we are bracketing the time-honored language of individual interaction, that is, the extensive discourse that views each individual as at least partially a product of others' inputs (e.g., socialization effects, modeling influences, attitude change influences) and in turn, a stimulus who influences the lives of others. Although an extensive discourse, and of certain value in shifting attention away from the otherwise autonomous individual, this orientation nevertheless retains the view of the individual as an integral whole. Relationship, in this frame, is a byproduct of interacting individuals rather than a process sui generis, as we are proposing.

11. For a more extended account of theories pointing toward a thorough saturation of self by society, see Burkitt (1991).

12. See, for example, Spector and Kitsuse (1977).

13. For more recent applications of systems theory to human action, see Ford (1987) and Olds (1992).

14. Can we extend the boundaries of our common intelligibilities and play in the pastures of multiplexity? As Kuipers's (1993) study of the Weyewa people of Indonesia indicates, with sufficient immersion in the ritual practices, we can even come to appreciate how responsibility for our present actions could be traced to the words of our ancestors. As Hill and Zepeda (1993) also demonstrate, our common forms of accounting contain multiple and continuously sliding allocations of responsibility.

15. Here, we distinguish our perspective from that of Habermas (1979, 1992). Although we share with Habermas an interest in understanding how to construct, in conversation, a sense of community, we depart from his reliance on community as a byproduct of some normative ethic. Our point of departure hinges on our own attempt to celebrate the distinctive voices in any particular conversation or community, whereas Habermas places his own concern in locating how distinctive voices have a normative social fit. To Habermas, reliance on the notion of community norms serves to justify his conversational ethics. We do not attempt to offer justifications for relational responsibility. To us, the challenge is not how to achieve consensus or intersubjective understanding. The former we see as silencing, whereas the latter we view as impossible. The challenge, as we see it, is one of coordinating multiplicity, which requires curiosity and respect for the relational construction of meaning. We prefer to value the imperfections, contingencies, and uncertainties of relational life to any form of normative clarity.

16. Our position here is similar to that of Rorty (1989) in that we argue for historically and locally contingent realities where, in Rorty's terms, a sense of solidarity is constructed. His question, and very much our question, centers on how to talk about the ways in which people with diverse discursive resources can generate some sense of responsibility in relation to one another. Is it possible for incommensurate communities to coordinate their activities with one another? Yet Rorty's argument for solidarity is premised on "the ability to see more and more traditional differences . . . as unimportant when compared with similarities with respect to pain and humiliation" (p. 192). We prefer to avoid essentializing any features or characteristics of persons in relation, such as pain and humiliation. Our own attempt here is to articulate the relational ways in which we create our sense of humanity and thus to garner respect and appreciation for the contingent, indeterminate, historical, and local nature of our communion with others.

17. See, for example, Billig et al. (1988).

18. See Burr (1995) for further discussion of positioning (especially pp. 140-158).

2

Relational Responsibility in Practice

So I am searching for the threads—
Like the many textures and colors of a vast Persian rug.
Similarities of wonder, and goodness and love,
Commonalities of wishes, and hopes and dreams—
Lines of light that weave us together
Lines of love that whisper of oneness

—Patricia L. Jobling

We have now outlined a rationale for a process of relational responsibility and offered a range of theoretical resources for animating such a process. We now move in a more practical direction. Given these various lines of reasoning, how might a process of relational responsibility proceed? What would be different if we framed our talk, our descriptions, our explanations about self and social life in relational rather than individual terms? What new conversational opportunities might a relational orientation offer? How might we talk differently about ourselves, our relationships, and our everyday interactions, politics, policies, education if we foregrounded these assumptions and their implications?

Earlier, we characterized the individualist tradition as one that treats relationships as artificial and oppressive. By offering a way of talking that emphasizes relational process, perhaps we can remove the thrall of individualist discourse. Simultaneously, we hope to move beyond the objectification of relationships as the binary opposition to individuals. We are attempting here to essentialize neither individuals nor relationships but rather, to create conversational opportunities that facilitate our getting on in a world of enormous and ever changing complexity. To objectify is to freeze the conversation.

Katha Pollitt (1994) suggests that life in the global village of today requires a kind of flexibility for knowing how to find out how to act rather than how actually to act. Similarly, we wish to avoid dictating specific techniques or practices, a "knowing how to act" on specific occasions. Rather, we draw attention to a variety of practices that may variously be placed in the service of relational responsibility as circumstances suggest. These explorations into relational practice are open to further elaboration and invention. Some of these practices will momentarily objectify the self-contained individual; others will suggest the reality of intentional action. However, the point of relational responsibility is not to abandon all previous forms of conversation. Rather, we strive toward a sensibility in which any way of describing, explaining, or acting may serve in some relational context as a fruitful resource for participants. What forms are useful at what particular times cannot be specified in advance. For the sake of coherence, we will focus on practices congenial with our earlier emphases on internal others, conjoint relations, relations among groups, and systemic process.

SPEAKING THE INTERNAL OTHERS

If I feel insulted or abused by someone close to me, I often go into a "slow burn." I seldom initiate conversation and if I must speak, do so with only a minimum of words in monotone. I can go on with this punishment for days. However, if the victim of my silence would only point out, "your performance is now more skilled than your father's," I would probably break down in smiles.

My friend and I argue relentlessly on this issue. Why can't he see my logic; how can he be so obtuse; why must he persist in arguments that are so obviously flawed? A week later, I find myself at loggerheads with a colleague from another department. He is so aggressive. I argue forcefully, but slowly begin to realize that I am indeed using the very same arguments I had opposed the week preceding. Now, I am speaking in my friend's voice.

Although in most instances I try to act reasonably, I must admit to my penchant for pushing the boundaries of caution a bit. I continue to react against the voice of my safety-conscious father. And yet I now hear his words of caution as I speak to my young son. When I hear those words, I try to counter with encouragement for risk with the voice of my mother.

These are but a few moments in our own experience in which consciousness of self moves ever so slightly toward inclusion of another. In each case, the critical element is the realization of our embodiment of others. The challenge posed by the present analysis, however, is to develop from this consciousness new alternatives for action and especially, alternatives to replace the traditional habits of personal blame. We can fantasize a range of such possibilities. But it seems more fruitful to draw from and extend a range of existing practices. Various practices already exist that move effectively in the direction of opening the internal voices. How can these be made relevant to the specific development of relational responsibility?

The early writings of transactional analyst Eric Berne (1964) opened one relevant avenue. Berne depicted the self as multiply populated and outlined ways in which therapists could bring these voices (for example, "the child within") to expression. Self-help books on "codependence" (Beattie, 1989; Mellody, Miller, & Miller, 1989) guide people through their internal dialogues with others who populate the interior. Advocates of the codependency movement "understand one's colloquy with oneself as the dialogue that gives shape to one's destiny" (Greenberg, 1994, p. 29). Yet although both transactional analysis and the codependence literatures offer a range of powerful metaphors, their practices are also problematic. Although our attempt here is to celebrate the multiplicity within—in the service of expanding the range of others who share in the responsibility for one's actions—the self-help works tend to see such voices as contaminating. The alien voices must be shed to realize a pure, unified self. Therapy functions to control or banish these imported influences and to help the individual to achieve full autonomy.

More helpful for our purposes is the therapeutic work of David Epston (1992) and Karl Tomm (see Chapter 12, this volume) on exploring the internalized other. Here, clients are asked in various ways to explore the voices, born of previous relations, that presently inhabit their being. Such inquiry enables participants to recognize and legitimate the often competing intelligibilities available in con- fronting problem situations. The individual may, for example, find inner support in the internalized voice of a close friend, relative, or colleague. These internal- ized others may invite and applaud untoward actions. The same person might locate other voices representing self-doubts about that position (perhaps the voice of a friend, relative, or a competitor). A third voice might suggest an alternative option to be explored. Because it is credited to an internalized other, such a suggestion is depersonalized—not really me—and as a result, can be evaluated less passionately. From Epston and Tomm's standpoint, giving expression to these various intelligibilities aids participants in creating a sense of their own multiplicity. They stress the advantages of multiplicity as a useful resource for living rather than as a character flaw. Participants find new ways of moving in and out of various identities and new ways of acting in relationships because they have created a sense that each of these selves is legitimate in some relational context.

Epston and Tomm's explorations have substantial applicability to the practice of relational responsibility. Consider cases of blame, for example, in which family or organizational problems are traced to an individual's nasty temper, brutal disposition toward others, or single-mindedness. We are tempted to see the individual as flawed and deserving of correction if not punishment. However, one may inquire, what voice is speaking through the individual on these occasions—a mother, a father, a domineering brother? And what voices within this person might find these actions praiseworthy, marks of strength or autonomy? To recognize these voices is to diminish the tendency to blame what we otherwise presume to be a unified and autonomous individual. With further inquiry, we might also find that the same person carries voices that find his or her own actions reprehensible, not at all desirable. To learn of such doubts would still further diminish the tendency toward individual blame. And last, if given an opportunity, perhaps we would find that the person carries voices that recognize alternative possibilities, that would recommend other courses of action. These voices might well point the relationship in other directions.

In addition, relevant is Penn and Frankfurt's (1994) therapeutic work with client narratives. Drawing on Bakhtin's (1981) dialogism, they reason that the construction of self requires the other. "Voice . . . is generative; it is unfinished and awaits a reply. . . . It invites the other into what one might call a dialogic space" (Penn & Frankfurt, 1994, p. 222). Using these ideas, Penn and Frankfurt have found that different voices can be invited into the therapeutic conversation via letters written by the client to others. Because writing takes place at a different pace than talk, they find that it makes room for the "thickening" or "layering" of sensitivities and reactions and thereby stimulates the creation of multiple readings of self, other, and relationship. Writing, as they say, "encourages us to develop many different readings of our experience" (p. 230). It also invites clients to consider otherwise silent voices as possible resources for relating. To extend the implications of this practice, in a work setting, managers might write hypothetical letters to a host of significant persons whose voice in the organization is generally absent (e.g., parents, mentors, neighbors, citizen groups, clients, and so forth). In so doing, those others are brought into the organizational setting, thereby vitally expanding the range of those to whom a decision is responsible.

One important feature of this letter-writing work is that it brings into focus the way our own voice is affected by the identity of the person to whom we address ourselves. In this sense, our actions are always for another, always directed to a particular audience. The shaping of a message for an audience doubles back to shape the self. Thus, as we begin to recognize that the particular audience whom we are addressing is only one audience among many, we can see possibilities for expanding our sensitivities to the multiple potentials within ourselves. Consider how a couple locked in argument might respond to each other if each were to project him- or herself into the future or back to the past in conversation with another, perhaps a close friend, relative, or work associate, about the current disagreement. Just a momentary consideration of "how I would talk to them about all this" can introduce a new or different voice, description of events, or set of actions—new discourses to inhabit. In addition, as the descriptions are altered for these various audiences, the "hard reality" of the present becomes relativized. The embattled couple may see how they were arbitrarily limiting their potentials for description and explanation—building unnecessary walls that prevented escape.

In related work in organizational development, David Cooperrider (1990) observes that most organizational development takes a problem-solving approach that privileges conversation focused on problems—discovering their causes and planning remedial action. Discourse is effectively built around organizational deficit. As he proposes, organizational participants also harbor voices of appreciation, that is, positive views of the organization, their colleagues, and various company policies. In his work with organizations, Cooperrider displaces "problem-solving" discourse by using interviews and group discussions to elicit voices of appreciation. As participants describe positive practices, not only is the problem "dissolved," but conflict is typically replaced by more positive relations among participants, and concrete images emerge of positive organizational futures.[1]

Cooperrider's (1990) emphasis on voices of appreciation has implications of far greater scope than the organization. Again, relevant to the tradition of individual blame, this work suggests that for many actions we hold in contempt, we also harbor voices of approval. If we could but access these voices, we might find positive qualities that would open new avenues of conversation. We can see the rude as resolute, the hostile as forthright, the thief as rebel, and the deviant as creative or brave. Such awareness may also enable us to locate a broader range of voices within the other. If our knee-jerk reaction is not that of blaming, we open a space for the other to respond with something different from enmity or defense. All such voices may blunt the force of otherwise punitive and divisive relationships.

Last, we may draw from the therapeutic work of Mony Elkaim (1990). As the client describes his or her problem, Elkaim suggests that the therapist should listen internally to his or her own voice of reply. The therapist listens by asking himself or herself a series of questions: What is the client's description inviting in the way of a response? Is this description asking me to speak as a father, a combatant, an admirer, and so on? Elkaim theorizes that, if a long-standing pattern is to be broken, it is important that the therapist avoid responding in the invited way. Rather, as therapist, he or she explores alternative voices available to him or her that would not fortify or sustain the well-rehearsed patterns that may themselves contribute to the individual's anguish.

Again, the implications for relational responsibility are considerable. Sometimes, we are faced with a person whose barbarity or hostility draws us into confrontation. We feel a strong urge, abetted by the joy of righteous indignation, to attack and correct. The result is reasonably predictable: Our effort only incites the other's antagonism. Realizing the rocky route on which we are now embarked and drawing on a repository of alternative voices, can we locate an alternative reaction to the other's failing? Could we in the face of attack, for example, imagine responding with a comment that constructs an image of the other as important, loved, respected, valued? Could we invite the other to work with us in creating an opportunity for his or her "success" in the present situation? Can we invite him or her to collaborate with us in a construction of ourselves as helpful, kind, concerned and himself or herself as important, respected, and so forth? Should we locate such possibilities, the relationship would be transformed.

As we find, there are rich resources available for thinking about and accessing internal voices in the service of relational responsibility. Our aim here is not so much to list a set of techniques as to outline a rationale and a range of provocative conversational moves. The moves outlined here can and should be expanded. For example, we find ourselves drawn to the metaphor of the silenced interlocutor. That is, we may ask of any situation in which individual blame is invited, Who is silenced by the ensuing interchange? When we blame an individual, what voices are suppressed, kept at a distance, and why? Is my blame attempting to cover my own culpability? Or when I act aggressively or dishonestly, whose voice am I trying to silence? Is it possibly the voice of self-doubt, for example, that I wish to vanquish? By locating silenced interlocutors, we again open new paths of conversation.

In the same way, we find that exploring the dominant discourse can also be useful. We may ask, for example, Why is the voice of judgment and punishment the prevailing discourse? Why is this one so compelling, as opposed to all others? Who gains and who loses by joining the dominant discourse? Again, new avenues of exploration are invited.

CRAFTING CONJOINT RELATIONS

He was such a depressed old man, sitting there with his long-suffering wife. She complained that he had been chronically depressed for over a decade. We invited him to walk the beach with us. He walked sluggishly, his shoulders stooped, his head bent toward the sand. But as we walked and talked—about the beauty, about personal relations, about politics—he began to brighten. Periodically, he asserted an opinion; we listened—and replied. Soon, we were approaching the end of the strand—where the nude bathers gather in security. As we approached, his voice became increasingly animated, his gait more lively. As we thought to turn back, he told us a funny story. He was alive! Yet as we turned back and moved again down the beach, his words became fewer, his stride more weighty. When he finally settled heavily, dully next to his wife's beach chair, he was again "himself."

We were driving on a dangerous cliff-side road on the French-Italian border. The rain was heavy, visibility was impaired, and the traffic was treacherous. We were both very tense, and as my driving was less than flawless, my wife became increasingly critical. The tension mounted. Soon, it was not only the road we had to fear but ourselves as well. We then took a new turn in our interchange. Rather than view this as "my driving," and "her critical interventions," we decided to share the roles. *We* would drive and *we* would criticize. She became extra eyes on the road; I developed a self-critical posture. The remainder of the drive was not only uncomplicated but yielded a great sense of satisfaction with our relationship.

Watching my young son experiment with language and with life has been an engaging preoccupation. One afternoon, in the midst of our play, he turned to me and asked, "Mumma, are we having a good time?" To him, a good time is a communal achievement.

Having met in graduate school and consequently joining the same faculty at the same university, we find ourselves in silent competition. Rarely do we actively compete; yet we frequently talk about our disappointments when one has received fewer invitations, honors, and so forth. For years, this competitive edge worked like a wedge between us. Any comments on a draft of an article or conference paper would be seen as attempts to one-up the other. Seeing how damaging this conversation is to our relationship and to our identities, we created a ritual. When our conversations take competitive turns, we stop ourselves and say with laughter, "We do competition so well!" Our recognition of this as our achievement interrupts the destructive scenario.

These cases all revolve around a discourse of interdependence. For purposes of relational responsibility, we move from a language of individual resources to that of relationship. The discourse of relationship invites us to lay aside the question of individual blame and to shift attention to the ways in which the reprehensible actions are accomplished within relationships. Concentration is on joint achievement. Again, we find richly provocative examples in existing work.

Of early prominence, the therapeutic conversations of the Milan Team, well summarized by Boscolo et al. (1987), were significant in underscoring the relational production of family problems. As their work demonstrated, actions typically traced to individual motives can be reconstructed as relational accomplishments. Often, the vehicle for achieving such reconstruction is circular questioning, particularly questions about relationships (Palazzoli, Boscolo, Cecchin, & Praae, 1978). Rather than accept participants' descriptions of the situation (e.g., "My husband is always rejecting me.") as potentially photographic—to be compared with the facts of the case and thus yielding a "problem to be solved"—the Milan Team devises questions that embed the descriptions within the relationship. Through circular questions (e.g., "When is your husband most likely to reject you? Are there times when he doesn't reject you? What are you most likely to be doing at those times? If you knew he was going to reject you, do you think you would be able to prevent him?, etc.) the simple description of rejection is embedded within a complex fabric of interchange. The motive for the rejection, in this case, is removed from the head of the husband and placed within the patterns of interdependence.[2] Through successive comparison and contrast, participants are encouraged to transform accounts of individual wrongdoing into stories of complex interaction.

Circular questioning is scarcely the only (or even the preferred) means of shifting the focus from the individual to the relationship. We find it especially useful to focus on patterns of complementarity and most especially, pairs of actions that mutually invite, warrant, or support each other. Among our common patterns of complementarity are attack-defense, anger-anger, critique-counter-critique. As the patterns are recognized as relational dances, we are encouraged to locate alternative and more promising steps in the dance. In an organization, for example, a supervisor may feel outraged by his uncooperative employees. However, if he can turn his attention to how well he plays the autocratic leader, he might begin to applaud his employee's outstanding rebellious performance as a logical complement. His performance invites and grants intelligibility to the rebellion, and their rebellion testifies to the skill of his performance. A married couple might discuss how each sustains his or her discredited role (nagger, perfectionist, hysteric, critic) in their repeated conflicts through the effective performance of the other. To play the critic would be useless if not for the other's enactment of inadequacy, and it is only through the performance of inadequacy that the critic gains permission to crow. Means of bringing about discussions of complementarity of action are to be sought, then, as a way of generating relational responsibility.

In related work, Pearce and Cronen (1980) illustrate the relational nature of unwanted yet repetitive patterns of interaction. Their research describes how each participant in a relationship may individually detest a given action (e.g., hostility, abuse), strongly desire a different kind of relationship, and can even document his or her attempts to bring the alternative to fruition. However, despite the individual desires and attempts, the same unwanted pattern ensues. It is interesting that all participants in Pearce and Cronen's studies report that their partners are personally to blame for their inability to break out of the pattern. Yet as they cogently argue, these seemingly inescapable patterns of interchange are the result of the conjoint actions of the participants. To illustrate, Harris, Gergen, and Lannamann (1987) show how a husband's minor criticism of his wife sets the stage for her "natural reaction" of punishing him. The punishment is experienced as a gratuitous insult and leads to a more caustic attack. The latter, in turn, is just cause for more forceful retaliation and so on, until the husband finds that violence is "what any normal man would do under the circumstance." Neither wish the violence, both regret it; but once the familiar pattern of interchange is set in motion, it is difficult for either to avoid the escalation.

The practical implications of this work are broadly apparent. For anyone working with troubled and recurring patterns, the stage is set for inviting participants into dialogue on how their own actions form interdependent sequences and how each move by each participant may seem justified but at the same time, contributes to the pattern of the whole. This places a premium on locating ways to "act unnaturally"—to step out of the "natural" sequence and thus subvert the sequence as a whole. The unnatural act may be as simple as moving to a metalevel of conversation, in which either participant asks "Why are we doing this again?" or "Is this the way we want this to go?" To initiate this form of conversation is to step out of a debilitating sequence and into a more promising form of interchange.

Further avenues of intervention are suggested by Pearce and Cronen's (1980) observation that participants in these unwanted interchanges typically embellish them with stories. For example, they can describe how their actions fit with their broader understanding of themselves, their relationships, and their cultural life more generally. "I am not the kind of person who stands for this kind of abuse," a participant might relate. "My father was so aggressive, and I didn't respect her for not standing up to him. I'm not going to have this kind of life." Typically, each participant can justify his or her actions in just these kinds of narratives. In terms of practical implications, this suggests that further discussions can be initiated into the broader understandings that support the unwanted patterns. Attention may be focused on the deeper logic into which otherwise irrational actions fit. To frame the other as acting intelligibly within a given way of seeing the world changes the focus of conversation and the meaning of irrationality itself. It is not the "evil other" with whom one contends but an externalized logic that could be negotiated. In effect, participants step out of the sequence to focus on their construction of the situation.

More generally, within the arena of conjoint relations, it is useful to envision a conversation in which the sense of independent individuals gives way to the dominant discourse of we. "We are attentive." "We are caring." "We did that argument well." "We don't do supportive conversations well." In arguing for just this sort of discourse, Shotter (1984) points out that once the we is asserted as a conversational reality, the problem of ascertaining individual intentions, motives, or responsibility becomes either uninteresting or impossible. In a similar vein, Pearce (1993) describes a dialogic perspective where the central concern is with how we coordinate our activities so that we can relate more adequately. As he proposes, "This perspective gives rise to questions about what kind of person I will become if we produce this or that form of conversation" (p. 80).

In other sources, Pearce (1989) has referred to this emphasis on conjoint relations as *cosmopolitan communication,* which he claims "results from a commitment to find ways of achieving coordination without (1) denying the existence . . . of 'other' ways of achieving coherence (and without) (2) deprecating or opposing 'other' ways of achieving coherence" (p. 169). With these descriptions in place, we are well on our way to participating in forms of relationship where joint accomplishments are substituted for individual agency.

INVOKING GROUP REALITIES

We are careful now about who we spend time with as a couple. Sandra and John share with us all their antagonisms; we join sides and soon find ourselves angry with each other. Fred and Nancy seem so deeply loving; their devotion for each other is worn on their sleeves. In their company, we soon find ourselves doubting our own feelings toward each other; our relationship seems superficial by comparison. Don and Rhoda have developed such constraints on what we can all talk about together—no politics, no abstract ideas, no gossip—that within an hour, we find ourselves desperately bored. We shoot barbs at each other for the banality of each other's remarks. When we chose our friends, we seemed to fashion ourselves.

As a young faculty member, I used to feel fiercely fractionated. I seemed to be several different people: there was my scholarship, my teaching, my committee work, my family, my friendships, my life in my community, and so on. I began to feel overwhelmed by the conflict. My writing seemed to conflict with committee meetings; class preparations suffered because of the needs of my family; I couldn't honor my friendships because of the demands of my scholarship. Life began to change when an administrator told me he was pleased with the work I had been doing for the University community and that he felt it was an effective extension of the theory I was working on in my writing. The reframing was marvelous. I began to see all these otherwise compartmentalized activities as drawing importantly from each other, with each site offering resources for the others. Each relationship enriched the next.

Not long ago, I was asked to facilitate a discussion among members of a community-based health practice in which hostilities were rampant. To begin the discussion, I asked the members to describe how they came to join the practice and to summarize their own backgrounds and specific interests as they related to the practice. As the stories unfolded, one could see that the room was populated with representatives from disparate "professional communities." Each community had a strong but very different investment in the health practice, its purpose, and its rationale. As we later talked about the way in which the members' decisions reflected these professional communities and the interest of the communities in the well-being of the health practice as a whole, antagonisms began to wane. The practice no longer seem dominated by bad characters, individuals making unwise and selfish decisions, but by people doing their best according to their communities of origin. And their best was intended for the benefit of the organization as a whole. I left the session very encouraged.

We shift focus now to relations among relations—to relational responsibility as generated by expanding our scope of dialogue to relations among groups. If we treat a problematic action not as an outcome of individual intent but as a manifestation of a group (or the relations among groups), we open alternatives to the reflex of individual blame. To press this line of argument into action, we again draw on several existing resources.

Initially invited are practices that enable people to appreciate the meaning of so-called bad actions from within the perspectives of the groups that give them birth. "Can I understand what you have done in terms of the group to which you belong?" Here, for example, traditional role-playing practices may be useful. As outlined earlier, we carry with us multiple intelligibilities, some of which contain an appreciation for actions we find ourselves publicly abhorring. We may detest the roar of an unmuffled teenage car, the beer bottles tossed on the roadside, and the wanton damage to other's property, but suppress in our anger the remembrance of the untamed excess that stimulated the epiphanies of our own youth. Parents positioned as admonishing agents in relationship to their own errant offspring may be particularly sealed from these potentials—just as their children may not be able to recall the voice of adult responsibility that they have absorbed so well from the ambient culture. For the therapist, guidance counselor, or family friend, there is an open invitation for both the parents and their young to explore the group realities of the "adversary."

In a related vein, it can also be useful to think in terms of invoking the presence of off-stage groups. That is, various practices may make the absent groups more vivid and salient. Participants can be invited to consider and identify who has commissioned them. In other words, what other persons have some investment in their participation in the current undertaking? The ensuing conversation typically makes manifest the views and values of absent groups to which the participants are related and that affect their actions in the group. Often, one finds that individuals are commissioned not by one group or individual but by several. In this way, participants begin to see more clearly the complex tensions expressed in their behavior together. Furthermore, participants can begin to understand their group itself as a relational product—not the responsibility of any one alone but of the interaction among them. Some consultants work toward a similar end by having a chair placed in the current setting to represent absent others who have a stake in the issues under discussion.

There is an alternative approach to invoking the presence of outside groups, one that uses intergroup conflict in the culture at large to explain local conflicts within a relationship. By framing an interpersonal antagonism as a manifestation of larger group relations, the tendency is reduced to see each other as personally faulty. Rather than blaming each other, participants may come to see themselves as playing out group antagonisms—puppets to outside forces. The stage for such conversations is already set by the strong tendency within the culture to personalize groups. Thus, for example, popularized accounts of gender differences—such as Tannen's (1990) *You Just Don't Understand* and Gray's (1992) *Men Are From Mars, Women Are From Venus*—have the effect of framing otherwise individual conflict in terms of group relations. To shift the conversation from faulty individuals to problematic group differences moves the topic of conversation outward to cultural issues and raises the possibility of rebelling from the norm and "becoming an exception."

Expanding on the idea of group presence in an interesting way, Tom Andersen and his colleagues (Andersen, 1991) work therapeutically by physically bringing an outside group into the problem situation. Specifically, they ask a team of individuals to observe family therapy proceedings. At a certain juncture, these observers are admitted into the presence of the family and are asked to talk about what they have heard and seen. When the observing group has finished offering their reflections, those who have come for therapy are invited to talk about what they have heard. This shifting from what Andersen calls "the listening position" to "the reflecting position" continues throughout the therapy session. This practice not only brings fresh voices and otherwise absent perspectives to the therapeutic conversation. More important for our purposes, it allows clients to see the constructed character of the realities in which they live, to see them as group constructed rather than individually produced. In addition, Andersen finds that one group frequently invites the other group into direct conversation. The result is that the family increasingly sees itself as forming a singular unit.

As we have reasoned, by seeing individual action as commissioned by others or as manifestations of intergroup relations, the tendency to blame the individual is mitigated. At the same time, however, the result may be an intensification of group blame. One may conclude that it is the entire group that is "rotten," including the single member. At this point, the emphasis must turn to means of bringing conflicting group realities into coordination. How, then, can people tell their stories in such a way that they stimulate interest rather than inquisition and enable alien groups to live more peacefully with each other?

One useful example is furnished by the Public Conversation Project in Watertown, Massachusetts (Roth, Chasin, Chasin, Becker, & Herzig 1992). Here, issues of broad social consequence—such as abortion and homosexuality—are discussed by "conflicting" parties in a manner we would consider relationally responsible. To achieve productive dialogue, rules are preestablished: Individuals will not be interrupted, no disparaging commentary is allowed, and each participant will be allowed full opportunity to speak. Furthermore, each speaker is encouraged to make himself or herself intelligible through personal stories. Thus, the reasons for one's feelings about the abortion issue, for example, are personalized and concretized. A participant who explains her own abortion following a rape is not attacking the opposition on the grounds of abstract principles; rather, she is inviting them to share her life experiences.

Yet it is not only the personalized and nonaggressive nature of participants' stories that seems effective in these conversations. In the wake of asking about each person's unique relationship to the issue, two additional questions are addressed. Each participant is first asked to identify what is at the heart of the matter for him or her—why commitment to the issue is truly important—and second, to comment on the foggy or gray areas of this issue. Typically, participants find they can agree with the stated motives (e.g., "I think it will improve our lives together") of the so-called opposition. And by sharing doubts, the groups replace a posture of attack with the admission of vulnerabilities. By locating each person's rationality within their own stories and by structuring the situation such that each person can be heard, the project creates a conversational context with lessened risk. The broader communities of "prochoice" and "prolife" move from postures of mutual annihilation to exploring possible affinities.

ENTERING THE SYSTEMIC SWIM

So little seemed to function well in this Italian city—the transportation, police, sanitation, and power systems all seemed to operate sporadically. "People don't pay the taxes," my Italian friend explained. "Because so many cheat on their taxes, there is no money for these public services." Immediately, I felt a sense of irritation at this irresponsible attitude. "But," my friend went on, "they don't pay their taxes because so many of the government officials are corrupt." My ire shifted to the government officials. How can they be so irresponsible? "They are corrupt," he explained, "because so many people get various favors and payoffs—political functionaries, businessmen, and even organized crime. All prosper, and this prosperity trickles down to others." I sighed. Who is to be punished, when the people benefit from the very system that so ineptly serves them?

A fast-foods store recently closed in a nearby neighborhood. I asked the proprietor why it was necessary to close, because the store was one of the few in which young people from the predominantly black district could get work. "I can't hire help with enough education to do most of the jobs," he complained. "And there is a lot of theft; I can't make a go of it." I then remembered last year's report on the city educational system and the fact that a great proportion of the youth scarcely attend classes. The report, in turn, blamed the poor educational productivity on the lack of stable homes to give the children the kind of support and guidance needed for school success. As a colleague in sociology explained, home life is unstable because the males cannot find work; they don't have the education. The situation is worsened by a general public who really doesn't care much about life in these conditions—unless they are victims of the resulting crime—in which case, they simply vote for more police and prisons.

The faculty claim the administration is inept. Administrators claim that their attempts to respond to the faculty needs are thwarted by the Board of Trustees. The Board is constrained by the state government that must allocate limited funds among competing demands (welfare, education, etc.). The state responds to the conservative vote of the public, who simultaneously demands inexpensive public education and extensive social support services. The voters continually vote against a state tax, thus limiting the amount of revenue the state government can allocate for public services. Many parents and children of the state bemoan the relatively high cost of public education yet feel sympathetic to the underpaid faculty, although others view life at the university as irrelevant and easy.

These fragments of daily life move our concerns outward into the full domain of cultural life. Here, we explore the ways in which even the simplest of actions is embedded within an infinitely expanded domain. There is no event in itself—no individual action, no family interaction, no community—nothing that is not simultaneously a constituent of just possibly all that there is. Practically speaking, however, to think in terms of all that there is provides little rationale for action. In the face of "everything is related," what is there to do? We thus propose the following imagery: We have at our disposal numerous ways of categorizing the social world. We distinguish among individuals, couples, families, clubs, organizations, nations, and so on. Furthermore, let us imagine the possibility of relations among various units—let us say, between the couple and the extended family, the family and the community, the community and the regional government, and so on.

As we variously generate pairs from this extended domain, new questions and curiosities emerge. How is family life related to the regional government, how is community action related to national policy, how is individual action related to international economic relations, and so on? Each relationship, in effect, shifts the topic of the conversation or inquiry outward. As we broaden the range of relationships under consideration, we move increasingly to a sensitivity of the systemic whole. Most important, as we come to appreciate the worlds produced by these various conceptual connections, new practical options become available as replacements for the tradition of individual blame.

At the initial level of relating configurations, consider for example, the early work of Murray Bowen (1965). Bowen was a central figure in the move from individual psychotherapy to a more relational form of family therapy. In his early work, Bowen abandoned therapy devoted to individual problems, not to replace it only with family discussions but with full community participation. At the level of family involvement, Bowen launched an unusual program whereby the family of hospitalized schizophrenics literally moved into the hospital with the patient. In treatment, Bowen included not only family members of the hospitalized patient but the hospital staff and significantly involved others. In many of his sessions, family, friends, medical professionals, and other stakeholders participated in discussing "the problem." How are we involved; what is our role in all this; how can we work together to create change? All become significant questions.

Another early illustration of expanding our focus beyond the unit of the individual or family is demonstrated in the work of Boszormenyi-Nagy (1966). His concern was less with individual problems and more with survival of the group. Employing the metaphor of accounting, Boszormenyi-Nagy invited participants to explore debts and payments incurred in past generations or in related groupings that might come to bear on the present so-called problem. For example, the in-law's expectation for a wife to raise a family might create marital tension despite both spouses' agreements to each other to pursue professional lives. Individual action is no longer the possession of the individual in these practices but of the full set of extended relations. The therapist simply creates an atmosphere where participants can address what they see as their debts or undue payments.

In more recent extensions of this orientation, therapists in Finland (Seikkula et al., 1995) have developed a practice of bringing members of the community together to discuss problems that have traditionally been cast as the property of individuals. Whether there is concern with school performance or delusional episodes, therapists working in teams invite a host of participants to join in discussion of the problem. Included might be school officials, medical professionals, neighbors, friends, family members, and sometimes even more distant relatives or acquaintances. This conversational format aids in the construction of their understanding of locally defined problems in terms of broader relational configurations. For example, an unexpected consequence of a meeting among mental health professionals, a psychotic patient, and the town planner might be the generation of a new sensitivity on the part of the town planner to the patient's daily living constraints. Also initiated might be the mental health professionals' understandings of the complex issues faced by the town planner. A pragmatic discussion by this group about the quality of life for all members of the community not only shifts the discourse away from further pathologizing of the patient's situation but gives voice to other issues of relevance and importance to that patient. These sorts of conversations may be significant building blocks for future relational networks that may, in the long run, benefit many members of the community. As in the illustrations offered by Bowen (1965) and Boszormenyi-Nagy (1966), the sense of responsibility for individual action becomes spread throughout the community.

In a similar vein, bold experiments on large-group decision making are being conducted in organizations (Jacobs, 1994; Owen, 1992). Organizational consultants have introduced several models that bring all members of an organization together in revisioning the organization. One such model developed by Harrison Owen (1992) is called *open space*. As part of Owen's program of events, he invites organizational members to post topics or issues of interest in a central place. Over the course of his workshops, members survey the topics posted by their colleagues and are free to add their names to the topic that interests them most. At a designated time, groups are formed around the proposed topics. Owen assumes that whoever is present in the group is who should be present and whatever happens in the group is supposed to happen. The groups discuss the issue and often propose strategies for change. After some hours, the groups convene and share their work with the entire gathering. Owen's intent is to draw on the rich resources already available within the organization and to allow participation in reorganization by members at all levels. In this way, problems that were previously identified as local or germane to one unit or level of the organization are seen in a broader, more extended context. Different voices are given a hearing and consequently, different organizational possibilities are generated.

Under the umbrella term of *systems consultation,* there are also movements bringing family therapists into consultation with medical organizations, community groups, social service systems, the military, and business (Campbell, Draper, & Huffington, 1989; Fruggeri, Telfner, Castellucci, Marzari, & Matteini, 1991; Wynne, McDaniel, & Weber, 1986). A central assumption in this work is that treatment of an individual or family cannot be understood apart from the political and economic climate of a community, region, or country. For example, mental health professionals have moved their drug rehabilitation efforts away from treatment of individuals toward forms of practice involving entire communities. Professionals might, for example, solicit a group of students to work as partners in the development of rehabilitative and educational programs. The resulting discussions often include not only students, teachers, and parents but might call on community leaders and other concerned and interested citizens. The programs that evolve are very closely linked to the political and economic constraints as well as the potentials of the community. Given the broad investment in these programs, greater success is likely.

Fruggeri et al. (1991) describe how drug addicts, who have made use of the local social services, are employed as volunteer "social workers." With support from the community services, these volunteers go to the streets and encourage other drug users to attend informational sessions. Here, the clients themselves become the therapists providing peer education and building relationships to encourage rehabilitation.

Not only do these creative efforts redistribute human and financial resources within the community but in addition, they draw members into relationally responsible forms of practice. There is great potential in these practices for tracing microsocial processes (e.g., couples, families) to broader contexts, such as business and industry. Are there ways, for example, in which local industries can join forces with schools to develop programs to give teenagers career skills and simultaneously reduce the amount of time for gang-related activities? What other contributions could businesses make to the financial well-being of the communities in which they reside, thereby reducing some of the strain on community members' finances? These are just a few of the ideas suggested by this creative group of systemic consultants.

In a broader sense, each of these single practices operates as a disorienting device. Each of them unsettles one or more ways of explaining who or what is responsible for a given outcome and suggests an alternative frame. Each brings to the moment an alternative discourse and thus, a new way of moving in conversation and action. We are disoriented in particular from the vocabulary of individual blame and inner subjectivity and launched into the broader spectrum of potentials. At the same time, however, we should view each of these practices as simultaneously isolated—holding in focus one particular set of relations while excluding others. Although each is a useful intervention—an innovative contribution to the process of relational responsibility—we should never forget the boundaries drawn around the focal set of relations and the myriad possibilities that are created by lifting these boundaries. Thus, we may ultimately envision a broadened inquiry in which each of these practices is viewed in terms of still further constituents of the whole. How are the extended family and community relationships—so central to Bowen, Boszormenyi-Nagy, organizational consultants, and to the Finns—related to broader systems of media, economics, or cultural values, for example: How is organizational action interdependent with governmental policies or the values of customers in other countries? Ultimately, we might hope that these kinds of questions, and resulting practices, would also come to embrace issues in ecology. Relational responsibility should not cease with considerations of human action alone.

CONTINGENT CONCLUSIONS

To conclude, we are placing a strong value not on products but on an immersion in process—continuous processes of comprehending, adjudicating, and adjusting within relationships. We are deemphasizing final products—fixing blame, correcting errors, solving the problem—in favor of continuous engagement in relational inquiry. Yes, there are momentary conclusions, clearings, and resolutions, but each gives way to further immersion in process. We achieve, then, not a harmonious conclusion or final stopping place but continuous engagement in the process of generating meaning. At the same time, we are placing a strong value on relational life itself, that is, a condition in which actions are coordinated with the vast surrounds from which they derive their identity. We are suggesting a move beyond formalized, stable identification of responsible action toward a sensibility that sustains a relationship. Our ultimate hope is for an open-ended process of world coordination, which, in effect, constitutes relational responsibility in its most extended form. We now turn to an illustration of relational responsibility in practice. This illustration is followed by our companions' voices.

NOTES

1. For additional work on generating positive organizational futures, see the list of offerings and materials provided by The Taos Institute (http://www.serve.com/taos), which is dedicated to applications of social construction in organizational and therapeutic practices.

2. For reviews of the Milan Team's circular questioning techniques, see Tomm (1985) and Penn (1985).

3

A Case in Point

We have now treated four conversational logics, each favoring a shift from individual to relational responsibility. We do not propose that it is a simple matter to abandon long-standing patterns of exchange in favor of more novel moves in conversation. Even we who write about such matters continue to be enticed by the pleasures of blame and individualized understandings. Yet even though our experience does suggest that these conversational shifts hold substantial promise for the normal give and take of daily life, what can be said about those cases in which the moral fiber is deeply disturbed, in which we not only wish to blame but feel that we would indeed be morally remiss should we not? Is a shift to relational responsibility even plausible under such circumstances? Let us explore this question by considering what for us is a very difficult case, one in which we are impulsively drawn toward individual blame. And in considering the case, let us bring to bear the four logics developed in Chapter 2. Can they make a convincing difference? Our aim here is not to offer concrete evidence that relational responsibility will, does, or could eradicate our traditional tendencies. Rather, our goal is to explore departures that have potential for valuing, sustaining, and creating forms of relationship where common meaning can take wing.

There is little that elicits more profound public outrage than child molestation. The impulse to punish the perpetrator is intense and seemingly unmitigated. If not quintessentially evil, he (typically) is viewed as morally corrupt or degenerate. In the most enlightened context, he may be seen as emotionally perverted, or mentally ill. In any case, he is to blame. Long-term incarceration and possible hospitalization are common. In what sense would an advocate of relational responsibility have it otherwise?

At the outset, it must be recalled that by advancing relational responsibility, we are not attempting to eradicate the individualist tradition. Rather, we are opting for a space of critical reflection, to ask about the limitations of this tradition and possible alternatives. Here, it is important to underscore the difficulties in justifying individual blame in these cases on grounds that the perpetrator chose to act in a given way. Virtually the entirety of the behavioral science and mental health movements of the present century serve as prominent challenges to the assumption of free agency. Nor is there any ultimate warrant for the presumption shared within these latter quarters that the individual's actions were determined by environmental and hereditary causes. These, too, are constructions whose warrant is derived from evidence already produced and understood within these frameworks.

Nor is it fully clear that punishment for wrongdoing functions as a significant deterrent. The controversy over the effects of the death penalty for capital crimes continues even today. In fact, there is an ironic way in which the righteous urge toward castigation lends itself to an increment in child molesting. As our ire turns to desire for prevention, so do we become increasingly sensitized to the possibilities of abuse. The newspapers, courts, schools, churches, and the populace at large go on alert. As we search, so we shall find. For the very categories of understanding that motivate the search for justice and prevention also become the means by which we index otherwise ambiguous events. Our indignation creates the very conditions for constructing a world in terms of abusers and victims. And as we construct the world in these terms, an increasing number of people are rendered guilty. The recent epidemic of purported recovered memories of abuse is a case in point.

Important from our perspective is also the way in which the traditional mode of individual blame moves toward a truncation of the meaning-making process. When we presume that individuals are simply to blame for their crimes and that the execution of justice (and possible therapy) is sufficient for our returning to normal life with a clean conscience and sigh of relief, then the cultural dialogue comes to a close. We have a tidy means of settling difficult problems, and further discussion is unnecessary. On the practical level, the termination of dialogue means the erosion of sensitivity to context, to the many differing meanings of an otherwise similar act as performed in various settings by different persons. It also closes discussion of the multiplex web of conditions that might favor what we call child molesting. We cease being curious, searching for cooperative means of creating a livable future together. Most pointedly, we remove ourselves from the case; we need do nothing, alter our actions one whit, for the case has nothing to do with us. We simply go on with life as usual . . . until the next atrocity.

It is in this light that we turn to the concept and practice of relational responsibility, not as a means of removing punishment, adjudicating more accurately, or spreading the blame, but rather, of broadening and enriching the conversation and thus, our options for action. Consider first the search for internal others. Significant openings can be generated by inquiring into the many voices that "speak the guilty party." At the outset, such inquiry breaks the stranglehold of the unified ego. By this, we mean that our traditional tendency to see the individual as a singular mind—and in this case an evil one—is undermined. There may be evil, but there is more. We find the person constituted by many voices, some dear and valuable, thus subverting our reflex to rage. This move is already prepared by forms of therapy focusing on the early home life of the perpertrator. Many therapists have found that men who sexually abuse children have been sexually abused themselves. Their abuse, in effect, may speak the voice of their elders. And if we inquire into other voices within—for example, those aspiring to be a responsible parent and a loving spouse—we open a door to recementing family relationships otherwise permanently sundered.

There is further value in exploring voices within. First, within therapy, these other voices may be used as means of generating internal dialogue, dialogue that could have preventative effects. By inquiring, for example, into what the perpetrator believes his victim, his spouse, his father and mother, his friends, his legal adviser, or his neighbors would feel, their voices are made increasingly salient. If means can be located of sustaining this salience from day to day, then the context of construction is altered for the person. The internal dialogue functions as a preventative. On the broader societal level, inquiry into internal others may give us an enriched grasp of the more subtle entries into individual meaning. For example, there is a subtle way in which the media discussion of child abuse contributes to its frequency. As the various news media thrive on reputed cases of abuse, so does the very intelligibility of the act become crystallized. Steeped in such stories, people who had never before considered children a source of erotic arousal begin a new pattern of viewing. Through the voice of the media, the realm of the erotic expands, and increasingly, child molesting becomes "a choice" as opposed to an absurdity. Inquiries into the way such voices speak the perpetrator open new conversations about media responsibility.

Let us turn from internal others to conjoint relations. Here, it is essential to recognize the constructed character of child abuse. That is, child molesting is not simply there in nature, to be recognized for what it is. Rather, we are dealing here with culturally constructed categories, and to where and to whom they apply and with what implications are matters of cultural and historical situation. Does fondling a child, sponging his or her genitals, or rolling naked together in a bed constitute molestation?—many would answer in the affirmative, others would not. To put it otherwise, the existence of child molesting requires conjoint relations. The actions in question may have meant one thing to the participants at the time and another thing as they later spoke about them. And as further conversations take place, they may be additionally constituted. In terms of relational responsibility, the point is not to locate the truth so much as to sustain enough ambiguity that the door to meaning making is never finally closed.

In this context, there is wisdom in exploring, with those involved in a potential case, the multiple meanings that may have been at play for them. What interpretations were made of various words and actions and even silences? How was the abuse brought about or made possible, in action and interpretation? How were the actions and inactions of those around made intelligible? Nor should such inquiry be limited to narratives of an earlier time or voiced to a single interlocutor. What story could be made conjointly intelligible in dialogue with one's parents, siblings, or friends or perhaps a therapist or a lawyer? Each conversation may raise new issues and insights through which to ramify "the event(s)."

Let us turn to the possibilities of invoking group realities. It is difficult to think of participants in child abuse representing or acting on behalf of broader groups in society. Again, however, it is important to remain curious about such possibilities. To what extent, for example, is a male offender representing or acting on behalf of males more generally? Why do males believe they have the right to abuse a child? Is it partially because of the male mythology of paternal ownership of the family? By dint of tradition, the male is encouraged to view the family as "mine," living in "my castle," and "I am the lord and lawmaker of what takes place." Such mythology also furnishes insight into why the probability of a child being molested by a stepfather is much higher than by the progenitor. The stepfather is obligated to take care of another man's property, for which no recompense is provided. On this symbolic level, that he should ask the offspring for special indulgences is his unspoken right. In effect, child molesters may speak for a male tradition that itself requires challenge.

The possibility for exploring a multiplicity of group realities also emerges after accusations of abuse occur. Different family members may each live within separate enclaves of meaning—family circles, friendship groups, police, attorneys, and so on. There will be many different stories to tell under these circumstances, multiple creations of the purported event and its significance.

Unfortunately, the press toward individual blame holds such powerful sway in contemporary culture that there is no easy means for sharing meaning across the different groups. There is typically the realist question of guilt or innocence to be resolved and if potential guilt, there is blame and defense. Once the contours of conflict are established, our forms of deliberation scarcely permit more than attack and defense. Ultimately, in the service of relational responsibility, we must search for new modes of dialogue.

Last, we must consider explorations of the systemic swim. Given the enormous problems inhering in the view of the person as an originating source of action, how can we broaden our understanding of contributing factors? If we can view child abuse not as a personal action but as a cultural achievement, what aspects of culture lend themselves to such actions? These are particularly important questions, because they open options for changing the cultural conditions. They prevent the easy resolution—"He is evil, and it has nothing to do with me"—and ask us to consider our own unwitting contribution to the ethos of abuse. Opening discussion on these matters may lead in many significant directions. We have already mentioned the media's role in generating the intelligibility of molestation. This role may be small in comparison with the more general media reliance on erotica. The media create an ambience in which sexuality is given a prominent place in life and in which inactivity is treated as failure, loss, or unnatural. Furthermore, because the same media furnish models for dress and manners of young women, the salience of sexuality is reasserted in all walks of life. And of particular significance, as young girls, even children, model themselves on these figures, they become increasingly Lolita-like in their appearance. JonBenet is a case in point. Contributing to these trends are parents, clothing stylists, clothing manufacturers, and beauty pageant directors, among others. All join the media in generating a context for child molesting.

At this juncture, we wish to reassert that our discussion of child sexual abuse is not directed at providing solutions. Nor is it intended to convey some masked approval on our part for such activities. Our hope is to expand our resources for action and thus for understanding—and to do so by demonstrating how a fluid movement among the four conversational logics we have proposed earlier might expand our possibilities in such difficult scenarios.

In the following section, we move to the voices of our respondents. As mentioned earlier, our desire has been to create a book that in some small way put relational responsibility into practice. The responses that follow represent significant relationships—in varying forms—and expand, critique, and limit the meaning of relational responsibility.

PART **2**

Expanding the Dialogue

4

When Stories Have Wings

How Relational Responsibility Opens New Options for Action

David L. Cooperrider
Diana Whitney

Has social contructionism any practical use? What might it mean in practical terms to address the myriad issues related to "responsibility" in America's inner cities—where the issues of housing, crime, poverty, education, and fractured family relations dominate our media and sap the hope of the most idealistic citizens and optimistic new leaders? Can anyone really argue that traditional ways of talking about and nurturing responsibility—in which the individual serves as the originary source and to whom we apply devices of correction and restoration—is the way forward in the future? What alternatives open up to us when responsibility is constructed in relational terms, where responsibility is an emergent sociogenic achievement, born and renewed daily in the conversational search for the "good" and the "possible?" What alternatives open up when we take seriously the pathway suggested by Sheila McNamee and Kenneth Gergen where there is a "deemphasizing of final products" (e.g., final definitions of responsibility) and instead an emphasis on "keen appreciation of relationships—intimacies, friendships, groups, communities, institutions and cultures" (p. 10), and

> immersion in process . . . toward a sensibility that sustains a conversation of the many. . . . We believe that the attempt to bring our varying identities, partners, relationships, and communities into conversation situates us within a open-ended

process of world coordination, which in effect constitutes relational responsibility in its most extended form. (pp. 47-48)

Presented here is a fascinating story regarding the linguistic space where consensually crafted positive accounts of responsibility are shared, reconstructed, and ultimately embodied in practice. It is a story that grows out of the soil of social constructionist thought via the practice of appreciative inquiry (Cooperrider, 1996; Cooperrider & Srivastva, 1981). And it is a story of hope—it is located in the heart of one of America's troubled and divided cities.

Although lessons from the narration are many, we will place prominence on two particularly exceptional features of this story. The first has to do with the power of intergenerational conversation as a particular relational site that holds great promise for inspiring new images of relational responsibility. The second has to do with relationally constructive vocabularies. What the story illustrates is that intergenerational relationships thrive where there is an appreciative voice giving rise to conjoint valuing—where young and old see the best in one another's life experiences and histories; where there is a sharing of dreams and ultimate concerns in mutually affirming ways; and where the generations are connected in full voice to create not just new worlds but better worlds. Conspicuously absent from this effort to create communitywide change, where the children figured prominently as catalysts, were the traditional and highly professionalized vocabularies of human deficit. As the reader will see, there is much in this story that is counterintuitive—and inspiring. It brings the social construction of reality into the realm of practice in a reflexive, relationally expansive, and intergenerational way.

IMAGINE CHICAGO: HOW WOULD YOU APPROACH RELATIONAL RESPONSIBILITY WITH 7 MILLION PEOPLE?

We want to tell you about a successful businesswoman—a corporate banking executive for 16 years at First Chicago—who one day decided to leave it all to devote her next 10 years to transforming the city's future. Trained in organization development (OD), savvy in action research methodologies, and a visionary in her own right, Bliss Browne asked the question, What might happen if all of Chicago's citizens were mobilized to give public expression, continuously, to their imagination about a healthy future for the city as a whole and were invited to claim their role in bringing that vision to life? Could it be that we human beings create our own realities through imagination and conversational processes and that the creation of positive images on a collective basis in our 3-million-person city might well be the most prolific activity that individuals and organizations can engage in if their aim is to help bring to fruition a positive and humanly significant future?

The story begins with a conference where community and business leaders met to discuss how imagination, economics, and faith could make the city a better place. But there were major concerns: surveys, for example, showing 85% of U.S. citizens losing faith in the future of our cities as well as in the institutions that govern them; images of cities as hellholes (just look at the demonized picture of urban America in our movies and the nightly news); and the malaise of our young where the negative images have been correlated with apathy, cynicism, fear, discrimination, and other damaging behavior. Ways were needed, agreed the participants, to rebuild essential connections, to renew hope, and to reinvigorate human creativity and leadership at all levels. Browne believed that how one conceives of the city shapes how one lives in the city. Cities echo creation. They are a living symbol of our ability to imagine and create, to turn our visions into tangible products. They are an inventory of the possible and incarnation of human capacity and diversity. Cities concentrate forces of darkness and light and hold the world in miniature.

Imagine Chicago, now a 4-year-old, nonprofit organization, was born out of that and subsequent meetings. Imagine Chicago is a catalyst for civic innovation, working to bring people who live and work in Chicago to the realization that they are the owners and creators of Chicago's future. The MacArthur Foundation funded the first several years' pilot project. And when theories and practices of change were sought out, appreciative inquiry (AI) was selected as the approach most likely to help serve as a catalyst for civic innovation.

The outcomes have been dramatic. The pilot included more than 800 individuals in more than 40 neighborhoods, with involvement of more than 100 community organizations and schools. For example, Imagine Chicago, in collaboration with Barbara Radner, the Director of the Center For Urban Education at DePaul University, developed a citizenship curriculum now being used by 4,000 Chicago public school students. Though only a young organization, Imagine Chicago has already attracted broad recognition: a national award in 1995 from Eureka Communities in Washington, DC, for its exemplary work on behalf of children and their families; citation by the Mayor's Youth Development Task Force in 1994; and perhaps the most profound recognition, that of being emulated—

there is now an Imagine Dallas organization as well as plans in other cities and in other parts of the world, including an initiative called Imagine Africa.

A Most Extraordinary Learning

The process of AI unfolds through a cycle of four phases that together comprise a 4-D model: discovery, dream, design, and destiny. At the core of the cycle is the frame or forestructure for the inquiry—the topic(s) that are chosen and will ultimately guide the formulation of questions for discovery. AI begins and ends with valuing that which gives life to a community or organization. In this sense, the broadest topic behind any AI is the constructive discovery of the community's or the organization's "life-giving" story. Focus is first placed on what the community or organization has done well in the past and is doing well in the present. Participants are asked what factors give life to this organization when it is and has been most alive, successful, and effective. Second, participants are invited to dream about and design a better future. What are the possibilities, expressed and unexpressed, that provide opportunities for more effective (vision-congruent) forms of community or organization?

Using these two broad questions as guides, communities and organizations "home grow" their own more specific topics. The topics, to begin with, are bold hunches about what gives life to the human system. Most important, the topics (usually three to five areas for inquiry) represent what people really want to discover or learn more about and that will likely evoke conversations about the desired future. It is commonly said in doing AI that the seeds of change are implicit in the first questions that are asked. As human systems often conversationally construct realities in the directions they inquire into, people are encouraged to select topics of those things they most want to see grow and flourish in their communities or organizations.

One of the important logistical questions for Imagine Chicago had to do with scale: How to create an appreciative 4-D cycle with such a large system. When we first met with the design team, they asked about "mass mobilization" methods for each of the phases. There was talk, very early on, of wanting to conduct appreciative interviews with 1 million people—at least one interview for every household in the city. Now it appears, as the whole thing is blossoming, that many more than that will happen as new requests, programs, opportunities, and technologies are multiplying. But more important than scale was the other key question: Who should do the interviews? Should data collection be done by professors? OD consultants? Doctoral students from the University of Chicago? How much training would be required?

This is where the remarkable learning happened. It continues to leave us breathless. The pilot's very best interviews—resulting in the most inspiring stories, the most passion-filled data, the most textured and well-illustrated examples, the most daring images of possibility—were all conducted by children of Chicago. The most powerful interviews were when young people with scarcely any experience in interviewing sat down and held dialogues with the city's elders—priests, CEOs, school principals, parents, entertainers, artists, activists, mystics, scientists. Although the radically appreciative questions were of course one input into the conversations, there was something more important happening in this process. Clearly, it was not the training. Nor was it previous expertise in data collection. What stands out is the relational configuration—it was the intergenerational dynamic of the dialogue that made the data collection stage soar. (One is reminded of Margaret Mead's hypothesis that the best societal learning has always occurred when three generations come together in contexts of discovery and valuing—the child, the elder, and the adult parents.) Let's look further.

Appreciation and Discourse

An observer described the chemistry in the interviews as magical. One 72-year-old respondent said at the conclusion of his interview,

> I really thank you for this conversation. You got all of me. That hasn't happened too often in my life. You valued me. You forced me to share my visions and crystallize them into clear images. This has given me tremendous hope. Now that I can articulate clearly, I know they are doable.

In the classic interview, for example, a 13-year-old requests a time to meet with his principal. As interviewer, he raises many questions: "As you reflect on your career, can you tell me the story of a high point; a time you felt most alive, most impactful, most successful in terms of contribution to this school and community?" The principal scratches her head, even starts a bit slowly, but soon is in full voice. The young person, listening to the drama, gets so excited with the story of courage and conviction that he cannot sit quietly. He interrupts the flow and blurts out, "So what was it about you that made it a high point . . . what are your best qualities . . . can you tell me what you value most about yourself?"

A little later, the topic switches to more volatile topics, such as race relations. Again, the positive query: "Thinking about your school's contributions to building higher quality multiracial and multicultural relationships, what have you done in this area that has made the biggest difference? What one thing are you most proud about?" The stories are told, one after the other. The interview lasts an hour longer than planned. Later, an evaluation team follows up with the school principal to get feedback on the dynamic of the interview. Typical comments included

> "I've never been asked these types of questions by youth in this school; when I do converse with the students, it is usually for disciplinary reasons."
>
> "That night, after the interview, I laid wide awake. I could not sleep. I kept replaying the conversation. I got back in touch with a lot of things important to me. . . . I also articulated some ideas of a better world I never put words to before."
>
> "You know, during that interview, I really felt like I was on the pulpit. I got animated. I was literally looking into the face of the future, exploring the essential elements of the good society. This conversation mattered."

Barbara Radner's (1993) studies at Loyola University show that when the appreciative civic inquiry methods are brought into the curriculum (in 13 Chicago Public Schools), children's achievement in all areas (including math, reading, writing, etc.) rises significantly in comparison to controls. In doing the interviews, children began hearing stories they would never hear on the news, on TV, or even in the more common cynical discourse of society at large. They connected with community elders in new ways and found themselves part of new networks. They began hearing experiences where change has happened for the better and developing their own images of possibility. One young person, Willie J. Hemple, was so excited and moved by his experiences, he started volunteering his time to Imagine Chicago every day after school:

> It was during my interview with Ed Brennen, CEO of Sears, that my dreams and hopes were ignited. You find you have so much in common in terms of hopes for our City. And you find out people like Ed really care, not just about money but social justice causes, about me as a young person and about our future. . . . My ideas about people like Ed and the politicians I interviewed all changed, and so has my life. That is why I want to volunteer my time now, it is all about making change happen.

Hundreds of stories akin to Willie's suggest something like this: *Where appreciation is alive and generations are reconnected through inquiry, hope grows and responsibility through relationship expands.*

To be sure, the appreciative approaches—where people were actively engaged in gathering data into the strengths, potentials, achievements, and visions of the Other—did not create a rose-colored world or a wonderful utopia free from conflict. Indeed, although the vast majority of people did experience being valued, listened to, and included in substantive ways, there were other tempests in the making. One person put it like this, after a conversation of broad sharing of perspectives: "There was so much, I just was overwhelmed, it was a sense of vertigo, like the bottom had fallen out. . . . I went into the interview with my elegant and clear priorities and came out quiet . . . and restless."

This person heard stories and visions that challenged her to get off the sidelines of complacency. She talked about certainties lost and experiencing something like a sense of vertigo. Some people, as they talked about the varieties in perspectives, began to swim in the sea of competing intelligibilities and began to acknowledge the validity of the Others' realities. It appears they simultaneously were made more conscious of their own limited assumptions and contextual biases and perhaps how parochial their own visions of the good and the possible really were. For many, this reflexive turn, this sense of arbitrariness of priority and point of view, was like the ground underfoot beginning to unexpectedly give way. Some came away embroiled in doubt.

The whole relational process was telling. The deeper the appreciative interchange (that is, the more people felt valued and in turn opened up in increasingly substantive ways), the more it appears the listeners became self-reflexively aware of the culturally conditioned approaches of their own "true" worlds. One's so-called truth, therefore, seems to become relativized by new consciousness of compelling alternatives. And not so incidentally, the alternatives in this case were all the more compelling because people were telling each other success stories. The appreciative approaches were inclusionary and valuing but also, for some, deconstructive, dislodging, and creative of reflexive doubt.

Today, Imagine Chicago is taking the lessons of its pilot into six major project initiatives: (a) The Urban Imagination Network, (b) City Dialogues, (c) Creating Chicago: A Citizens Guide, (d) City Connections, (e) Citizen Leaders, and (f) Sacred Places. In all of these, the spirit, if not the actual process, of the intergenerational conversation and appreciative forms of joint valuing will lead the way. Our own next major involvement is to help Imagine Chicago, with the support of the Kellogg Foundation, to bring the intergenerational pairs into large group interactive forums (anywhere from 100 to 1,000 people in a Future-Search-type conference) to share stories from the appreciative interviews and to construct new images of the desired future. The whole thing is exciting and is, we believe, an example of McNamee and Gergen's vision of expanding domains of relatedness, moving from conjoint relations to relations among groups to the whole system invitation of entering the systemic swim.

CONCLUSIONS

There are myriad questions to be raised about the Imagine Chicago initiative and the potential for a pragmatic social construction of future worlds where relational responsiveness and responsibility guide human action and destiny. Imagine Chicago suggests that when intergenerational inquiry and dialogue succeed in bringing forward the best of what has been and is, it simultaneously sparks a collective anticipation of an equally vital and meaningful future. Intergenerational conversations provide opportunities for a community's values and best practices to be shared and passed on. Elders are honored and renewed and members of the younger generation are inspired and moved to serve the creation of a positive future. The positive power of intergenerational inquiry and storytelling has become a lost art for much of the modern world. As follow-up to the splendid success and learnings of Imagine Chicago, we must ask ourselves two questions: How might we restore the power of intergenerational storytelling in our communities and organizations? And in addition, how might we pragmatically and consciously, through the selection of appreciative topics for inquiry, use intergenerational inquiry and dialogue to further the well-being of communities, families, and organizations around the world?

The story of Imagine Chicago suggests a need for the further development of a language of positive potential and for conversational techniques that invite a better future into being. It suggests that one approach to community-based relational responsibility includes the social construction of inquiry based on a language of positive potential. It asks us to study and to create relational resources to shift the language frame of our institutions, including education, health care, government, and business from the currently dominate discourse of human deficit toward a discourse of positive potential.

The extraordinary power of inquiry and dialogue to transform personal and community realities emerges from the story of Imagine Chicago. Imagine Chicago has been liberating and generative. In providing new images, it created new avenues for action and new hope for a better city. For some, the process was disconcerting, creating a confusion of personal priorities and an invitation to speak, act, and live in a new city changed only by conversations with a previously unknown Other. Flowing from these many examples of personal and community transformation, we must ask ourselves, How as educators, consultants, and social change agents do we really make a difference? Might it be, as Bliss Browne (1996) professed, that helping others to create positive images and discourse on a collective basis is the most important activity that we can engage in to create a relational responsible and humanly significant future?

5

Collaborative Learning Communities

Harlene Anderson

I agree with McNamee and Gergen's rationale and contrast of the implications and limits of individual responsibility and the potentials and constraints of relational responsibility. They suggest that from a social-construction perspective, responsibility is relational; it cannot be anything else. One person does not make another person relationally responsible. It occurs through and in interactions between people. I also agree that "relationally responsible inquiry has transformative potential for the participants" (p. 27, this volume) involved in any joint endeavor. As I read their words, my thoughts continually shift between the premises and the practices. My interest hovers around the question, How can I position myself with, think about, act with, and talk with others in a way that puts relational responsibility into action?

As a clinician, teacher, and consultant, I have found that relational responsibility or what I think of as shared responsibility (accountability and consequence) is inherent in collaborative relationships and processes, the essence of which is dialogue (Anderson, 1997). By dialogue, I mean a dynamic generative kind of conversation in which there is room for all voices, in which each person is wholly present, and in which there is a two-way exchange and crisscrossing of ideas, thoughts, opinions, and feelings. Likewise, learning and the development of knowledge is a dynamic generative process.

Transformation occurs in and through dialogue, and intrinsically, relationships transform. I am reminded of two questions that a colleague, Glen Boyd, (1996) posed: "What if the kinds of conversations we have are the kinds of relationships we have?" and "What if coming together in conversation creates something larger than both of us" (p. 6)?

In my capacities as a teacher, therapist, and consultant I want to invite and engage the people I work with into a dialogic space and process. Here, I focus on those aspects relevant to the discussion of relational responsibility. I will illustrate how, as a teacher, seminar leader, or supervisor, I create collaborative learning communities in which joint responsibility is invited and emerges. This involves creating learning spaces and processes in which people can connect with each other, in which there is a collaborative atmosphere, and in which people can be involved in constructing knowledge.

Because I value the concept of relational responsibility, I want to invite others to experience it in action. I believe that to invite another person into this kind of process, I must first act relationally responsible. This requires that I position myself in a particular way that demonstrates and encourages relational responsibility. I take a collaborative position. Toward this aim, I enter each learning situation maintaining an awareness throughout that cultural and organizational discourses bestow authority on teachers, placing us in hierarchical and dualistic positions. I hold the personal freedom, however, to choose how to accept and exercise that authority.

I keep in mind that the purpose of the joint circumstance and the expectations of how I will accomplish that purpose is influenced by at least three investors: the institution, the learner, and me. Each is embedded within other relationships and expectations—licensing boards, professional associations, credentialing agencies, professional settings. Each brings preformed assumptions about the learning purpose and how it will be accomplished.

Setting the stage for and sustaining collaboration commences with the first contact, usually face to face in the classroom. I have found that being open about myself and inviting others to do the same is an important first step. I begin, therefore, any course of learning by introducing myself, previewing my agenda for the course, and summarizing information and assumptions of my understanding as to why I was invited to teach and why I accepted the invitation. I am open that I am influenced by my imagined assumptions about the educational institution's purposes, by my past professional and personal experiences, and by the prejudices that I hold. These influence what I think others expect me to offer, what I think I can offer, and how I can best share that.

I want to create and facilitate a learning environment and process where participants can access, elaborate on, and produce their own unique competencies. I want each person to generate his or her individual seeds of newness and to cultivate them in the personal and professional lives that take place outside the organized learning context. I want to invite and encourage participants to take responsibility for and to be the architects of their own learning. To these ends, I want to ensure that each participant has a voice, contributes, questions, explores, is uncertain, and experiments.

To further set the stage, I might ask participants to form small conversational clusters or to talk in pairs, depending on the size of the group, to address such questions and to discuss with each other their reasons for enrolling in the course—their learning agendas, expectations, and questions or dilemmas that they want addressed. I tell them that I have many ideas and experiences to share and have access to other resources but that I do not want unilaterally to make the selection for them. Instead, I need their input as to what they want me to select out. To help me, I need to know about them, the learners: Why are they here? What are their expectations of the course and of me? What are their individual learning agendas? What are their preferred forms of learning? How do they learn? I might also ask them, "What do each of you think is the most important thing for me and the others to know about you and your everyday contexts that would help us best meet your learning agenda and match your learning style?" Each group is given a large pad on which to record the generated material, a small pragmatic action that enhances engagement.

We reconvene. As each conversational cluster recounts their talking, I ask questions to clarify or to make sure that I understand, which often expands and adds agenda items. I record the material on a large pad for all to see. At the next meeting, I distribute copies of the beginning agenda to the participants. Each meeting thereafter begins with a checking-in to see what new items we should add to our agenda and what old ones are still hanging.

Inviting and providing opportunities for all voices continues throughout a course of learning. In addition to frequently forming conversational clusters, I give students a reflection sheet at the end of each meeting, asking them to share their internal words and thoughts with me. Sometimes, I ask for general reflections. Sometimes, I pose a question such as, Do you think that you are learning anything new, and if so, or not, how do you know? What are you learning about yourself and how you learn? Are your original expectations being met, and if so, how? Do you have new expectations? Or, We have two meetings left: Please let me know what you think we should address in these meetings. Although I have to create each reflection sheet ahead of time, questions or issues to address come from the content and process of the particular course, group, and our relationship and workings together. Learners bring the reflections with them to the next meeting, signed or unsigned. I read them and take them seriously. I also share my reflections on our last meeting.

The reflection process furthers several interrelated purposes. It consistently builds in continuous self, other, course, and teacher evaluation. I can learn more about the participants and their needs. In response, I may emphasize or deemphasize course content or expand or fine-tune the agenda. It gives me an opportunity to improve my teaching methods and to adjust my style to serve their individual and combined needs. Through their initial lead and continual reflection, I accommodate to what each group, occasion, circumstance, and relationship calls for. Through a weaving of voices—theirs, mine, and ours—we create and immerse ourselves in a process of development and transformation of knowledge.

The process encourages learners to be active in their learning and to determine its direction. It makes learning more purposeful and self-directed. It provides opportunities for learners to think about, to expand, to reconsider, to question, and to understand differently. It promotes an opportunity to develop an awareness of and to develop habits of focusing on, thinking about, and tracking their learning and professional growth.

Learners report multiple effects of the conversational cluster and reflection processes. They report feeling safe to share. They report that they develop a trust in the other person's capacity for self-agency and an inherent trust in the process and relationship. They report becoming aware of the richness of their own internal conversation, their self-dialogue. They report that their reflections trigger a self-reflective process that translates and continues beyond the formal learning arena to their unique everyday settings.

Learning from this perspective is not standardized. As it becomes collaborative and participatory, it also becomes individualized and self-directed. Students begin to experience, recognize, and value their expertise, competencies, and talents. They become more thoughtful and active in delineating what they want to learn, in determining how they best learn, and in requesting a teacher's and fellow students' participation in their learning. They develop a sense of confidence as their voice is invited in, as they realize their own multiple inner voices. They develop an appreciation of the richness and possibilities that come from difference as they move from a need for consensus to an openness to uncertain and yet-to-emerge possibilities.

In their reflections, learners consistently comment on their individual learning styles, my teaching style, and the group process. They report amazement at the richness of the small-cluster conversations. They are aware of the generativity of the conversations, including the emergence of new learning—the way their own thinking changes and the way they interact with what they are listening to and hearing. They express appreciation for the opportunity, although an unfamiliar and challenging one, to think about how they learn and what they want to learn. They express excitement that builds with feelings of having and expressing their voice and being listened to and heard by me and their peers. They express pride of ownership in the course and their learning, feeling accountable for their own learning and feeling responsibility to each other.

The following words are drawn from student reflections:

I sensed a part of myself growing and emerging—a self that I knew was within but rarely allowed others to see.

The atmosphere beckoned to me, "Take a chance."

Wow! Today was really exciting for me to feel free enough to actually participate in conversations about questions and ideas that I've only really discussed with myself. . . . Unfortunately, not all places of learning start at the point where the students are. . . . I remember feeling a shift in my self as a result of talking.

I'm beginning to recognize now how my potential for learning is enhanced through the process of shared inquiry. As I'm writing this, I am becoming aware that I have always known this about myself and have held myself back with the idea that, "No one wants to do this with me."

I am shy and quiet, and actually a bit nervous, so I tend not to talk in class. . . . The small groups and reflections process have helped me get more comfortable, and I am able to more freely give my thoughts and ideas without having to be asked.

Some of the silence which often follows your invitations for comments and feedback is because we, as students, are not used to such openness for freedom of the type of conversations that you allow.

As usual, I'm always humbled by the minds of others. . . . The consultation on my case helped me reflect on my own inner dialogue and also free myself from a very stuck position. . . . I don't think the class knows how important their feedback and conversations are for me.

I am intrigued by how asking questions to learn more about and clarify leads to—could lead me to a change in my perception of the case and how relieved I am by that (referring to the previously mentioned consultation process).

In my mind's eye, what these learners say support McNamee and Gergen's notion that as one positions oneself differently with an other—as I position myself differently with learners—I no longer hold sole responsibility for their learning; it is shared. When responsibility is shared, the relationship is more mutually rewarding.

As I reflect on McNamee and Gergen's words, I am aware of the incongruence and awkwardness I experience in trying to explicate a belief in the inherence of something such as relational responsibility and then trying to create situations and processes in which it can be accessed and enhanced. As I reflect on my own biases and experiences, I am left with these questions: How can these ideas be communicated, and in what language, to an everyday ordinary citizen? How can they be relevant, for instance, to a Spanish-speaking immigrant mother involved in the legal and child welfare systems and who is accused of child abuse? In other words, the important question that I believe needs to be addressed is, How can the concept and practice of relational responsibility move from the academic discourse to everyday ordinary life?

6

Relational Moves
and Generative Dances

Ian Burkitt

The present move to a relational notion of selves is one that is most welcome in the social sciences. As Sheila McNamee and Kenneth Gergen so rightly point out, the whole idea of responsibility and justice in the West is based on the assumption of the isolated, rational actor whose agency is entirely a subjective matter. This notion of agency centers on the figure of a lone individual whose intentions, plans, understanding, and control over actions apparently takes place in a world without others–at least at the point where these inner deliberations are taking place. Instead of this view, what the project of relational responsibility suggests to me is a new way of making human agency intelligible by under-standing it as movement and dialogue within the ever present relational matrix.

This, however, raises other questions and problems with traditional ways of thinking based around the notion of discrete selves, particularly with ideas of freedom and determination, which are indelibly connected to blame and respon-sibility. The judicial systems of the Western world tend to work with the idea that a person can only be punished and blamed for their actions to the extent they are judged to be responsible for them, which is to say, that they are fully in charge of themselves and their actions. If it can be shown that a person was fully in control of an action, then they can be held entirely responsible and be made to pay for it. If, on the other hand, it can be shown that the person was in some way suffering from diminished responsibility, then the extent to which they are punished for an action will be mitigated. Yet all these notions rest on the fundamental belief in an individual cognitive system functioning in isolation from all else. Holding someone fully responsible for an action suggests that he or she, and he or she alone, is the author of the act and that it stems from an internally rational process of decision making. Pleas of diminished responsibility are usually made on the grounds of psychiatric evidence that suggests some psychological impairment, cognitive malfunctioning, or personality disorder. In other words, decisions as to whether or not someone can be held responsible revolve around questions of the degree to which the person is in charge of his or her own mental faculties. If it is decided that an individual has about them all these faculties, then it is reasoned that the person can always have done otherwise—that their decision to act in the way they did and not in some other way was entirely within their own powers. But all of this revolves around the notion of an isolated individual who is guided only by the organization of his or her mental processes and the degree to which, through these processes, he or she has control of their actions.

In the scheme of relational responsibility, however, this model is fundamentally critiqued and deconstructed. Instead, we envisage a world of relationships and interdependencies in which each individual is a nodal point of intersection and connection. Activity takes place within interrelationships and only has sense, meaning, and purpose within that context. Actions are always preceded by other actions, relationships by other relationships, and the individual self by the selves of others. There is no action taken by a rational consciousness in some mythical rarefied stratosphere above relationships and interdependencies. All actions take place in the context of other actions and within the realm of interconnections. Every act or practice is always preceded by other acts or made in connection with others. More often than not, individuals are in dialogue so that practice has a joint authorship: An example would be a book that bears the name of a single author and yet is the result of the many books that the author has read and been inspired by prior to writing her or his own. Relations and joint activities are multiauthored and multivoiced, a dialogue rather than a monologue. In any joint activity, responsibility is always shared so that a single individual is never entirely to blame for a situation or event.

Because we are always in networks of interdependence, this means that the lone, rational individual is a chimera. Relations and interactions are what constitute persons and selves so that no person can ever reach a decision, formulate a plan or strategy, using only the bare bones of rational laws. Each person is socially constituted and moves through relationships guided by a prior sense of being: this, in turn, is constituted by tastes, preferences, interests, and desires, all formed within embodied beings located in the interconnecting webs of interdependence. Indeed, without these things, how would it be possible for people to choose between different options? Decisions ranging from which political party to vote for in an election to what foods to eat for dinner are impossible to make solely on the basis of rational principles. Instead, choice is made on the basis of who one is or considers oneself to be—on the basis of values, beliefs, or identifications with others. This is also true of morality for, as McNamee and Gergen point out, what is moral in one context may well not be in another. To act morally and responsibly is not, therefore, to choose a course of action based on rational laws or categorical imperatives but to negotiate a way through the complexities of various relational contexts.

This means that notions of freedom and determination on which much traditional thinking about responsibility rest (see Glover, 1970) is a dichotomy that needs to be overcome. Unless one is a determinate social self located within cultural and historical networks, then one has no choice and no basis on which to choose. To have latitudes for free choice and action, one must be, to an extent, determined. The notion of relational responsibility faces us with the need of abandoning this dichotomy. As Anthony Giddens (1979, 1984) and others have argued, social action always takes place in the context of unacknowledged conditions: that is to say, in conditions that a single person will not have chosen or designed. Although Giddens tends to see these unacknowledged conditions as the social rules that structure activity, I think these can more profitably be seen as the relational networks that precede us. These are the social structures that are continually made and remade in social interchanges, a process that Giddens called *structuration.* It can be claimed, however, that what structures social activity is the relational network in which it takes place and that the outcomes of such activity are transformed relationships. Yet the point is that no one ever completely chooses the position from which they start, the relationships in which they are bound. As such, these are at the root of the meaning that actions contain and play a large role in structuring them: In turn, these actions have a part in reshaping the relational configuration so that in no way could they be described as "determined."

In this sense, relationships are characterized by what Bourdieu (1991) has called *generative structure,* which is a structure continually being reformulated and reconstructed through the process of social practices. Generative structure is a form of regulated improvisation in which people make innovative moves in their practices, often without realizing or planning what they are doing. It is a similar process to the one a jazz musician may be engaged in, producing endless improvisations from the same standard tune and an increasingly trained and refined musical technique. In terms of relationships and the effect of joint practices within them, there is a continual and constantly ongoing reconfiguration. I would like to suggest that this process is best characterized as a generative dance, a constant repositioning of individuals through relational changes, all brought about by the participation of persons. This entails a play with conventions in a similar way to that which Bakhtin (1986) has identified occurring in language. That is, through utterances related to the actual situations in which they occur, persons not only draw from the systems of meaning and the structure of language contained within their culture, but they also change that structure and those meanings by using them in practice. Again, a similar thing occurs with the jazz musician who, in the context of the jazz club and in front of an expectant audience, can take the familiar notes of a well-known song and end his or her solo playing something entirely different from the expected configuration of notes they started with. Each different night will bring new improvisations from the springboard of the same standard themes.

It seems inappropriate to talk in terms of "structure," however, because this brings to mind a fixed framework closed off from change, whereas relationships are constantly changing through the joint action of those involved in them. It is for this reason that I prefer to talk of movement or dance, because persons in relationships are constantly repositioning themselves like dancers engaged in fluid but patterned formations. In relationships, people are always repositioning themselves in respect of others and also in respect of previous relationships and their outcomes.

This relational form of generative dance must influence our views of responsibility, for no action or event occurs outside of it. There is no individual thought, intention, or action that is unrelated. It is in this sense that McNamee and Gergen rightly say that all so-called evil actions are intelligible in a context and that they are related to the actions of others—even if this is only silent approval. This idea is illustrated quite clearly in Zygmunt Bauman's (1989) work on the Holocaust, in which he shows that the German people did not become hate-filled anti-Semites rushing to do the bidding of the Nazi leaders but that the racist ideas in circulation had made them indifferent to the fate of the Jews. This allowed people the possibility of looking the other way or looking on without too much care while Jewish people began to be removed for "resettlement." Bauman's account of the Holocaust has often been criticized for not putting enough emphasis on the role of the Nazi party and its leaders, but in many ways, this criticism is misdirected because Bauman is concentrating on the wider social conditions that allowed the genocide to occur. Looked at in this way, it is inappropriate to blame particular groups or individuals for what happened during the Holocaust because many shared responsibility for what occurred. The event happened in a context where ordinary people who were not evil became bound up in evil actions through their silence.

The realization that an action is intelligible in a certain context and was not just the result of the pathological condition of certain individuals does not make that action or event any the less immoral, however. Just because we understand the context in which the Holocaust occurred does not make it in any sense moral and does not mean that people will not be held to account. But what a relational understanding does attempt is to shift the focus away from a desire to blame and redirect it toward a concentration on the conditions that allowed such horrific events to occur—conditions that may well implicate us all with some portion of responsibility. The questions, then, would no longer simply be, Who is to blame, but also, How can we prevent the possibility of such relationships reconfiguring again in the future, and How is it possible to create and sustain relationships in which everyone figures as a person toward whom we all have moral responsibility? In turn, this would involve fostering a sense in which we could all see ourselves as related and, thus, as fully human.

What theorists of relations and dialogue are claiming, then, is that responsibility is not a force, a characteristic, or a substance contained inside us but a feeling constituted in the interdependency of social life. To illustrate this, Bauman (1989) has used the work of Emmanuel Levinas (1989), who believes that sociality and moral responsibility is a primary factor in social life. For Levinas, responsibility for the "other" predates self-consciousness and bypasses rational, calculating thought, existing as an openness to others, a willingness to respond to the "face" as a summons that cannot be ignored. This responsibility is unconditional and involves the recognition of the other's face as one that is different but nevertheless has legitimate moral claims on us. Responsibility for others is therefore lodged in face-to-face relations of everyday sociality. This openness to others and recognition of their claims on us is achieved because our identity as individuals is constituted through them so that the other is always already in the self—something that a viable ethics must take into account.

The key to understanding Levinas's (1989) notion of responsibility lies in his ideas about proximity, which contain all the goodness of an original sociality. In such face-to-face encounters, we are in a state of being-with-others that is outside all the formalized structures and institutions of a given society. This does not mean that such sociality is lost in our highly institutionalized modernity but that we must constantly work to build a society in which the integrity of the self-other relation is reinforced. In a so-called good society, we must be able to surmount the particularistic interests of the egocentric self and the in-group and open ourselves up to the other (Gardiner, 1994).

This style of relational responsibility would also encourage us not to externalize moral problems when they occur, blaming them on the other. For example, it is all too easy to explain an event such as the Holocaust in terms of the history or characteristics of a group of people belonging to a different nation or race—whether that be the German or Jewish people. Perhaps we should instead ask, To what extent do the conditions for inhumanity reside within our own relational groupings? If responsibility for others rests on our relationship to them, then we have to take seriously the suggestions of those such as Richard Lichtman (1982) who argue—quite correctly in my view—that in the West, we tend to repress the understanding we have of ourselves as interrelated and interdependent. This is because within our culture, it is seen as strong to be self-sufficient and self-reliant and weak to be dependent or reliant on others. Because we do not emphasize the importance of relationships and the way they constitute our lives, it is easy to look at life only in terms of isolated individuals so that when something goes wrong, it is particular people who can be blamed and there is no need to examine the fabric of our social relations and institutions. Again, we often seek pathology in the psychological makeup of those who are blamed for events rather than searching for answers in sociological terms (see Adorno, Frenkel-Brunswick, Levinson, & Sanford, 1950).

And yet, as Levinas (1989) and Martin Buber (1970) have said, the only way in which people have the possibility of being moral in the first place is because they are socially interdependent agents. George Herbert Mead (1934) extended these ideas by claiming that we can only have the capacity for morality and responsibility to the extent that we can place ourselves in another person's shoes and see things from their perspective. This involves being capable of genuine dialogue, of being able to temporarily abandon one's own embodied position as a person and to see how the world looks from the position of someone other than our own self. We have to be able to take on the position of many different selves to imagine how others will think and feel. Only then can we take another person into account and be a fully moral agent, capable of responsibility for others. The notion that to be fully responsible, we must abandon our own position and see things from another perspective, thus moving toward new possibilities, can be illustrated by many examples. One of the most telling has been the very tenuous attempt to achieve peace in Northern Ireland, where Loyalist and Nationalist movements and parties, along with the British and Irish governments, are attempting to move slowly and painfully toward the hope of some lasting settlement to the armed conflict. In this process, the different factions and parties must move to some point at which they can begin to see things from each other's perspectives, thus being able to imagine a future where Catholic and Protestant communities can live together in peace. But this means letting go of the desire to blame one another for the problems and for the acts of violence committed and, instead of hankering after retribution, planning for a future in which conflict can be settled through dialogue. Seeing things from the perspective of another is important because no one vision of the future can dominate in this process if it to be successful, and no one set of recriminations for the past can prevail. A future without armed conflict in the relationships between Loyalist, Nationalist, and the British will necessitate an ability to appreciate different positions, avoid blame, and begin to feel responsible for people who have hitherto been seen as other (that is, as different, as the enemy).

A successful peace process would depend on the acceptance of all voices into the debate but also on the acceptance that these voices would have the power to change current political institutions. The institutions and organizations that govern the province, along with those that oppose this government, will also have to change. So voices in a dialogue are only one, albeit important, aspect of relational change. Other factors involved in relational changes and the distribution of responsibility include the political and economic aspects of relations and their institutional sites. This is one of the ways in which interdependence comes to take on a reality that sometimes feels as though it is immutable. No network of relations is ever independent of other networks, stretching out into an ever expanding web, and this infinite series of relations can be mutually supporting as well as a source of potential conflict. There is no functional system at work in the span of interrelations, no organic plan that ensures the interconnection between different networks of interdependence; yet, as they configure, various relations and their institutional sites may begin to interlock in a mutually supportive or oppositional way. Although many voices make up these interdependencies, they are not composed solely of voice, and those vocalizing for change or stability in their relations may find their entry to the dialogue futile.

This is where the question of power enters the frame. As Michel Foucault (1982) has claimed, power is a relation and, as such, certain people in relations will find themselves in different positions of power or domination. Those who are marginalized or dominated will struggle to have their voices heard with the dialogue and may well find an alternative voice imposed on them. Foucault, of course, illustrated how those who are labelled as mad have their voices suppressed, and other voices given to them—those of medicine, science, or law. The mad are the other, the voices of unreason who cannot be heard or who are prevented from being heard and instead have other means of expression forced on them: In the case of madness, this has been the medicalized model of insanity that emerged within the asylums of the 19th century. However, in the latter part of the 20th century, the reliance on a medical understanding of madness has been chipped away, and another approach is beginning to emerge that welcomes madness into a dialogue. Here, as P. J. Bracken (1995) has pointed out, a different type of ethics is emerging that is "not about codes and rules, but about the development of an ethical sensibility which respects difference, transgression, and disorder" (p. 11). However, it could also be said that this is about developing a sense of relational responsibility, in which a person labelled as mentally ill is not the other, whose experience is to be interpreted by a superior model, but is a fellow human being to be welcomed into the circle of reciprocal relationships and whose voice must be heard. A person's own interpretation of his or her condition is of as great, if not greater, value than any other.

To reach such a position, however, many aspects of contemporary power relations and institutions will need to be challenged. This does not mean that we have to return to some idealized notion of an original sociality, as Levinas (1989) suggested, because the highly mediated relationships of Western society may well be in the process of transforming themselves through their own double-edged natures. Although there is validity in the notion that mediated social relationships break up the proximity between individuals, interfering with their sense of responsibility for one another, it can also be argued that the widening of social networks that is made possible by the mediation of institutions and global communication systems also increases the span of mutual identification between people. Anthony Giddens (1991) has said that mass media and communications technology allow social relations to be disembedded from particular spatial locations and time zones and reconstituted on a more global level. This means that in modernity, relations are more globalized and with them, so are feelings of responsibility. We may feel more closely related and responsible for people living half the world away than we do for people who live next door. As Gergen (1991) has claimed, technologies of social saturation are making it possible for many different voices from various locations to enter our dialogues, adding to the voices that populate the self. But this new form of global relatedness has its price, certainly as far as the mass media is concerned. In the reporting of wars or famines, some people are given a voice while others are denied it. The media can open up channels of communication and create feelings of responsibility between people—as happened in the Vietnam war when images of the victims created a sense of responsibility among Americans for the Vietnamese people—while also being able to close such channels off—for example, during the Gulf war when images of people suffering were very carefully controlled. As far as relational responsibility goes, the high levels of mediated relations in modernity are double-edged.

Responsibility, then, does not arise from within people nor can it be imposed externally by some supraindividual body. Rather, it depends on the structure and form of our social relations and the way people are located within them. An understanding of responsibility can be achieved through the idea of social selves: that is, persons who are related and interdependent with each other and whose actions cannot be removed from such a context. To supplement Levinas's (1989) notion of responsibility located in the recognition of the other's face, we can say that this is not just the bare face of human physiognomy but a face superimposed with social identity taken from the way the person to whom it belongs is situated in social relations. A human face is meaningless and empty, devoid of all moral demands, if it is not recognized as one belonging to a social self, one to whom we are related and with whom we can recognize and respect differences and similarities. If such a relation fails to be established, then terrible consequences can follow, yet the source of that terror lies not inside the individual but in the relation between social selves. To say this is not to absolve individuals from blame if they are irresponsible with the lives, safety, or dignity of others; but it is to try to focus attention on where the real difficulties in relations and selves may occur, to try to prevent or help repair situations where responsibility is lacking.

7

On Being Relational in an Accountable Way

The Questions of Agency and Power

John W. Lannamann

That my response was invited seems to me to be a good-faith effort to put into practice the notion of relational responsibility. All this talk about voices and internal others challenges the monovocal tradition of authority in the academic community. Bakhtin (1981) warns literary scholars against missing the "multiplicity of social voices and . . . their links and interrelationships" (p. 263). Of course, I can respond in my voice as husband of the first author (in a monologic tradition, this voice would be treated as my only one and as such would disqualify my response[1]), yet this voice is but one in a ensemble of voices, including my scholarly persona as a sometimes critical social constructionist.

The multiple voices at play in my response are not free-floating utterances hovering over an undifferentiated social landscape. As Volosinov (1929/1986) points out, all utterances are addressed to someone, and there cannot be an utterance without an addressee, real or imagined. He writes that this social situation

> shapes the utterance, dictating that it sound one way and not another—like a demand or request, insistence on one's rights or a plea for mercy, in a style flowery or plain, in a confident or hesitant manner, and so on. (p. 86-87)

So in addition to (or actually intertwined with) my options concerning the appropriate voice for this essay, I am acutely conscious of another set of questions. Who is my addressee? My academic community? My promotion committee? The mother of our 5-year-old son? My department chair? My wife? My wife's coauthor? My friend? My respected social constructionist colleague? Can a both-and logic work here?

I will try to juggle this carnival of voices and audiences by beginning with a story because, as Bateson (1979) points out, a story is a "little knot or complex of that species of connectedness which we call relevance" (p. 13). Perhaps, the story will offer something relevant to each of my conversational partners.

In the 1985 film, *Desperately Seeking Susan,* a film that for me is emblematic of painful awakenings in my own relationship with Sheila, Rosanna Arquette plays the role of Roberta, a suburban home worker patronized and silenced by her self-centered husband. The film follows Roberta as she makes her way through a maze of mistaken identities that allow her new voices and unusually responsive conversational partners. When her husband comes to "rescue" her from the bizarre circumstances of being identified simultaneously as a magician's assistant in a night club act, a (falsely) accused prostitute, and an underworld mobster, he discovers that he can no longer control Roberta with his monologues.

> **Roberta:** They thought I was a prostitute, that's why I got arrested.
>
> **Gary:** Roberta, are you a lesbian? Leslie told me that lots of prostitutes are lesbians.
>
> **Roberta:** Gary, you're not listening to me. (Raising voice) I'm not a prostitute or a lesbian . . .
>
> **Gary:** We'll get professional help, I don't care how much it costs. The important thing is, I want you to come home with me.
>
> **Roberta:** Why?
>
> **Gary:** (Softly) Why? Why? What do you mean "why?"
>
> **Roberta:** I mean why do you want me to come home with you, Gary?
>
> **Gary:** Come on, don't get excited, all right? Don't get excited, jjsh, what are you, on drugs or somethin' now?
>
> **Roberta:** (Whispers) God. Look at me.
>
> **Gary:** I looked at you. You look ridiculous.
>
> **Roberta:** I mean look at mee, Gary. (Softly) Look at me. (Pause) I'm not coming home with you.

Gary: You're just tired. Ah, why don't you get changed and we'll talk about it at home, all right? Come on, Com'on. (Pause) Fine. That's fine, ahh, I, I'm gonna go outside and I'm gonna wait for 5 minutes, and if you're not there, I'm going to leave without you.

Roberta: Goodbye, Gary.

I watched this scene 10 years ago with some ambivalence, with one voice celebrating Roberta's independence and the other voice urging caution and possible reconciliation. Theorists interested in the dialectical aspects of relational life (Baxter, 1990; Baxter & Montgomery, 1996; Rawlins, 1989) suggest that this tension between celebrating connection and preserving autonomy is what produces relational change. The tension returns to me now as I read Sheila and Ken's discussion of relational responsibility. I found myself agreeing with their Zen-like transformation of dyadic struggles and their celebration of connection, but I wonder what Roberta would say about a more relationally responsible alternative to her autonomous action. I suspect that she would prefer unilateral action to continued relational engagement with Gary.

Now, certainly, one could argue that Roberta was acting in a relationally responsible way, a way that interrupted the monovocal and patriarchal narrative rehearsed by Gary. Yet to make such an argument, it is necessary to expand the notion of what counts as "relational" to include virtually everything done or said by a person. Such a move makes a certain kind of sense, because to the extent that we are born into a preexisting language community, any use of language or even nonlinguistic forms of communication might be termed relational or multivocal. From such a perspective, blaming and victimizing actions become relational acts because these actions can only be accomplished in the process of social interaction.

Part of the power of Sheila and Ken's analysis is that it shows us the relational character of apparently individualistic acts. Their analysis calls attention to the ways in which the rhetorical trope of individual responsibility is socially constructed and then hidden from view. Thus, one take on the relational responsibility argument is that it is not simply a move to counter the modernist faith in individualism but rather, that it is an attempt to dissolve the dichotomy of individual versus relational identity entirely. They subsume the individual within the domain of the relational processes. Thus, their project can be seen as a form of consciousness raising, an attempt to liberate us from the constraints of a false dichotomy.

However, this consciousness-raising element in their project, like other metanar-ratives of liberation, runs the risk of invoking a form of abstract idealism that, paradoxically in this case, separates persons and relationships from the situationally specific interactions that constitute persons and relationships. It would be hard to get Gary to see Roberta's moves as a relational process, to see the "function of such process in the relationship," putting aside how "the individual 'really feels' " in order to "consider the relational repercussions of portraying one's emotions in terms of being saddened or disappointed, for example, as opposed to irritated, or outraged" (p. 21, this volume). Somehow, this process seems to fit the seminar better than the street. Why?

Perhaps it is unfair to juxtapose an angry Gary with Sheila and Ken's prose. The two vocabularies access different forms of life, and calling for equivalences between the two would impoverish both spontaneity and understanding. I think the reason that the two seem to be incommensurate discourses has to do with the differing moral orders they imply. Gary is living in a world of "shoulds, oughts" and "musts" that looks and feels very different when translated into Sheila's and Ken's proposed ethic of relational engagement.

Sheila and Ken seem to want to transform the moral vocabulary of relational life by moving away from the notion of individual responsibility, a key element in most individualistically oriented moral philosophies since Kant. But if the shoulds and oughts that constitute our conversational identities are dominated by a tradition of individualism, then what are the relational alternatives? Can we still play the language game of accountability once we move away from an individualist ontology? Or is the notion of accountability inseparable from the tradition of individualism that Sheila and Ken have deconstructed?

Answering this question returns us to the problem of incommensurate dis-courses. In theory, it is possible to deconstruct the notion of accountability and demonstrate that it is an invention of a particular social and historical epoch. In the practice of our everyday life, though, it is hard to deny that relational engagement has hooks. The emergent moral force of conversation can still hang us up. That we feel these hooks suggests to me that accountability should not be thought of as relevant only in an individualist orientation. The interactively negotiated oughts and shoulds that structure our ongoing relationships are the basis of a kind of accountability that is more like an emerging melodic theme, the "hook" of a tune, than an individual note in isolation. The contour of the relational activities both constrains and enables future activity.

Although it is difficult to account for our actions from within a relational form of life without appealing to concepts such as individual intentionality, it is worth the effort. For when we venture into the terrain of accountability, we bump into some important issues that have a direct bearing on the practical implications of what Sheila and Ken are proposing. Does it make sense to talk about relational processes devoid of first-person agents who initiate actions? And confronting the issue of accountability raises what I would like to call Roberta's dilemma: When does forgoing the fiction of first-person intentionality in favor of relational process become a form of accommodation to a dominant discourse? Thus, I hope my contribution to the relational responsibility project is to offer a few supplements and provocations to expand the range of Sheila's and Ken's important ideas so that the concept engages issues not yet rehabilitated from their modernist exile: the problems of accountability, agency, and the politics of interaction.

ACCOUNTABILITY AND AGENCY

Sheila and Ken propose "abandoning the ontological question of agency" (p. 11, this volume). Such a move makes sense as long as *agency* is understood as a description of a natural category in the world, and this may be what they mean by the use of the term *ontological.* Yet such an understanding makes sense only if language is seen as a system of representation rather than as a performative practice of bringing forth various social realities. I take Sheila's and Ken's orientation to language to be a performative one. They are explicitly interested in asking "What social functions are served by attributing intentions to self and others" (p. 21). Certainly, one of the functions is that of accountability; the invention of individual intention as a category of things in the world allows for a particular form of accountability. Thus, from a constructionist perspective, actions can be explained in terms of individual agency as long as the individual intentionality is not reified as something apart from the conversational reality sustained by the interlocutors.

In an earlier article, Ken offered a useful framework for understanding the origins of the psychological concept of intentionality (Gergen, 1985). He suggested that the principle of intentionality should be understood as a linguistic practice that resolves the difficult problem of trying to describe the continuous processes that make up human action. The use of the term *intention* allows the speaker to construct endpoints that stand in for the nameless minutia of the ever changing living moment. Intentionality, and the related notion of agency, then, are conversationally sustained inventions that solve practical problems and do important work. Like any other category used to describe mindful behavior, agency is not a description of an inner mental state. Rather, it is a category that arises in discursive practices. More like a dance than a seizure, it is jointly performed, not foreordained.

Yet this constructed and performative aspect of agency is pursued in Sheila's and Ken's treatment of relational responsibility only as a way to diffuse or deconstruct the idea of agency in the service of reducing conflict and keeping the conversation going. The constructed fiction of agency becomes a trope used to dismiss the term. But this deconstruction of agency results in an accountability problem. Once agency is dismissed, accountability disappears as well. Sheila and Ken are left in a position similar to the party game, "Taboo," in which one player tries to get others to guess the hidden word without using key words related to the hidden word. It is hard to recognize responsibility without the crucial clues of accountability.

There are two ways to handle the problem of accountability without being seduced by individualism. One way is to simply recognize that we already have the linguistic resources for talking about collective agency. For example, we have no trouble talking about organizations as agents, as in "The university does not discriminate based on race, ethnicity, sexual orientation, or religion." The recognition of this collective agency allows for a form of collective accountability. There are many examples of organizations held legally accountable for various unlawful acts even when no single individual is identified as the culprit. This form of collective accountability, however, falls short of Sheila's and Ken's radically social orientation to relational responsibility. Collective accountability simply imports the language of individual agency into the realm of interindividual groups.

A second and more satisfying way to put accountability back into relational responsibility is to recognize that our notions of agency and accountability are socially produced in situations that we participate in but do not control. Shotter (1984) refers to this mindful, but not determining, aspect of social life as "joint action." He writes that, "I have called this kind of activity 'joint action'; . . . it is productive of outcomes unintended by the individuals involved in it" (p. x). The unintended nature of joint action constructs the "institutions within which [people] make sense of their activities to one another" (p. x). Shotter's notion of social accountability does not rely solely on a concept of individual agency. People act into an emerging flow of conversation that is neither determined by their own intentions nor completely random and formless. Joint action produces the conversational resources that enable people to account for their actions. Based on joint actions (including occasional surprises, flare-ups, and other events beyond my control), my family has developed ways of making sense of things so that we can account for our behaviors. I am accountable to the family as a member whose "individual" identity is interwoven with the ongoing, conjoint relations constituting the family and constituting me as husband, father, professor, and chew toy for the dog.

Sheila and Ken include conjoint relations in their discussion of the four domains of relational intelligibilities. But they opt to replace the presumption of individual, interacting selves with conceptions of "we." Although this move to the "we" is consistent with their interest in relational processes, it short circuits the relational process because it ignores the fact that the individual 'I' is always, necessarily, a social construction, one that plays a central role in the production of joint action. They go on to write that it is "we who generate the hostile remark, the sense of injury, the cruel retort" (p. 14). The difference between this orientation to joint action and Shotter's is that Shotter, by preserving space for socially constructed agents (social I's), leaves more room for the messy possibilities of unintended consequences.

The problem with the move to the "we" can be illustrated using the *Desperately Seeking Susan* example. Roberta would have a hard time finding her voice in the patriarchal "we" narrative enacted with her husband. She leaves the relationship because to stay in it would have required her to continue to account for her behaviors using a discourse of "we," a discourse dominated by her husband's insensitivity and one that ignored the possibility of her own agency. As Shotter (1984) puts it, "our ways of accounting for things have a coercive quality to them; only if we make sense of things in certain approved ways can we be accounted by others in our society as competent, responsible members of it" (p. xi.). As long as Roberta was held accountable to the "we," little would change because her "I" would appear incompetent and irresponsible. It is this tension between the two narratives that shapes the drama of the film. Novelty and change are produced through joint actions with other social "I's" whose practices contribute to, but do not determine, the unintended consequences of interaction. Thus, relational change is the consequence of interaction between social agents, not abstract relationships. It is a messy and sometimes contested process that cannot be transformed by simply shifting to a language of "we."

Michael White's (1994) therapeutic work with men who abuse offers an interesting example of a relational form of accountability that keeps an ear to the "I." White's work is firmly rooted in the relational tradition where actions such as abuse are understood as part of a larger discursive practice. He writes that

> To see these men who perpetrate violence as aberrant would enable me, as a member of the class of men, to avoid facing the responsibility that I have to take action, to contribute to the dismantling of men's privilege that perpetuates inequality of opportunity and that supports domination. (p. 70)

This sensitivity to the reflexivity of relational practices seems consistent with Sheila's and Ken's project to move beyond individual blame. Instead of engaging in discursive practices that isolate the perpetrator of the violence as an "other," White engages a social dimension of responsibility that goes beyond the isolated actions of the individual and locates him in a discursive web. Yet White does not ignore individual agency or individual accountability. He does not move immediately to the "we." He begins by meeting alone with the men who have abused to set the scene for introducing the processes of accountability. The preliminary tasks at this stage of the process include working with the abusers to help them take responsibility for perpetrating the abuse, helping them to develop an understanding of the experiences of those who were abused, and getting them to appreciate both the short-term and the long-term effects of the abuse (p. 68). These preliminary steps seem to call attention to an individual's agency, but it is an agency that is socially embedded in the "dominant ways of being and thinking for men in this culture that venerate aggression, domination, and conquest" (p. 70). Thus, White's approach yields a very relational form of accountability that is able to balance both agency and social accountability by keeping track of how the "I" is constantly in dialogue with the "we."

THE POLITICS OF
RELATIONAL RESPONSIBILITY

I am intrigued by the potential of Sheila's and Ken's project to bring about social changes. They suggest that relationships should be thought of as processes within which the economy, housing conditions, education, politics, and "broader relational engagements intermingle, are recreated, and transformed" (p. 23). Given the increasing gulf between rich and poor, between the exploiters and the exploited, and between those who label others' problems and those who are pathologized by the labels, a transformation of a nonviolent sort sounds like a good idea.

I would like to hear more about how transformations, even small ones, operate when the participants are on different footings. What kinds of transformations can be brought about by a relationally responsible move when the initiator of the process is in a subordinate position relative to the other? For example, it is hard not to applaud Roberta's move in separating from Gary, yet I am not convinced that her move satisfied the relationally responsible requirements of sustaining and enhancing forms of interchange. Could she have escaped the dominance of her husband if she had privileged the relational processes over her personal identity?

What happens when the relational responsibility model is applied to a conversation in which one member maintains certainty and is intransigent? If the relational process is prioritized, those not interested in playing the relational game are empowered because the relationally responsive member will attempt to move the issue in a way that favors the possibility of including rather than excluding the holdout. This is the logic of a focus on the "we," particularly when in the hands of communication theorists too sophisticated to fall for the trap of representationalism, where "content" is separated from metacommunication.[2] In a rapid shift to the "we," the consequentiality of "what" is said is obscured by the focus on the relational "how" it was said. But from a performative standpoint, a stance that I think Sheila and Ken embrace, the what and the how are both relational actions that bring forth our social realities. Downplaying one in the interest of keeping the conversation going runs the risk of obscuring the material consequences of the conversation.

When a stance on an issue is softened by a relationally responsive interlocutor who hopes to keep the conversation going to protect the sanctity of the relationship, the softened response nevertheless enters the stream of discourse and has consequences. If the situation is politically charged, the consequences contribute to a consolidation of power by the less relationally responsive member of the conversation. Thus, by using a relationally responsible rhetoric of incorporation and not denying the extreme demands of one party, the effect will always be a shift (even if relationally progressive) in the direction of the intransigent person's position. Many would say that this was President Clinton's problem during his first term. By trying to work with the opposition, he forfeited most of his game, and although something might have been better than nothing, the shift was unrelentingly to the right. There is little incentive to change for those not interested in relationally responsible action, particularly when they know that the other will practice relational responsibility. Thus, a potential consequence of the practice of relational responsibility is a humane but conservative drift.

I would like to close with an example of these concerns by pointing to the challenges relationally responsive interlocutors face when confronted with others whose conversational style is more domineering. In an intriguing, though misleadingly titled, popular article called "How to give orders like a man," Tannen (1994a) provides an example of a conversation in which an airline copilot attempts to warn the pilot about ice build-up on the wings of their plane. Tannen suggests that the copilot's indirect speech is sensitive to his lower status in relation to the pilot. She provides this transcript taken from the "black box" recorder recovered after the crash of Air Florida's flight 90 on January 13, 1982.

Copilot: That don't seem right, does it. (3.0) Ah, that's not right . . .
Captain: Yes, it is, there's 80.
Copilot: Naw, I don't think that's right. (7.0) Ah, maybe it is.
Captain: Hundred and twenty
Copilot: I don't know.

Instead of risking damage to relational harmony with a direct contradiction of the pilot, the copilot mitigates his response with tag questions and such qualifiers as "I think" and "I don't know." In this case, the dominant language style of the captain and, perhaps, his intransigence deflected the indirect suggestions of the copilot whose actions may have protected the relationship, but with tragic consequences.

Elsewhere, Tannen (1994b) provides a similar, though less tragic, example of how fragile relationally responsible action is when practiced in the presence of dominant others. Commenting on gender differences in conversational styles used in group meetings, Tannen writes that the skills women learn

such as linking one's comments to those of others, waiting to be recognized rather than speaking out, making suggestions rather than demands, supporting others' remarks rather than making all one's comments sound original, are very constructive *when everyone at the meeting is observing those rituals* [italics added]. (p. 301)

Yet when these relationally oriented styles are not practiced by all (read "the men"), women find it difficult to get heard in meetings. Although relational responsibility as Sheila and Ken have presented it involves more than communication style, Tannen's example is troubling because it suggests that, at least in the short term, dominance trumps relational overtures.

I recognize that Tannen's (1994a, 1994b) examples do not completely measure up to Sheila's and Ken's conception of relationally responsible practice. Clearly, airplane crashes and testosterone in the boardroom are complicated things and involve significantly different phenomena than Sheila and Ken set out to discuss. I have offered them as caricatures of interactive moments that hint at directions to extend the concept so that issues of dominance, power, and access can be refigured as relational processes.

What seems clear to me as I consider the examples is that accountability cannot be completely diffused into the relationship nor can it be reduced to a simple question of individual agency. In the Tannen (1994a, 1994b) examples, one speaker's willingness to trust the relational process–to diffuse accountability into the relationship–is sabotaged by a conversationally dominant other. What we need is a new language that allows us to tell the agent from the relationship, even though each is emerging interactively. The challenge that awaits us is to develop practices of accountability that are sensitive to the social and political origins of our uniqueness without losing an appreciation of dancer, the dance, or the music.

NOTES

1. It's interesting to note a related issue about the voice of academic authority: That authority is primarily accomplished through criticism and defensive strategizing rather than, as the authors of this text invite, through supplementation and extension. Readers would certainly suspect the legitimacy of a spouse's response written in the critical mode, because the relationship between the critic and the author would be seen an intervening variable confounding "independent" thinking. Yet from the perspective of this book, responses are always dependent on relationships, and once the ability to respond ("response-ability") is made relational and multivocal, then other voices can be heard in a spouse's response.

2. What is said and what is said about the relationship are not separable. It is tempting to think of relationally responsible action during a dispute as actions intended to maintain the relationship even at the expense of the issue or content at hand. Yet this temptation leads to an untenable container model of communication in which relational contexts are treated as existing apart from the communicative actions that constitute them.

8

The Uncertain Path to Dialogue

A Meditation

Sallyann Roth

I invite you to join me in a meditation. The questions to follow are not requests for information; they are invitations to experience the sense of human connectedness and shared responsibility that comes from allowing ourselves to wonder, to not understand, to participate in the repersonalization of the generalized and objectified, to open up space for the future, now-being-realized world, the world that we create together. Perhaps, too, the questions are answers in themselves, pointing beyond themselves.

Think of the "I" voice as yourself as you read and reflect.

Sometimes, I am in a conversation, or an argument, or perhaps even a shouting match that goes nowhere, an encounter that produces nothing

AUTHOR'S NOTE: The author is indebted to Michael Hjerth of Stockholm, Sweden, with whom she is working on an expanded version of this chapter, for contributing his thoughtful comments and ideas to this meditation. The meditation embodies many of the ideas developed in the Public Conversations Project (Becker, Chasin, Chasin, Herzig, & Roth, 1995; Chasin & Herzig, 1994; Chasin et al., 1996; Roth, 1993; Roth, Chasin, Chasin, Becker, & Herzig, 1992: Roth, Herzig, Chasin, Chasin, & Becker, 1995), for which the author gratefully acknowledges her colleagues and long-time teammates, Carol Becker, Laura R. Chasin, Richard M. Chasin, Margaret M. Herzig, and Robert R. Staines, Jr.

but heat. Sometimes, I feel certain that I know exactly what someone else is about to say and I anticipate, with great conviction, just how wrong-headed it is going to be.

Sometimes, I feel hopeless about ever being heard, understood, or adequately listened to by a particular person or in some particular conversation or on a particular subject. And sometimes, I just get tired of trying to make myself understood. I don't want to try to explain myself again, or I feel dismissive or perhaps violent. Sometimes, I want to run right over what others say.

At times like these,

> How can I keep from being taken over by hurt, hopelessness, anger, or disrespect?
> How can I keep from being taken over by the belief that the other person or group is really the problem?
> How can I keep myself from just shutting down?

But then, on the other hand,

> What do I do that shuts others down?
> What do I do that leaves others feeling insignificant, blank, out of place, silenced, walled off, unwilling to be open when they are with me?
> What do I do that prompts others to try to convince me of their rightness, of my wrongness, to will their assertions on me, to not speak directly to me, or to ignore my presence or even my very existence?

When I meet people who challenge my views, or my beliefs, or my values,

> What makes it possible for me to listen to them?
> What makes it possible for me to invite them to tell me more about what they think and feel?
> What makes it possible for me to ask them how they came to think and feel as they do?

When I feel challenged, or even threatened by others,

What makes it possible to wonder about, to be interested in, to ask about, how they came to believe what they believe or to "know" what they know when it is so different from what I believe and from what I "know"?

What kinds of actions and contexts encourage me

To speak with an open heart?
To listen with an open heart?

What kinds of contexts feel safe enough

To enable me to speak so openly and listen so openly to others that I may be changed by the contact, influenced by the conversation?

What kinds of actions and contexts make it possible for me to shift the meanings I make of my experiences of past and present events and of imagined futures?

How can I open up to explore our many differences, our stories, our lives, our present circumstances?

How can I speak fully even when speaking fully may reveal that we simply cannot understand one another?

What kinds of actions and contexts encourage me

To abandon assumptions that I know what others mean?
To turn my passion to inquiring about things I do not or cannot understand?
To reveal how much I do not understand?
To make space for differences in experience, in the meanings I give to that experience, and for every other kind of difference there may be?

What do I do

That calls forth from others that which is unusual for them to speak openly?
That brings forward responses of unusual complexity and richness?
That calls forward other people's reflections or their most passionate intentions?
That calls forward their readiness to speak of fragmentary thoughts, thoughts that are only on their way to being fully thought, or those that have been thought but never before spoken?

When I have thought that others would find my thoughts, feelings, beliefs, or perspectives "wrong," "off center," or just too different,

> What have others done that has allowed me to be open with them, to think of and speak of things I have not spoken?
>
> What have others done to call into voice that which I feared to say or perhaps even to think when I imagined, perhaps rightly, that open speaking might alienate the very people I cared about or depended on?
>
> What have others done to call into voice my full feeling, thinking, and speaking in a way that has permitted me to welcome confusions, to feel less certain, and to open myself to change through my connection with them?

When I feel that other people's thoughts, feelings, beliefs, or perspectives are "wrong," "dangerous," or just too different from mine,

> What might others do or say to prepare me to listen to that which feels intolerable to hear, too different, too confusing, too challenging, too incomprehensible, things I just don't want to hear?

How can I remind myself to speak for myself, from my own experience, and to not shore myself up by speaking as a member of a group as if I represented others?

How can I remember to listen fully, openly, with genuine interest, without judgment, and without argument to another's challenging or different ideas, feelings, beliefs?

How can I stay open to hearing fresh things even in other's familiar words?

And how can I listen just as fully, just as openly, and just as generously and without judgment to myself?

If I do hold myself open in this way, and if the other, the one who is "different," does the same,

> Might we then experience and speak of our similarities and refrain from defining ourselves strongly by our differences?
>
> Might we refuse to define each other as "other?"

And if I hold myself open in this way with "like-minded" people,

> Might we speak openly of our differences when we have previously defined ourselves by our similarities?
>
> Might we step away from seeing ourselves as an "us" that is distinct from the "them"?

How can we create a place where we experience our connection with each other through our very differences? A place where neither of us gives up central beliefs, values, and commitments but where the tension of our difference—and our meeting across that difference—generates a fresh experience of you, of me, and of us with one another?

What does each of us each need to gain the vision, the will, the strength, the simple doggedness to travel this path?

How shall we find the courage to make this journey?

———————

9

Relational Responsibility

Deconstructive Possibilities

Mary Gergen

A fax found in my study June 1996 contained this scribbled message:

> Mary, This is not anywhere near what I had hoped to send you . . . I keep running
> into life's dilemmas
>
> - chipped tooth—I'm off to the dentist for a cap this a.m. for 3 hrs!
> - well going dry—I am rationing water & getting a monitor
> - unexpected guests and the weekend went whizzing by
> - allergies/cold/reaction to dryness & fire fall out. What a life. This week I do
>   have time and will write write write. Oh how guilty I am! And how amazing to
>   have such a list of excuses!! . . . .
>
> W . . .

And so to begin with a familiar story: a litany of guilt, rationalizations, supplications, and remorse, from one friend to another, to justify some real or imagined offense for which she has taken responsibility. I preface this commentary with this note to give evidence for a traditional form of exchange, in which we all engage when we believe ourselves to be in the wrong. This discourse of individual responsibility runs deep, even among people who would yearn to deconstruct it. It is in this long, dark tunnel of the solitary individual, burdened with the obligations of guilt and shame for responsibilities unfulfilled, that the introductory chapters on "Relational Responsibility" serves as a light. It is not the end of the tunnel of individual fault, of course, but it offers some respite in the form of an alternative formulation, which, on the one hand, challenges the old burdens of individual responsibility but on the other hand (lest we get off the hook too easily), offers us a new obligation in the form of a revised understanding of how we live together and to what we owe our due.

In what follows, I will elaborate on themes that have arisen as a result of conversations with authors, responders, and some textual friends. Combining various threads of discourses, I hope to write my way out of the dilemma (which is probably shared by most of the respondents) of creating a relationally responsible rejoinder to work that is important to two people with whom many relational ties are shared. Writing an interesting supplement, which is both provocative and appreciative, to these exceedingly complex and creative chapters has been a difficult challenge. At the same time, it has been an intriguing exercise to react to a formulation that arrives fresh on the doorsteps of academic discourse.

PERSONAL RESPONSIBILITY:
THE DARK UNDERSIDE AND SHINY SURFACE

The problems of traditional notions of responsibility are well developed in the initial chapters. Sheila McNamee and Kenneth Gergen describe the discourse of individual responsibility as "severely limited—intellectually, ideologically, and pragmatically" (p. 3, this volume). In consort with this viewpoint, one can see life as composed of clots of conflicts and controversies, which are resolved by clarifying who is responsible for which misfortune. Whether it is the home, school, courtroom, highway, or high seas, distributions of responsibility, blame, approbation, and punishment persist. Tendencies for expanding horizons of individual responsibility are evident in news reports across the globe. In the United States today, we increasingly read accounts of young children tried as adults in criminal cases, parents held responsible for the actions of their offspring, company vice presidents on trial for the misdeeds of their subordinates, homeowners sued for the mishaps of their neighbors, and professional workers for malpractice. It is against this riptide of individual responsibility that the movers to relational responsibility suggest a systemic swim. Can one be optimistic given the current trends?

Before we begin to explore the theme of movement from the individual to the relational, we might briefly note that missing from the McNamee and Gergen account of individual responsibility is its upside. Daily life is also characterized by an emphasis on meritorious responsibility—Dean's List; Employee of the Month, Nobel prizes, MacArthur genius awards, Pulitzer Prizes, and Olympic medals for individual achievements. Who gets credit for successful enterprises is important enough in our society that people struggle over who gets the kudos. From CEOs such as Roberto Goizueta of Coca Cola, who earned more than $1 billion dollars since 1979, to coaches of NBA basketball, such as the Boston Celtics coach who tops the charts at $7 million, to the manager of the local hardware store, the bucks and responsibility for success stop at the same chair. Because society extends its highest rewards to those who are responsible for its outstanding achievements, the desire to maintain such a form of evaluation is high, especially among the successful and those who are orienting their lives to attaining these rewards in the future. *Responsibility* is a word worth hanging on to from the perspectives of the winners.

The tenacity with which people generally hold to the need for assigning responsibility to individuals is also fueled by the belief that an orderly society requires it (M. Gergen, 1992). Justice is done in that people responsible for bad things are punished, and people responsible for good things are rewarded. In everyday life, it is ordinarily believed that the obvious outcome of a withdrawal of this type of system would be chaos: Terrible crimes would be committed frequently and at random once "responsibility" and its consequences were removed from the grand calculus of social accountability; nor would people engage in prosocial behaviors, because there would be no credit for doing so. Part of the problem in relinquishing the notion of individual responsibility is that if attention to individual motives, goals, and actions is lost, there are no widely held reframings for considering human behaviors. The theoretical enterprise McNamee and Gergen have undertaken might be viewed as an effort to provide an alternative, once personal responsibility is lost.

Although the term *relational responsibility* at first struck me as an effort to undermine our understandings of individual responsibility, I discovered I had misread their intent. The authors seem reluctant to give up on the notion altogether, as they note that the process of relational responsibility "augment[s] the existing tradition" (p. 3, this volume), not replaces it. However, despite supporting the value of inclusivity of all forms of discourse, including individual responsibility, the paper's major argument is directed to creating an alternative type of responsibility based on an appreciation of relatedness as the source of all human meaning and thus, of human action.

NEW FRAMINGS:
RELATIONAL RESPONSIBILITY AND
THE PATHS TO NEW POSSIBILITIES

Contrary to the authors' inclinations to supplement individual responsibility with another kind of responsibility—namely, relational responsibility—I would like to consider what would happen if individual responsibility were absorbed into a relational framework. The restructuring of individual responsibility as relational suggests situating any action, positive or negative, in the emergent qualities of the so-called systemic swim. If we want to talk about responsibility for the Oklahoma City bombing, we do not point a finger at the one who set the bomb and let it be done with; or if our concern is to honor the creation of a new AIDS vaccine, we do not give the Nobel prize to one or two medical researchers and assume that they alone created this serum. To be relational, we become committed to forms of analyses that bring into focus multiples of contributing forces—human, elemental, serendipitous, and historical. The myopic thrust for the apprehension of the individual culprit or the homage to the lone hero fades along with notions of genius, creativity, autonomy, and personal choice, either angelic or diabolical. Beyond this orientation to the emergent quality of events and individuals, a shift to relational responsibility leads to other, more elaborated, discourses of human life.

According to McNamee & Gergen, "Relational responsibility is a dialogic process with two domains of transformation: first, in the interlocutors' understanding of the action in question, . . . and second, in the relations among the interlocutors themselves" (pp. 5-6, this volume). People come to recognize that it is through their relations with others—internal voices, friends, other associates, social groups, and mediated relationships, such as talk shows—that the world takes on meaning. Events are not motivated by the solitary processes of an internalized consciousness. Rather, everything we think, do, feel, and evaluate is in a crucial sense enclosed in the network of relationships. In turn, we recognize our interdependence with our relational partners in having a personal life and in knowing what that life is all about. Although it would be a lifetime project to illuminate all of the facets of this theoretical turn, one might suggest arenas in which radical changes could occur if relational responsibility were taken seriously. Imagine what new forms law, education, and all other competitive activities as well as cooperative endeavors, such as volunteering in community projects, would take. Using the discourse of relational responsibility, the attributions of responsibility might spread far and wide. A couple's argument might be attributed to any and all of the following and more: a prior relationship to siblings in which verbal abuse was the norm, excessive drinking the night before, early morning commitments, pressures at work, a crying baby, the general economy, or the last general election. A promotion at work could be the responsibility of childhood television fare, an assertive grandmother, good touching skills at the office, MBA training from Case Western Reserve professors, a good rapport with one's computer or one's boss (or both). By moving to a relational responsibility posture, ordinary social understandings would be thrown into chaos, and new forms of adjudication, perhaps along the lines of a multiple regression analysis, might be forecasted. One might imagine a judge declaring that the cause of the accident was $\frac{1}{16}$ driver, $\frac{1}{16}$ cellular phone, $\frac{1}{16}$ faulty traffic light, $\frac{1}{16}$ color of other vehicle, $\frac{1}{16}$ pavement surface, $\frac{1}{16}$ weather conditions, and so forth. However, my point is to suggest that once all the voices had been heard in the adjudication of an accident, not to mention a terrorist attack, decisions about responsibility would still be so embroiled in a tangled thicket of options that one might not wish to engage in the effort of sorting out the fractions of responsibility. Responsibility could be so embedded in so many complex interactions and thus spread so thin among various participants, it might just disappear as an interesting and useful idea. If giving blame or credit got to be that much trouble, people might just throw up their hands in dismay and never speak of it again.

THE DECONSTRUCTION OF RESPONSIBILITY

Despite the introductory chapter's title, the most vigorous theme in it is not responsibility but relational theory. Throughout various sections, arguments are made that we are born into relationships, carry them with us in all moments of life, and derive our identities from them. Less emphasized, perhaps, but also of importance, is the extent to which the individualizing forms we take on—that is, our selves born in the flux of relating—coconstruct the relationships. In this sense, and I wish it had been put more forcefully in the introductory chapters, individuals can be creative and agentic but still insinuated into a relational form.

For me, appreciating the transformative power of relationships, in two facets of the meaning of *appreciate,* is primary within their orientation. By this, I would suggest that these two meanings: to appreciate, in the sense of to apprehend, to recognize, to perceive and in the sense of to value, to prize, to be glad for, are the essence of a relational response. Arriving at this conclusion, I would suggest that *relational appreciation* rather than responsibility is closer to the spirit of the original text. We both perceive and value the power of relatedness in the creation of all that our lives are. I shall return to this point at the conclusion of this commentary.

Let me, however, return to the notion of responsibility to explore two other arguments against the use of this term, whether attached to individuals or to relationships. One objection I have to the term "responsibility" rests on its association with universal moral claims, and the other objection is to the claim of the authors that the term responsibility should be retained because of its popularity as a conventional means of understanding behavior. The first argument is simply a reminder that social constructionists regard all talk as nonfoundational, including all calls to moral obligation, duty, or responsibility. Framings such as "One must do one's duty to one's country," "Every person is responsible for his or her own welfare" or "We must be indebted to our relationships" suggest that there is some higher authority or transcendental plane of being that has deemed this statement a universal truth, law, or principle, which cannot be discussed, questioned, or disobeyed, at least without censure. Richard Shweder (1991) has called such statements *noncontingent universals*—that is, they hold at all times and all places for everyone. Every aspect of this assumption—that there are unquestioned higher authorities, that there are unrestricted foundational statements, or that there are universal truths—is undermined by social constructionist views on the creative powers of discourse. If language shapes the forms by which we describe the world, then moral claims about the world cannot exceed the language in which they are placed. Thus, moral claims are bounded and contingent on their sayings. Here, I am also in concert with the statement of Rajchman (1991): "The piety of moral theory is to try to say what is good for each and all of us, and where and how to find it" (p. 143). Thus, I believe, neither the authors nor I would want to make any universal claims as to the status of responsibility.

There is, however, a danger that in my argument I have created a critique of universal standards that is unnecessary. The authors might argue that there might indeed be standards, other than eternal verities, that would be helpful in stabilizing notions of responsibility so that it would not be necessary to repudiate the term altogether. The authors might argue that despite the lack of foundational principles in any ontological sense, it would still be useful for the well-being of a community to continue to use this construction as if it were indeed buttressed by foundational principles. Although others have argued for this strategy, it strikes me as patronizing because some members of the community decide for others which so-called truths to universalize and which to dismiss. Another strategy that I do support is that a community decides to adopt a principle, while at the same time acknowledging that the grounds for their doing so are forever shaky.

My second argument addresses the authors' views in favor of continuing to support the word *responsibility* in public discourse because it has such a clear and powerful place in conventional rhetoric. Hardly a moral discussion can be held but the notion of responsibility is highlighted, they argue. The authors suggest that it is foolish to struggle against this linguistic habit, arbitrarily erasing or attempting to exclude it from the public vocabulary. My argument is that words are not so concretized as all that. Rather, they can easily become overwritten, if not erased, through various social practices. Clearly, in ordinary language, it is commonplace that words slip into and out of prominence in fairly short order. (For example, words on the decline: modesty, chastity, virtuous, retiring, illegitimate children, mulatto, Mongoloid trait, moron, crippled, poetess, LP, hi-fi set, affirmative action; words that have more recently come into fashion: worst-case scenario; bottom line; borderline diagnosis, physically challenged; downsize; postmodern, hyperreal, "whatever," as well as many other words that have been related to the influx of new technologies).

Even when words remain intact linguistically, they can shift their meanings considerably. If one recalls the meaning of divorce in the 1970s, when couples in some states could only divorce if a specified act, such as adultery or physical violence, could be proven against one partner and where a case resembled a criminal trial, one can see remarkable shifts in meaning. In the 1990s, instead of a language based on who was responsible for the breakdown of the marriage, the discourse of divorce places an emphasis on psychological issues, social incompatibility, or in some cases, merely "growing apart." Divorce has become "no-fault." There is no longer the stigma of divorce, with its attending shame and guilt, although newer formulations have stressed the mutuality of emotional distress and loss connected to it. As divorces become increasingly commonplace, new meanings may become constructed. We see some efforts in this direction: Divorcing partners jointly send special greeting cards announcing divorce, divorce parties are held by a daring few to celebrate their new freedoms, and ceremonies of divorce conducted by therapists renew the family ties and separate the spouses. Changes in the term *divorce* may be such that by 2010 it could be construed as an experience similar to the selling of a house: stressful but, hopefully, profitable.

The experience of living through the recent "end" of the "cold war" is also a powerful reminder of the swiftness with which extensive vocabularies of understanding can be undermined. Even dying is not above reconstruction. Notions of assisted suicides and living wills shift the meaning of dying from a natural biological event to a group decision. Many other examples might be cited in which terms that were strongly entrenched disappear or are modified. To recall Marx, "All that is solid melts into air" aptly describes this view on the nature of language. I would argue that sustaining a word that undermines one's personal or political values because of its historical and social prominence or for its communication power and facility is not necessary or even wise. Perhaps, the authors will counter that my argument is censorious, and that all vocabularies should be allowed to proliferate. I do not agree. Although I appreciate aspects of the authors' argument that all discourses should be sustained, I have strong preferences for some kinds of vocabularies over others and will work to enhance the vigor of some discourses at the expense of others.

Despite the possibility that erasing "responsibility" might occur, the authors and others might be hesitant to relinquish "responsibility" because of dangers to society, such as those indicated in the introduction. Support for this position is found in Diane Elam's (1994), *Ms. in Abyme,* where she struggles with similar questions about the nature of responsibility or, as she calls it, a concern for justice. Elam is careful to point out that we face a paradox regarding our responsibilities for carrying out justice. "Even though justice is . . . impossible, one should not stop trying to be just" (p. 120). She suggests that "the call to responsibility to the Other [those that are different from the community in some unspecified way] comes from nowhere, is neither absolutely human or inhuman" (p. 110). She tries to locate a space for this responsibility between the notion of community solidarity favored by Richard Rorty (1989) and the notion of universal, or God-given principles. In her defense of responsibility, she quotes Derrida (1991): "Responsibility is excessive or it is not responsibility," (p. 108) that is, it cannot be justified; it goes beyond the knowledge of the moment. It is some obligation one has, beyond irrefutable arguments, as to why it is so. In this call for a nonfoundational demand for justice, a place for relational responsibility may well be seeded. McNamee and Gergen could claim that the discourse Elam lacks in order to talk about this type of responsibility is derived from the relational. This is the source of responsibility between the human and the inhuman or nonhuman world.

For Elam (1994), the demand for justice is insatiable. She argues, "Obligation to otherness is a debt that cannot be calculated; what single lump-sum payment could compensate non-whites for the history of racism, for example?" (p. 111). Although I affirm the efforts to locate a nonfoundationalist claim for an ethic of responsibility and the search for an always elusive justice, Elam's particular exemplification of relational responsibility is the downside of this formulation. It strikes me as both grim and, in the end, pointless to suggest an eternal and static relationship of responsibility between the victim and the perpetrators. The vision of human reparation as a life's work, without any progress, is much like the eternal punishment of Sisyphus, who each day must roll a boulder up the hill, only to have it roll back down again. In this view of striving for justice, I see a close parallel to the notion of relational responsibility. From a psychological viewpoint, such an orientation to life would do very little good for either the One or the Other. Although Elam tries to convince her reader that we are ineluctably responsible, for me it invites repugnance.

Beyond the impracticalities of convincing people of their endless responsibilities to serve the call for justice, my theoretical argument against Elam's version of relational responsibility concerns her construction of the terms of the One and Otherness. The extent to which McNamee and Gergen also depend on this binary is unclear, but it is a problematic aspect of pointing the finger of blame.

The spreading out of the responsibility for any deemed dishonor creates a deep dilemma of where to place it. If we are all responsible for everything and we have all been victimized, the term itself is deconstructed. In Elam's version, we find the limits of individual and pure group responsibility. Here, one can grasp the necessity of going toward a more collective and ambiguous notion of responsibility. Yet at the same time, one might wish for something other than the broadest notion of responsibility to bring us into closer harmony and a more perfect union with diverse and partially different others.

BEYOND RESPONSIBILITY TO RELATIONAL APPRECIATION

Once responsibility is deconstructed, we might want to explore other avenues for social commerce. Can we imagine formulations that might build on the notion of relational appreciation as a source? To begin, it seems to me that words such as *duty, ought to, must, should, be responsible for* serve to span a chasm between what might be thought of as natural "instincts" for self-interest, self-preservation, personal desires, and the like and the protection of the interests of others. When authorities want to prevent people from engaging in some so-called selfish behavior, the conventional practice has been to create a moral injunction, a law, a religious stricture, or a social code that enforces the socially beneficial behaviors over the so-called self-centered ones. The force of most negative aspects of individual responsibility seems to rest on this understanding. Be responsible or else! The shift to relational responsibility suggests that we recognize the generative powers of relationships to create the conditions of our understandings. Thus, one might argue that through relational processes one could alter this understanding of what one's desires, goals, and preferred behaviors might be. Within relational theory, a person is not innately desirous of dominating, defeating, oppressing, controlling, or destroying others. Even how one responds to situations of seeming privation and plenty is not preordained. The notion that the world would turn into a society as described in Golding's novel, *The Lord of the Flies,* is no more necessary than that it turn into some utopian vision of total harmony. Through relational processes, all options are opened. With others, we create what we are together (M. Gergen, 1995).

The present questioning of the concept of responsibility hearkens back to a theoretical controversy in the 1980s between Lawrence Kohlberg (1981) and Carol Gilligan (1982) regarding moral development and decision making. As I am suggesting, responsibility is a notion that has been dependent on principled arguments outlining a set of duties or obligations of an individual to other entities, the purpose of which is to ensure their protection. In this circumstance, the nature of the relationship among the parties is irrelevant. The significant aspect of responsibility I want to highlight here is that it is codified, thus standardized, and as such, insensitive to the nuances of any particular situation and the relationships developed therein. For a Kohlbergian, a highly developed set of moral principles concerning one's duties is required to lead an ethical life. Gilligan's (1982) approach required a more sensitive appreciation of the particulars of a situation. She too, stresses the notion of responsibility, but she has framed it within the context of caring and a concern for the hurt to others of any action. The flexibility she advocated is based on the possibility that one's actions in one situation might be different from those in a seemingly similar situation at another time. More central to her arguments are the notions of caring and of care. For me, Gilligan's conclusions stressed connectedness rather than rules; applied to the dilemma of relational responsibility, it is to suggest that a society that emphasized mutual affection, love, caring, and respect for others, qualities that are nurtured through rewarding relationships, would be much more desirable than one that stressed responsibility separated from care. Actions that could be described as responsible might well follow, but not from a principled stance. People who appreciate their relational involvements and who care about each other are likely to take care of each other. This community's discourse would emphasis relational appreciation, rather than relational responsibility, in its daily life.

Many of the arguments put forth by McNamee and Gergen in their introduction to relational responsibility would be applicable within the framework of relational appreciation. The understanding that relationships create individuality in a reciprocal relationship to the relations themselves would stand. So would the understanding that through relationships, realities are spawned and supported as well as diminished and erased. One's valuing of the centrality of relating would be connected to the outcomes of particular relations, as understood from an admittedly partial perspective. Although one might be inclined to value relatedness as a seemingly foundational element in the building of a life, the value placed on any particular relationships would be fluid and transient. Not all relationships would bear continuance but rather, should be destroyed. From my point of view, the slow passage of "responsibility" over the horizon of the linguistic landscape would be highly satisfying, as long as new forms of relational language would rise to take its place. The transformative potential of such a shift would be revolutionary. I think it would be very exciting to be a part of such a social experiment.

10

Relational Responsibility or Dialogic Ethics?

A Questioning of McNamee and Gergen

Stanley Deetz
William J. White

McNamee and Gergen ask, What kinds of worlds are made possible by alternative ways of putting things, specifically discussing responsibility in relational terms? This essay further pursues that question, suggesting, through the analysis of a specific case, that the language of responsibility, even with a relational focus, continues to limit the discussion. The language of relational responsibility makes it difficult to adequately consider power relations generally and specifically, the consent-and-compliance process that exists in relationships and communities. In contrast, the emerging language of dialogic or communication ethics offers a more thorough engagement in negotiation and mutually satisfying world creation.

This process of shifting the terms of discussion from the isolated self and the logic of responsibilities to the processes of communication entails the elaboration of new obligations to open conversation and provides more clarity to the importance of other voices and of alternate ways of being, knowing, and understanding. It is our argument that "responsiveness" to "otherness" made possible by open interaction is more critical to an emancipatory theory than is a notion of relational "responsibility" elaborated in terms of accountability, sensitivity, and obligations.

Consider this set of events: Each summer, a certain large Northeastern university runs a 4-week program for incoming first-year students from "economically disadvantaged families." The stated goals of the program include inculcating into these students certain skills (time management, writing, critical reading, and the like) as well as acclimating them to college life. The staff of this program is composed of administrators, instructors, and "residence life" personnel, including undergraduate peer counselors who are themselves alumni of the program. Each week, they meet to disseminate information about and discuss issues related to the program.

At one such meeting, in the context of a discussion about whether students are perceiving the classes as too difficult or too easy, a peer counselor raises the issue of instructors changing their syllabi with little advance notice. Students are concerned that they are unable to plan their time efficiently, he says, because the demands on that time are constantly being changed. A number of instructors respond: The practice is not so uncommon; "it is a fact of college life" to which students must adjust; "professors have a right" to modify their syllabi as they see fit. Then, an administrator interjects, "This is just griping by the students." It is "inappropriate," he goes on, to bring such gripes into the staff meeting. "Look, we're the instructors," he says. "You have to trust us." To do otherwise means that we would be letting "snot-nosed young kids" tell us how to run our classrooms. "I'm not jumping on you," he tells the peer counselor. "Don't take it personal." ("Try not to take it personal," amends one instructor, wryly.)

This scene, as routine and mundane as it may be, is filled with conceptions of personal and institutional responsibility. We will use it as a case to think through McNamee and Gergen's language of relational responsibility. What kinds of worlds, they ask, are made possible by discussing such events in terms of relational responsibility? What kinds of worlds are possible if discussed in other ways?

WHAT DOES THE LANGUAGE OF "RESPONSIBILITY" ENTAIL?

McNamee and Gergen choose to describe their normative concerns as a kind of responsibility. As a concept, responsibility has attracted the recent interest of a wide variety of scholars, from theologians (Smith, 1983) to philosophers (Johnson, 1993; Jonas, 1984; Lucas, 1993; MacIntyre, 1984) psychologists (Semin & Manstead, 1983; Weiner, 1995), political scientists (Ezrahi, 1990), and economists (Posner, 1981). The word "responsibility" itself is from the Latin, "I answer" (*respondeo*): Its very roots proclaim the primacy of the originary, unitary ego. The history, system of distinctions, and linguistic inter-connections of "responsibility" do not go away easily. Usually expressed within this idea of "response-ability" are three interrelated subordinate concepts: (a) causation, (b) morality (accountability and legal obligation), and (c) rationality or practicality. Causal responsibility for an event may be assigned to an entity to the extent that its actions (willful or otherwise) enabled the event to come to pass; we are allowed to speak of inanimate objects or forces being responsible for certain occurrences—"Gravity is responsible for the orbits of the planets."

"Moral" responsibility, as "accountability," suggests that a self-aware actor may be called on to explain (to account for) his or her actions by a boss, a court, a constituency, or a God: that is, by an audience presumed to have some capability or moral authority to pass judgment. Judgments of moral responsibility involve attributions about causal responsibility as well as the intentionality of the actor and the quality of outcomes; these judgments are then supposed to influence affective responses to the actor. Low perceived levels of moral responsibility for negative outcomes, for example, result in sympathy; high levels, in blameful anger (Weiner, 1995). As a type of moral responsibility, legal responsibility or obligation is constrained by the requirement that the law "decide in favor of one party or the other. . . . In morals it is possible to distribute the blame" (Roberts, 1965, p. 255). Roberts notes that "the moment one admits that blame may be bi-personal, or multi-personal, the path is opened for a long series of causal explanations extending back into the life histories of those concerned" (p. 255), which she regards with some trepidation but which McNamee and Gergen clearly relish.

Practical responsibility is a kind of trustworthiness indicating that an individual can be trusted to meet obligations that he or she has undertaken or been assigned. Ezrahi (1990) refers to this as the "technicalization" of action—action purified of personal ends and alienated (detached) from the public actor. Practical responsibility suggests that an actor is aware of the link between causal and moral forms of responsibility and will act accordingly. To behave responsibly, in other words, is to behave as if one will have to account for the occurrences one causes.

Let us return to the opening scene for a moment to indicate how this way of putting responsibility enables us to interpret what occurs within the vignette. The peer counselor, having undertaken the duty of advising and assisting a group of students, behaves in accordance with the dictates of practical responsibility, acting as the agent to the students' principal (as it were), raising their concerns in a setting appropriate to that purpose. To the instructors who responded, the events occurring within a classroom are their moral responsibility; to a certain degree, they feel the obligation to account for their actions (making syllabus changes). However, they are aware of the mechanics of blame to the extent that they are able to avoid attributions of causal responsibility, their actions are not blameful. And thus their response is to assert that syllabus changes are a (causeless and immutable?) "fact of life" to which the students must become accustomed. The administrator who interjected proceeds from a different set of assumptions. The peer counselor, in his view, behaves (practically) irresponsibly when he voices the students' "gripes" because teachers are not accountable to their students. He does not evade causal responsibility for syllabus changes; he embraces it. Instructors control what occurs within the classroom, and they are morally responsible for the students' learning, but the arrow of accountability points upward (to administrators, the university, parents, society) rather than downward (to students).

Both responses are problematic and limiting for precisely the reasons that McNamee and Gergen might suggest: Their language of personal and institutional responsibility asserts a theory (philosophy, ideology) that isolates human beings, misrecognizes their mutuality, and deprives certain members of negotiative voice. Such a language perpetuates the prescription of individual solutions in a world filled with systemic problems. Because we exist not as private, originary selves having linear effects but as selves constructed in interaction with others having interactional and mutual effects, the goal of interaction must be to ensure that this process of construction enables us to recognize alternative ways of being, knowing, and understanding as joint products. But have McNamee and Gergen escaped the traps of the language of responsibility?

SHIFTING THE LOCUS OF RESPONSIBILITY OR THE LANGUAGE OF RESPONSIBILITY

Irresponsibility, says Smith (1983), "is hopelessly bad, but responsibility is at best inadequately good" (p. 83). Responsibility, in other words, is not a high moral standard; an individual is responsible for an occurrence only to the extent that he or she (as a unitary, bounded self) intentionally acted to cause that occurrence. Events that cannot be attributed to such a self impose no onus; an individual is not obligated to remedy flaws that he or she did not create. Relational responsibility ups the ante. Relational responsibility moves us from "doing no harm" to working at reciprocal good; fortuitously, in interdependent systems, supporting the good of the other leads to self-benefit.

This relation apparently could not be recognized in the staff meeting case. The language of rights and responsibility left a nondiscussable, nonnegotiable situation where interdependence and complex rights and responsibilities could not be expressed and thus mutually conceived. It is interesting that if the university's total quality management officer had attended the meeting, he or she might have intervened by proclaiming the student as customer and introducing customer "rights." In doing so, another world with reassigned rights becomes possible, but those rights are no more relational than are the rights conceived by the original participants in the meeting. Different institutional and personal rights and responsibilities are assigned—but they are still personal and institutional. If the university had a relational responsibility facilitator, the new conflicts and discussions would be far different.

Like McNamee and Gergen, many of the attempts to shift the locus of responsibility from individuals to communities (that is, to various systems of relationships) rely on a shift in the residence of rights; such a shift seems necessary to lend rhetorical coherence to the responsibility argument. Jonas (1984), for example, suggests that the amplification of human technological powers and the resulting vulnerability of both nature and humanity's future to human action requires an acknowledgement of nature's rights and humanity's obligation to (the rights of) its future. There are correspondences between rights and responsibilities, in other words: The existence of a right incurs a corresponding obligation—a practical responsibility in all those who encounter (interact with) the rights bearer. By conceiving of new (or previously unrecognized) rights, we simultaneously conceive of new responsibilities.

In McNamee and Gergen's extension, these responsibilities have to be worked out in contexts characterized by indeterminant causal and consequent chains, high interdependence, and complex and conflictual institutional, community, and relational connections. The conception of definitive and substantive rights and responsibilities in such a context would be impossible. The answer, as McNamee and Gergen suggest, lies not in structural formulae but in procedural ones. As we become aware of the negotiated and constructed nature not only of identities but also of relationships and systems of relations, we begin to recognize the need to implement interaction processes that do not privilege particular ways of understanding and of being—to adopt an ethics of mutual decision making that requires us to engage in the negotiation of identities and forms of relatedness. McNamee and Gergen do not tell us about how to begin such a process—only that we must proceed. We are guided, however, by the idea that shifting the locus of responsibility requires the production of new obligations: to the voices within our selves, to the relationships in which we exist, and to the processes through which these are constructed.

But even accepting the tentative and initial parts of their work, we feel the world McNamee and Gergen inhabit is too benign, their sensibilities too middle-classed, and their hopes too academic. Their world seems filled with people who misunderstand responsibility but to lack the powerful, the petty, and the opportunistic. In their world, there are reasonable experimentations and minor jealousies but no passion or rage. They have people who wish to learn and grow rather than people who hate and fear that their world is fading.

Let us try a visual image to summarize where we are at the moment before we start another direction. In the 1930s, one of artist Saul Steinberg's (see Tillich, 1969) drawings captured an emerging sense of our mutuality and shared responsibility. He showed two people each balanced on an end of a seesaw (or teeter-totter). The fulcrum for the board, however, sits on a cliff with one person over solid ground and the other over the void. But the person over the void has a gun pointed at the one over land. The drawing provides a quick image of a kind of mutual responsibility, a responsibility built into the structure of the situation rather than the hearts and minds or even the language of the participants.

What is interesting about writing a description of the drawing rather than seeing it is the way causal chains and responsibilities shift as each detail is added. And we need not stop where Steinberg did. What if we now provide the person over the void with a "golden parachute" or safety net? Or we give the gun to the person over the land and he or she puts it to his or her own head? Any way we reconstruct the drawing, nuances of power, mutuality, and responsibility are placed in a different relief.

Without a doubt, the example staff meeting would have been different if each administrator, instructor, and peer counselor had seen themselves and others on that seesaw. But, and we think that this is a key challenge for McNamee and Gergen, the difference would not rest in a new language of relational responsibility but in an inescapable recognition of each individual's interdependence and interchangeability (the fate of person A would be no better in B's place). McNamee and Gergen add a couple of interesting twists to Steinberg's vivid sense of interdependence, which we think usefully complicate it, but we can envision further challenges to their conception.

First, imagine the Steinberg drawing as animated rather than static and, in McNamee and Gergen's world, let's give the drawing pens to each actor. One can easily imagine two tacks. One is for each actor to quickly redraw the picture to his or her own advantage and the other is to more cohesively wed their fates together.

A few observations: The one who pursues personal advantage and safety is clearly advantaged if his or her safety can be accomplished by individual action, regardless of what the other individual does. However, if personal safety cannot be secured unilaterally, but instead requires the joint action of both actors, then the need to think in relational terms might be more clear to each individual. "We," the figures on the see-saw might say, "are in this together."

All other things being equal, the value and desire for a relational language, as McNamee and Gergen recognize (counter the humanists), emerges in this second situation. But all other things are not equal. Some of our characters can draw faster than others, some draw to please the other, and others do not operate rationally. Power, consent, and ideology enter in. Why would either the powerful, the complicit, or the deceived enter into relational talk? Can a relational responsibility discourse replace one of personal advantage? What is the relationally responsible response that the student in the example meeting should make to the administrator? Why do we believe that this administrator would forfeit his identity for a more open interaction? How can the participants escape the initial asymmetry of sessions for "inculcation" and "acclimation?" Or are inculcation and acclimation important initial processes for developing a more productive language of responsibility?

Second, McNamee and Gergen present an even more complicated world for our actors. Let us imagine multilegged actors with feet on several seesaws at once and with the capacity to trade places with others across many different boards. Let us also start a clock that severely limits their stay on any board and give our actors veils that allow them only to see a small number of the effects of each of their moves, effects that are codetermined by the moves of others. The old conception of responsibility contained linear causal strings, capacities of foresight and rational choice, and accountability. Can the term responsibility carry any meaning in this new world, or does it carry only the moral force of the old term without any substance? If real interdependence cannot be calculated or even seen, when the world is filled with rude awakenings for even the most careful and best intentioned, can the language of responsibility in any sense inspire or even sort out? Would our example meeting be helped by offering a language of relational responsibility, or would its members invent relational responsibility only if their interdependence was visible and inescapable? Or perhaps a locus of responsibility is the wrong place to look.

A PLACE TO BEGIN

We would suggest that responsibility may be part of the language to be given up. At the least, it has become so connected to conceptions of individualism, rationality, and the psychological person to create endless misdirections in discussion. We have available to us another tradition that has long considered not only social constructivism and the social origin of experience but also power relations. This is the German moral philosophy tradition from phenomenology through hermeneutics and critical theory to contemporary feminism, the most relevant of which situates our mutuality in the communication process itself. Much of this literature is widely available and familiar, so we will not spend much time developing it here (Benhabib, 1992; Deetz, 1990, 1992, 1995a, 1995b; Deetz & Haas, in press; Habermas, 1984). We find it odd that McNamee and Gergen would turn more to a communitarian tradition than to a communication one.

Certainly, much heuristic guidance for their project could be gained by Habermas's (e.g., 1984) and Apel's (1979) grounding of ethics in the immanent conditions of communicative action. Rather than ethics being biologically or psychologically grounded in the person or sociologically grounded in the tradition or community, ethics can be grounded in the communicative micropractices of everyday life.

Critical theorists have been useful partly because their analysis of the rise of instrumental reasoning was complete and persuasive but perhaps more important, because they identified the key problem as the nature of the discussion itself rather than the participants. The difficulties arise from the process of talk itself rather than the language of responsibility (see Bauman, 1993).

McNamee and Gergen, like many who follow the more communitarian argument, hold a grossly untheorized conception of discussion and dialogue. Talk and "voice" are treated as surprisingly unproblematic. But the problem with their position is not only the weak dialogue mechanisms they posit but the consensual goals they seek—a weakness they share with critical theorists such as Habermas. Clearly, they go beyond Habermas. They avoid his faith in rationality but not his preference for agreement over conflict. Their solution to homelessness, insecurity, and self-interest does not rest in simply claiming the possibility for more rational foundations and social consensus. They accept the loss of community and foundations as a situation that can provide the freedom to seek more satisfying ways of living together (see also Giddens, 1991). They understand that we do not need more morality, we need better discussions. But their reclaiming of voices misses how these voices exist at all, the productive quality of fundamental conflict, the process of entering into decisions we make together, and the indeterminancy of all situations.

Feminists such as Benhabib (1990), in reframing Habermas's (1984) project, have simply been much better in understanding both the interconnectedness of people and the situated nature of power and discourse. Their avoidance of universalizing substantive or procedural claims yet advancing a communication-based ethics overcomes many of the weaknesses identified (see Deetz & Haas, in press). Habermas's ideal speech community, like McNamee and Gergen's world, assumes that all participants are considered to be equal. However, as illustrated by Benhabib, Habermas's theory of communicative ethics breaks down with the reality of gendered and racial inequities.

Habermas's (1984) ideal speech community and intersubjective communication can, however, be reformed in ways that foster the dialogic process in such contexts. Benhabib's (1990) concept of the standpoint of the "concrete other" focuses on a person's "concrete individuality" (p. 309). One does not start from a general obligation or an appropriate language but in relation with a concrete other, an other who exceeds any conception that can be had of him or her. This is an other with a genuine "otherness" that calls from us that which we do not give up easily: our own self-confident understanding of self, other, and world.

To the critical theorists, the attempt to reach mutual understanding includes a socially based method of morally guided dispute resolution and a description of communicative difficulties (i.e., those communicative processes that preclude mutual understanding). A "participation perspective" emerging from this position, and drawing as well on Benhabib (1990), also takes the pursuit of mutual understanding—but not necessarily consensus—to be its normative goal; it explores how communication difficulties arise from communication practices that preclude debate and conflict about values, that substitute images and imaginary relations for self-presentation and truth claims, that arbitrarily limit access to communication channels and forums, and that then lead to decisions based on arbitrary authority relations.

If we follow out this communication focus, the analysis attends more to interaction processes and language use than simply the vocabulary of action. When this is seen, then relational responsibility appears less like a virtue and more like a residual of a conflictual, demanded responsiveness. The question is not how to make interaction more responsible but how to make it more responsive. Voice is not granted by new concepts or elite groups but is demanded by those who have something to say in concrete situations. The best we can do as intellectuals is to provide more general analytic and expressive tools to disrupt the various processes by which discussion is closed off and conflict and voices are suppressed (see Deetz, 1992, Chapter 7).

For example, when the undergraduate student who served as peer counselor raised the question of changing syllabi, he was (potentially) beginning a discourse about how students and instructors should be or exist together—about what it means to be a student or an instructor. The various responses to the student's statement served as forms of discursive closure, suppressing potential conflict by closing off particular topics of discussion in a variety of ways. These include, in Deetz's (1992) terms, neutralization and naturalization ("Syllabi changes are a fact of life. Get over it"), disqualification ("That's just griping"), meaning denial ("I'm not jumping on you"), and legitimation ("We're the instructors. You have to trust us"). Recognizing these sorts of statements as products of communicative practices that close off avenues of discussion potentially enables a participant in the conversation to challenge them. The implication is that there are ways of communicating that open rather than close the domain of discourse; the question becomes one of identifying those ways. We are not sure we know how to convince our example staff members to be more relationally responsible. But we can offer guidance to the student on how to be responsive to the various concrete discussion blocks that emerge in practice.

This at least is another take. We have muddled through this, posing problems as they have arisen for us and using those problems both conceptually and practically as we address the discussion in our example meeting. Last, we have tried to consider other avenues that might foster the hope expressed by McNamee and Gergen. The conversation continues.

11

Responding and Relating

Response-Ability to Individuals, Relating, and Difference

Michael J. Mazanec
Steve Duck

Responsibility is a process that is taken and given, liberating and silencing, embraced and ignored—it has the possibility of being both our desire ("I want more responsibility at work") and our burden ("Don't lay all the blame on me"). We are interested in the interplay of multiple, although not necessarily equal, discourses of responsibility that grant meaning to daily life. We distinguish this approach from a hollow plurality of responsibility that is assumed to be equally available to anyone to participate in. Instead, we treat discussions of responsibility as prefiguring certain assumptions about everyday life. Being able to respond, assigning responsibility, taking responsibility, and silencing responsibility are all examples of the way responsibility is embedded in questions of power and material existence. In our contribution, we wish to explore, with McNamee and Gergen, the ways in which power and voice implicate discussions of responsibility in relational processes.

In and through a dialogue with the original manuscript, with each other as coauthors, and directly in writing to McNamee and Gergen, we aim to probe existing ideas, argue for different and sometimes contradictory points of view, and ask new questions that involve other relevant intelligibilities of relating that invoke important nuances of difference and responsibility.

POWER AND DIFFERENCE:
RESPONSIBILITY AS RELATIONAL

Sometimes, a relational moment permits a respondent to "blame the other." At other relational moments, one is socially positioned to do nothing other than "take responsibility." We agree with McNamee and Gergen that these constructions are meaningful within the conjoint realities of relationships. We begin to depart from their thesis, however, by suggesting that the construction of such realities as social and relational prerequires judgments that are embedded in questions of power and material resources. To illustrate this point, consider the following example about an event within a small Midwestern community attempting to construct meaningful intelligibilities of responding and relating. Each voice in the story is a series of overlapping conjoint realities invoking questions of power, constructed within multiple intelligibilities of relating and responsibility.

A bar, frequented primarily by students, was recently fined several million dollars for involvement in the alcohol-related deaths and injuries of several people. A young man, driving a car after too many drinks, injured himself and others. The questions of many in the community focused on the issue of who was responsible. The courts decided that the bar itself was responsible for selling the man alcohol over the legal limit. The lawyers for the bar argued that the man himself needed to take responsibility for his actions. Alternatively, it was also recognized that both the bartenders and the young man conjointly participated in the conditions that created this unfortunate incident. Such situations cloud the issues of responsibility, relational responsibility, and conjoint construction that arise in this volume.

We agree that meaning arises in conjoint constructions; however, we do not believe that these constructions are always equally accessible or possible for all parties involved. For example, the young man or the bartenders in this case were not relationally positioned to encourage (McNamee and Gergen's term) the court to see how it was playing the autocratic decision maker. Even the recognition of the conjoint nature of meaning (what McNamee and Gergen call a "complementarity of action;" p. 37, this volume) cannot displace our desire for responses that attend to differences in power and position and ultimately lead to diffuse constructions of responsibility. The intelligibility of responsibility is not solely the matter of its being situated within relationships of "complementarity" (if, indeed, such a place exists); but it is also the matter of how individuals and relational process are socially and intelligibly situated in relation to each other.

Simply put, "responsibility" seems primarily meaningful as a relational process only when it is embedded in hierarchies of power and materiality. Otherwise we would not be able to speak of "taking," "giving," "assigning," or even "sharing" responsibility. Thus, even positing that responsibility is best understood as a complementary of action implies an original difference in positioning that allows voices to be heard and legitimated.

To speak of responsibility is to remark that we live within a community where people have the ability to care ethically and morally for each other. Furthermore, it also suggests that we are able to assess one another's accounts that are offered and counteroffered when social exigencies prompt such ways of taking-giving-sharing responsibility. Nonetheless, to engage in a ritual of speaking that implicates relational responsibility is not neutral with respect to such usage. It invokes and warrants particular intelligibilities and simultaneously and inevitably silences others. As Burke (1985) noted, "Every way of seeing is a way of *not* seeing" (p. 20). The potential for silencing of voices or the engagement with confrontational or undesirable discourses is exactly what the concept of responsibility is called on to make intelligible in a variety of social relationships.

For instance, McNamee and Gergen use an example of how relational responsibility can be used to transform the "person whose barbarity or hostility draws us into confrontation" into an invitation to "collaborate with us in a construction of ourselves as helpful, kind, concerned and him- or herself as important, respected, and so forth" (p. 34). This position raises many questions for analysis. First, the tone of this argument, which appears to us throughout the text, seems to privilege a smooth, collaborative, and nonproblematic conception of relating over discourses of confrontation, anger, conflict, and other "anti" social enactments. Even if this type of smoothing over were possible, is it not desirable or responsible to invoke such a unitary construction of relating. Second, this position assumes that relationships occur on a level playing field where all start out equally responsible. As noted, this seems to mute the possibility of responsibility as a relational phenomenon and further ignores the social and material exigencies facing people on an everyday basis in which responsibility is understood. We are not advocates for constant hostility and conflict. Conflict and confrontation need no encouragement just as happiness and respect do not. We are interested in the complex interplay of different modes of relating that implicate particular ranges of response and those who have or are denied the ability to use certain parts of the range in everyday practices. In short, we seek to render constructions of relational responsibility relevant to the practice of everyday life.

SOME DIRECT RESPONSES
TO RELATIONAL RESPONSIBILITY

Guiding our response to other issues raised by McNamee and Gergen is the question of difference and how talk about rhetorical contexts warranting relational rather than individual responsibility is usefully informed by such concerns. The notion of responsibility per se is not treated by McNamee and Gergen as an inherently relational concept, given the discussed considerations. One cannot be responsible without being responsible *to* someone as well as responsible *for* something. The so-called bridging of multiple demands of responsibility by those in marginal social positions is the pull *to* someone and the push *for* something. There is an enormous contradiction in being a bridge (Anzaldua, 1983, p. 206). Thus, even those views of (individual) responsibility to which McNamee & Gergen react negatively are inherently and irreducibly relational concepts with implications beyond the relational walls (if the reader will, for the time being, excuse such language of containment) of the immediate dyad to social discourses of position, power, and marginality.

Rather than redefining the nature of relational responsibility as McNamee & Gergen propose, we believe that the matter is dealt with by considering the meaning of responsibility, by looking at the real-life implications of using the notion of responsibility in everyday contexts. It is not so much that the nature of responsibility becomes a relational rather than an individualistic concept but that one does not need to make that redefinition in the first place because the concept is already inherently social and relational. One needs instead to spend more time working out the ways in which individuals construct rhetorical responses to the situations where individual and relational positions of responsibility are called to account. One needs to explore the situations and strategies that people use to negotiate the manner in which relational responsibility, or responsibility for individual action and difference in relationships, is managed.

We find it problematic that the same inconsistency of terminology is used by McNamee and Gergen. They refer to the concept of contained identities becoming part of a third entity ("when any two persons enter a new relationship," p. 23) and so confuse the reader who was following the traditions of the argument against self containment. However, the matter is one of the use of language. Scholars have not yet managed to construct a terminology of relationship that avoids the pitfalls of individualism or speaks in ways that do not automatically place one in the role of talking about relationships between two objects that are soon unavoidably discussed as autonomous self-containments.

RELATIONAL RESPONSIBILITY OR
RESPONSIBILITY AS RELATIONAL?

Other issues in the McNamee & Gergen proposal that we would like to address are less in terms of its contextual relationship to other work but more directly in relation to its own terms. We use the analogy of the invitation to write this response as a way to demonstrate some of the points of concern that we perceive to surround the concepts proposed by McNamee & Gergen. It is interesting that McNamee and Gergen suggest that their hope is to "develop from this consciousness new alternatives to action, and especially alternatives to replace the traditional habits of personal blame" (p. 31). This alternative involves a shift to "relational responsibility-blame," which embodies and implicates the voices of relational others in complementary action. The construct of relational responsibility/blame is one that McNamee and Gergen argue will bring forth new responses that invite more inclusion and collaborative relational experiences. Although it may be assumed that a ubiquitous presence of collaboration or other prosocial communicative resources move toward less burdensome relationships where responsibility is "equally" resourced, this is not always the case. To be invited to write this response involves a number of relationships that simultaneously burden and liberate us, where equality of responsibility is not a possibility nor even the central force of action.

Each of the authors of this response had a number of other commitments to fulfill to other people in the time frame that was offered to us. A full professor invites an emerging graduate student to read and construct a response to a piece of writing on relationships. During the whirlwind of midsemester experiences, both are obviously embedded in a variety of relationships that invite or demand response. Course work, family, colleagues, (hoped for) romance, and so on are all relationships that seem to be within the "patterns of independence" that McNamee and Gergen suggest are where various other dimensions of relating get done (p. 36). We argue that these competing patterns are more than so-called conjoint realities but result in certain relationships being marginalized, although others are centralized to meet particular demands that exist within ideological constraints of choice and responsibility.

Indeed, the responsibility for completing the written response may not be with either Steve or Michael, but according to a relational responsibility approach, is placed with "anyone working with troubled and recurring patterns" (such as a writing partner who does not come through on time) (p. 37). According to McNamee and Gergen, one can look to patterns of relational interdependence to applaud other relationships for doing their part in the conjoint performance of an event such as writing a manuscript (p. 37). Following this theoretical line of thinking, one has to wonder who (or what relationships) would be applauded or blamed for helping not write the response? Lover? Roommate? Friend? Boss? Yes, we agree that it is not always useful to position the individual as the center of the blame (e.g., "Mike, what is wrong with you?"). All the same, do we point to relational resources (Do we applaud a roommate or mom for a good performance of distraction from writing?) of responsibility as if they were all equal in an attempt to change the construction of blame? Not all relational constructions are equally implicated or intelligibly responsible in a particular interactive moment but in questions of power and the rhetorical, local exigencies that construct such differences.

Discursive processes implicate hierarchy, difference, and power, which make responsibility a meaningful relational experience. If relationships are treated as only within and between individuals, then the interconnections of those individuals with other individuals are—must be—overlooked while such an analysis is carried out. The fault lies not with the analysis itself but with the failure to complete it by reconnecting the target relationship to that from which it was stripped for the sake of a particular sort of analysis.

The choice to coauthor a response placed us in a tension between multiple individual voices and a multivocal process of negotiated unity that increased the likelihood of suppression of voice and nuance. It also raised some issues of power and hierarchy given that one of us is the other's doctoral committee member. The shifting of the burden from individual to relationship thus simultaneously constrains and liberates rather than only being liberating in a number of ways that are critical to relationship functioning and to the expression of "voice." "There is no *neutral* [italics added] place to stand free and clear in which my words do not prescriptively affect or mediate the experience of others" (Alcoff, 1995, p. 101). This mediational quality of language leads to the appropriation of voice of others, and by engaging in discourses of responsibility, we potentially run the risk of doing injustice to other relationships. We are not suggesting that we deny relational responsibility, noting, however, that "ignoring the plight of the other is a blatant form of injustice, but addressing it is no guarantee of justice either" (Elam, 1995, p. 235). The assumption of equality of expression further violates the rhetorical principle of hierarchy (Burke, 1966) and overlooks the power dynamics that are inevitably built into the negotiation of relationship voicings—and also incidentally are implicit in the notion of contexts of warrant that give voice (or perhaps, give ear) to others as if they are hierarchically superior by virtue of their role of judges or audience of accounts.

Thus, the objection made by McNamee and Gergen to the unjustified, hostile, and self-promoting results of holding one person responsible can equally be made to the shifting of responsibility to the relationship, because it apparently ignores the dynamics involved in constructing the relationship and the resultant suppression, muting, or preferring of some voices over others.

We agree, in part, with McNamee and Gergen, that people trying to speak only for themselves would be seen as a retreat into individualism with the implication that this "isolation represents the negation of humanity" (p. 19). We recognize that a retreat from speech (or to individualism) is of course also not neutral because it allows the "continued dominance of current discourses and acts by omission to reinforce their dominance" (Alcoff, 1995, p. 108). Isolation and individualism do not need to be so passively conceded but rather recognized as potent social and cultural resources of intelligibility that implicate moments of new insight about relating and responsibility. For instance, we could ask of the examples used in this response (the drunk-driving case, coauthorship) what contexts and resources make possible the retreat to individualism. Did the lack of material resources to hire competent lawyers sustain the possibility of blame for the bar in question? Or, how do we engage in a complementarity approach to responsibility in writing this response when one of the authors has far more scholarly experience, and the implications for the decisions made about career futures is more intelligibly in the hands of one of the authors and not the other. The individual becomes one site among many where responsibility is invoked and provides a position of analysis where power and materiality are usefully explored. The concept of the "individual" is not necessarily bad nor does it entail a total negation of humanity but rather, is one of many social resources that is relevant to relating.

The hierarchical structure of responsibility is a requisite of the maintenance of social and relational systems (Sampson, 1993). A connective-relational framework is dependent on constructing others as connective (and thus denying others their own subjectivity), which is a structure made intelligible from a particular social position. Working from a place of connection implies that choice was involved for those making the move for connection, although those who may want to end such subjugations are not a part of the dialogue and are usually dismissed as buying into rampant individualism. In addition, the autonomous self also lives a lie—for the autonomous actor is dependent on constructing others as dependent to maintain the fiction that they are autonomous. In either case, autonomy and connection are not separate domains of the individual and the relationship but are meaningful social discourses that inform the desire for multiple intelligibilities that McNamee and Gergen argue for.

The shared agency that McNamee and Gergen seem to advocate can lead to the denial of difference, the deferring to pressures from networks (and hence the antiliberating and constraining effects of belonging to a relational group), and to gender and secular assimilation as a society forms and ultimately imposes the prevailing views of such things as marriage and relational form on the unwilling and the different or the unconventional. Thus, cultural authority creates a burden of responsibility that is ultimately constraining and not liberating either for minorities or oppressed groups (Huston & Schwartz, 1995; Moraga & Anzaldua, 1983). Authority also contains an inherent contextual pressure for normality to be more than the norm (in the statistical sense) and also conform to the norm in the sense of expectation. The notion of a responsibility to be reflexive also is burdensome in that the dialogue with an internal other requires self reflection that is intellectually class based and privileges some forms of thought or styles of behavior over others. Even the cultural privileging of politeness and collaboration over rudeness, hostility, and independence is a form of silencing of some voices because responsibility is itself grounded in the cultural authority of the notion of getting along and avoiding conflict (another form of difference).

CONCLUDING REMARKS

Just as we cited Burke's aphorism earlier, that "every way of seeing is a way of *not* seeing," so responsibility relationally also suggests that we envision not only ways to engage what we have in common but to engage in dialogue that is necessitated by difference and hierarchy. For dialogue to occur, difference *must* exist and become focal. Indisputably, such difference is often sustained both in hierarchical structures that limit responses and also in social contexts that are in need of further dialogue with the McNamee and Gergen proposal. However, it is also the goal of our response to forge a view of the relational world filled with complex and contradictory ideas of responsibility and difference that begin to unfold the tale of ourselves. In this sense, identity and difference is invented and contingent, not autonomous. As Trinh (1989) argues, the " 'I' is, therefore, not a unified subject, a fixed identity, or that solid mass covered with layers of superficialities one has gradually to peel off before one can see its true face. 'I' is, itself, infinite layers" (p. 94). The ability to respond and speak within and between these layers is the complex site of relational responsibility and difference.

12

Co-Constructing Responsibility

Karl Tomm

I applaud the initiative that Sheila McNamee and Ken Gergen have taken in proposing that we extend our notion of responsibility to its relational basis. Before describing some examples of relevant practices in my clinical work, I would like to provide some personal background to locate myself in this conversation.

I am a psychiatrist who became interested in family therapy almost 30 years ago during my residency training. Several early clinical experiences suggested to me that close personal relationships profoundly influenced the kinds of individual behavior, such as confusion, agitation, violence, withdrawal, suicidal action, and so on, that were considered manifestations of mental illness or mental disorder. As a psychiatrist, I was expected to diagnose and treat individuals behaving in these ways. Most of my professors, fellow residents, and psychiatric colleagues described these persons as "ill," that is, as having individual "mental disorders." I wondered whether they were living within "relationship disorders" instead. Subsequently, I came to distinguish specific interaction patterns within those relationships as problematic. As I pursued my interpersonal focus over the years, I found myself on a path that became increasingly divergent from the mainstream of my profession.

My psychiatric colleagues claim that compassion is involved in describing persons who manifest problematic behavior as mentally disordered or ill. They point out how our culture does not hold people personally responsible for being sick. It is assumed that illness is always unwanted and comes over a person without his or her intentional participation in being ill or becoming sick. Consequently, designating certain behaviors as manifestations of illness helps reduce blaming practices with respect to certain unwanted behaviors. My point, however, is that the effects of labelling persons as mentally ill can be devastating to their personal identity (as having legitimate worth) and to their place within the community (as having respectable status). The process of blame is, in fact, replaced with the more sinister process of stigma accompanied by loss of worth and status. When one becomes aware of the profoundly disqualifying effects of social stigma, the compassion entailed in the diagnostic labelling quickly evaporates. Social stigma tends to demoralize and paralyze persons who are objectified and categorized according to labels in the *Diagnostic and Statistical Manual (DSM)* of the American Psychiatric Association. This demoralization and paralysis undermines possibilities for constructive change in the lives of these persons. Indeed, their problematic patterns of behavior often become stabilized through the labelling and consequently become more difficult to alter. In other words, as psychiatric professionals, we carry a great deal of relational responsibility for stigmatizing persons and contributing to the maintenance of difficulties in the same persons that we are purportedly trying to help. This dismal state of affairs in my profession leaves me with feelings of outrage at some times and profound sadness at others.

My awareness of this iatrogenic pathologizing process emerged through conversations with family therapy colleagues who also saw individual behavior and its meaning as closely connected to the interpersonal systems of relationship in which persons are embedded. As my awareness of this grew, I came to rely less and less on psychiatric diagnoses and the biomedical and individualistic explanations associated with them. Instead, I focussed more and more on relational and cultural explanations to guide my work. Over time, my patterns of psychiatric practice changed quite dramatically. I now prescribe far less medication than most of my psychiatric colleagues and give much more attention to respond to the social networks in which my clients live. It should come as no surprise then that I have a strong bias in favor of the perspective on relational responsibility being proposed by McNamee and Gergen.

How do I go about implementing a relational view of responsibility in my day-to-day work? As is the case for most psychiatrists, my clients are usually referred because of "individual" symptoms. Because I regard these symptoms as heavily influenced by the pathologizing patterns of interaction that these persons are (or have been) living in, I orient myself to respond to them (and their significant others) by seeking to find and maintain alternative patterns of interaction that lead to a greater sense of well-being along with a concomitant decrease in personal and relational turmoil. I begin by engaging them together with their significant others in therapeutic conversations to co-construct relational healing and wellness. Part of this work might focus specifically on co-constructing greater responsibility.

The intended growth in responsibility may occur in three domains: within the client, between the client and her or his significant others, and between the client and myself as therapist. My initiative in valuing my clients' potential to respond constructively and in applying my therapeutic efforts to bring forth and expand their abilities to behave responsibly constitutes a here-and-now enactment of social responsibility in my relationship with them. I work on co-constructing client responsibility by focusing on bringing forth specific awarenesses that enable preferred choices to be made by them. I conceive of personal responsibility as more fundamentally social than individual. As a general human phenomenon, responsibility may be seen as first generated in social interaction and then secondarily internalized within persons so that at a later point in time, it can be enacted by the individual in relation to others. In other words, I see a generative process moving from relational responsibility to individual responsibility. Although responsible individual action may be the desired endpoint, it is only feasible for therapists or others to work at the social interactional end of this phenomenon to enable the eventual emergence of what could be called individual responsibility.

I use a specific definition of *responsibility* to guide my work. I see responsibility as "living consistently within an awareness of whether one likes or dislikes the consequences of one's own actions." This definition leads me toward fostering awareness as a means to co-construct responsibility. Conversation is a major means to create this awareness. It is important to note that three levels of awareness are entailed in producing responsibility: First, there is an awareness of the actual effects of one's behavior (as opposed to one's intentions); second, there is an awareness of whether one likes or dislikes these effects; and third, there is an awareness of one's preference for internal coherence and consistency. With respect to the latter, I assume persons naturally tend to drift toward greater consistency among their thoughts, feelings, and behaviors. So when a person becomes more clearly aware that he or she does not like the actual consequences of his or her behavior, he or she is less liable to repeat such behavior. When a person lives consistently in this awareness, he or she strives to avoid performing the kinds of actions that have the kinds of effects he or she does not want. If, on the other hand, a person likes the consequences of his or her behavior, he or she is more liable to repeat similar behaviors in order to have similar effects.

From a clinical point of view, then, one can proceed to generate responsibility by engaging clients in conversations to co-construct the awareness required to support a preferred direction for ongoing choices. This can begin by asking the kinds of questions that invite clients to reflect on the nature of their actions and on the effects of those actions (on others, on themselves, or on the environment). They can then be asked how they feel about these effects. If they don't like these effects, they could be asked about what they might want to do differently. By asking these kinds of questions selectively, a therapist invites the relevant awareness to emerge in clients, that is, an awareness that supports choices for more responsible action. A crucial step in this process is to introduce or expand on an awareness of the difference between the intended effects of one's actions and the actual effects of one's actions. Priority must be given to learning about and attending to the actual effects. Attention to the intended effects alone will not enable growth in one's ability to be responsible. Indeed, undue attention to intended effects tends to support more of the same and leads people down a path of justification for past actions rather than responsibility for one's choices to act in a particular manner.

Given that my intentions are to enable the client to become more responsible and that I also want to be responsible as a therapist, I need to monitor the actual effects of my own behavior in asking questions. The effect that I want is to open space for the awareness of the client to grow. It is possible, however, that in response to some of my questions, the client feels constrained and experiences a closure of space, instead. This tends to happen when the client experiences my questions as blameful. The most probable effect of blaming is for clients to close down rather than open up, because blame tends to be experienced as a threat. Thus, if I want to be consistent in my intentions and be responsible as a therapist trying to facilitate more responsibility, I need to avoid blameful questions.

In my therapeutic efforts to co-construct responsibility, I try hard to begin selectively with positive responses and create some safety through affirmation of my clients to generate a relational context that is more liable to be consistent with my intentions. The affirmation I work toward is both general and specific. It is general in the sense that I always try to establish a positive emotional relationship with my clients. My affirmation of a client becomes specific when I adopt the assumption that there was probably at least some positive intent, however small, behind whatever action was taken. Thus, after finding a basis for some general warmth and respect for the client, I ask about what the person's good intentions may have been in acting in the manner that they did.

The third step is to ask questions that bring forth an awareness of the client's feelings about the actual effects. These questions open space for clients to still honor their good intentions while they recognize and acknowledge unintended negative effects. The distinction between intent and effect goes a long way to enable clients to experience genuine regret for their own actions without disqualifying themselves. One can go even further here and help clients recognize the constructive effects of feelings of shame or guilt (or both).

The last step is to invite reflection on alternative actions that could have been taken that might help them prepare themselves for similar situations in the future. Answers to these questions often help clients toward living with more consistency between desired and actual effects.

Because the knowledge about the relevant event and their experiences are brought to the conversation by the client, the work is co-constructive in nature. My contributions as a therapist have to do with how I guide the conversation to foster selective awarenesses about certain actions and their consequences for the client and others. The awareness that is brought forth makes it easier for the client to anticipate alternative pathways of response and to choose a more responsible course of action.

The indirect methods I use in therapy to generate greater responsibility have to do with fostering greater understanding and insight into the general dynamics of human relationships. Such understanding usually provides conditions for responsibility to emerge spontaneously. I refer to these methods as indirect in that my immediate intentions are not focussed on co-constructing responsibility per se but are on co-constructing greater awareness and understanding of how certain actions in human interaction influence interpersonal relationships in specific ways. These indirect approaches may conveniently be grouped along the lines of the four categories that McNamee and Gergen use in their essay, namely, internal others, conjoint relations, relations among groups, and systemic process.

Over the last several years, I have evolved a process of "internalized other interviewing," during which I interview another person within the self as a method for helping clients get in touch with the experiences of the other. I do this by addressing the internalized other by name while speaking to the client. To prepare a client for this, I invite them to speak from the "I" position of the other person and express his or her (the client's) experience of the other person's (the internalized other's) experience. To orient myself in this work, I conceive of "the self" of the client as being constituted by an internalized community of persons that are significant to the self. I assume that as we grow and develop within our relationships, we make distinctions about others and retain (within ourselves) our understandings of their actions and feelings and our experience of their experiences as memories, perhaps in the form of concatenated internal conversations about these persons. When asking questions of an internalized other in a client, I'm not asking the client to role play the other person. I am asking the client to speak from his or her experience of the other's experience, that is, from as deeply as he or she is able to enter into the other's experiences. To emphasize this, I might suggest that when responding from the "I" position of the other, he or she feel free to articulate intuited experiences of the other that the other person may never have expressed (perhaps because the other was unable or unwilling to do so) but that the client feels is an authentic reflection of the other's lived experience.

There are many possible effects of this kind of interviewing, but one of the more significant ones with respect to the issue of responsibility has to do with enabling the client to become more fully aware of the actual effects they may be having on the other. When answering from the embodied experience of the other as internalized within the self, the client makes a shift with respect to awareness of certain interactions. The effects of the interaction between the persons involved becomes more apparent. Indeed, the whole process is an invitation to move into the "intersubjective" space. When trying to foster personal responsibility within this mode of interviewing, I would ask the internalized other questions about the effects of actions by the self. "What did it feel like for you, (name of the internalized other), when (name of the self) did . . . ? What happened deep inside you, (name of the internalized other)? Which of those feelings did you disclose and which did you keep inside? What held you back from revealing more of what you experienced?" Such questions open space to bring forth in the client an enhanced awareness of the actual effects of certain actions on the other in contrast to the client's intended effects. At the very least, these questions orient the client to become more interested in the impact his or her behavior might be having on the other. Their subsequent listening to these effects from the other tends to be much more acute.

Another way to develop a greater general awareness and understanding of interpersonal relationship influences is to differentiate specific patterns of interaction between persons (McNamee and Gergen's "conjoint relations"). I have been elaborating a concrete model for describing such patterns within important relationships. This work has been an attempt to shift the focus in clinical assessments from describing persons to describing types of interactions between persons. Indeed, specific qualities often attributed to a person can be redefined as a component of a recurrent interaction pattern. In my efforts to clarify different kinds of patterns, I have distinguished pathologizing interpersonal patterns (PIPs) from healing interpersonal patterns (HIPs), and wellness interpersonal patterns (WIPs). The emphasis in conceiving of and identifying these patterns is on the coupling of behaviors of interactants that tend to be mutually reinforcing. The behaviors become structurally coupled (Maturana & Varela, 1987), and the pattern tends to become repetitive and a relatively stable aspect of the relationship. The clinician, together with clients, can tease out the kinds of behaviors that might constitute a particular PIP and, having identified this PIP, can then postulate an antidote in the form of a HIP or a more general alternative pattern that promotes wellness (WIP). The coupling of behavior in these patterns is conceived of as "mutual invitations." With this description, space is opened for change in the sense that it is possible to turn down an invitation to engage in an old pattern and instead to enact a different kind of behavior and invite the other into a different kind of pattern. Participants are invited to see how they share responsibility for remaining within a particular pattern by accepting invitations to continue in it or for declining the invitations to do so and for offering invitations into a different pattern.

Relations among groups of persons become important in my clinical work when I find myself analyzing and disclosing the power relations between general categories of persons, such as between males and females, parents and children, whites and people of color, the rich and the poor, and so on. Certain presumed qualities of persons may be seen to derive from the group or category with which a person is identified rather than as inherent to that person. When individuals identify themselves or others as members of a particular group, they often tend to attribute qualities or patterns of behavior associated with that group, such as maleness, femaleness, parenthood, childhood, race, class, and so on, to themselves or others. This tendency can be very limiting with respect to behavioral options for oneself and for others and is often misleading in one's understanding. On the other hand, when one is able to see certain qualities or behaviors as a reflection of the larger social system in which the grouping is embedded, far more flexibility and possibilities for change arise. For instance, gender relations are extremely important, and certain patterns of behavior and interaction may be assumed to be based on the person's gender. Through a process of locating these behaviors as part of a cultural gender pattern, it may be easier for persons to recognize a space between themselves and certain behaviors and to decide either to continue to accept the cultural specifications for their gender or to reject them. Thus, a male might come to recognize how his domineering practices are a reflection of cultural expectations for maleness in a patriarchal system. This realization, along with an awareness of the unwanted effects of domineering or intimidating practices on his partner (male or female) could orient him to find alternative ways of responding to others. For example, he could orient himself to identify with ways of being male that privilege humility, sensitivity, and respect toward others.

The final area of systemic process outlined by McNamee and Gergen is quite general, yet it informs much of my thinking as well as my patterns of practice. One of the most important steps for me as a developing clinician has been the move from working in the domain of first-order "observed systems" to working in the domain of second-order "observing systems." I have become increasingly fascinated by the politics entailed in the act of drawing a distinction and making an observation. I keep asking myself, What are the consequences of drawing this distinction as opposed to some other distinction that could be equally viable? For instance, becoming aware of what one includes and excludes in distinguishing a system and in choosing how microscopic or macroscopic to be opens space for greater relational responsibility with respect to the distinctions that are drawn and the effects that these distinctions might have on the persons involved. It is one thing for the psychiatric profession to develop the *DSM* and use it to diagnose persons with the intention of implementing the appropriate treatment. It is quite another to develop an understanding of the stigmatizing and social control effects of the profession as a whole in developing and applying a nosological system of diagnosing and categorizing clients.

This issue of the systemic politics of drawing and using distinctions can also be applied to this project of exploring the notion of responsibility. One could raise questions about McNamee and Gergen's priorities in proposing greater attention to relational responsibility. I am in favor of this direction, but I do see some possible irresponsible consequences. By giving priority to looking at the origins of a particular behavior in its interactional context or history, one can justify a process of taking people "off the hook" and releasing them from responsibilities they should carry. Given that one can probably trace relational factors indefinitely when trying to understand the origins of any particular action, there must be some point of diminishing returns in such an exploration. There is likely some point at which the exploration actually becomes counterproductive and pathogenic. There is also some point at which it seems important to make a choice to act and to take personal responsibility for having done so. Where are these points? Is it useful to try to define them, or is it better to avoid making these kinds of distinctions? How could these points be defined? Who should be entitled to define them? Clearly, McNamee and Gergen have made a choice in favor of giving greater privilege to relational responsibility. I would be interested in hearing about their concerns when an exploration of relational responsibility becomes problematic. In not specifying or at least pointing to some limits, are they recruiting us into an interminable process of infinite regress and ultimately inviting us to become grounded in groundlessness? What are the effects of groundlessness with respect to making choices? Are those who accept groundlessness more vulnerable to exploitation by those who claim to be grounded? Can we identify some criteria to orient the direction and activity of a relational exploration that would reflect relational responsibility in itself? Can we specify points of danger in such an exploration, for instance, when the notion of relational responsibility supports a justification of destructive behaviors? In my opinion, an unreflective drift toward such patterns of explanation and justification could be extremely problematic and irresponsible in our communities and culture. I personally am not comfortable with being grounded in groundlessness: uncertainty yes, but not groundlessness.

My preference would be to collectively honor some natural biological cleavages in our ecosphere and acknowledge that some points of view and choices for action are clearly preferred over others. Our biological nervous systems probably do have limits with respect to what distinctions can be drawn with any degree of coherence and authenticity. Indeed, I find Maturana and Verden-Zoller's (1996) focus on the biology of intimacy and the biology of love as a basis for humanness quite compelling. Like them, I see a need to take more responsibility for my personal preferences. In the process of doing so, I also need to open space for others (especially for those who have far fewer privileges than I do) to challenge my preferences or to elaborate on them in ways that would increase my awareness of their effects and hence contribute to my ability to become more responsible. The Just Therapy group (Tamasese & Waldegrave, 1994) are currently developing some innovative methods of social and cultural accountability toward this end. I find their work very encouraging in that it appears to offer some concrete steps for movement toward relational responsibility that are grounded in actual performances of relational responsibility.

13

Inspiring Dialogues and Relational Responsibility

Eero Riikonen

A DIALOGICAL PERSPECTIVE

Even if it does not explicitly focus on problems and challenges of health and social care, McNamee and Gergen's text is extremely interesting and useful from the perspective of these fields. In developing explicit alternative conceptualizations of individual responsibility, the text also implicates alternative views of well-being and their associated practices. In what follows, I attempt to connect some of McNamee and Gergen's themes to my own actual interests regarding a dialogical perspective to the reproduction of well-being.

My thinking differs in some respects from theirs. I agree with McNamee and Gergen when they express their belief that a solution to the isolation and individualism of our societies can only come from the renaissance of relational forms of intelligibility. However, I see that their text reveals a limited array of cures for this ill: mainly, a combination of corrected language (in this case, language favoring connectedness) and a more intense and widespread systemic reflection. In my view, the idea of re-forming our language so that it would be difficult to speak of individual blame—or credit—sounds very problematic indeed.

Expansion of we-speech and we-thinking can also lead to horrendous results as we have seen during this century. For me, it is more promising to cultivate a general sense of irony regarding (a) causal thinking, (b) absolutely dichotomous concepts (like individual-social), and (c) identities in social life rather than create new criteria for correct speech.

Roads opened by more dialogical concepts like *voice* and *internal others* are not developed by McNamee and Gergen as far as I think they deserve. One of the limitations of their treatment in the text is the (not explicitly expressed) view that voices and internal others are identifiable and can be (relatively well) controlled by therapists or clients. Reading Bakhtin (see e.g., Morson & Emerson, 1990), to whose conceptualizations these ideas have strong ties, reveals that voices are extremely complex phenomena that can be consciously managed only to a minor degree. A related difficulty that I see concerns expressions such as "moving in and out of identities." After my inoculation with Bakhtin's dialogism, I can only wonder in what sense we ever really are in one identity from which we could move to another clearly defined one?

There are still some additional reasons why McNamee and Gergen's starting point, which admittedly is promising in many ways, still does not feel optimal for me. One of these hesitations has to do with the tendency toward increasing reflection and intellectualism, so central for our postemotional, postmodern societies. There is no limit to how far and how long discussions of systemic interconnections can go. As I see it, the *living* interaction that is the source of connectedness uses living everyday words and expressions. It is a true process of social poetics. Most people, including myself, seem to have only limited interests in abstract systemic deliberations and issues of this kind. It would not nurture their relationships in practice—systemic reflection, be it in speech or writing, just is not very revitalizing for most people. Conversations of this type are easily experienced as exclusive.

Still an additional difficulty: I am not a believer in abstract motives when it comes to really making the world a better place to live. I am convinced that issues such as "enhancing relational responsibility" are too academic to be able to influence people's hearts and souls on a mass scale. For something positive to (really) happen, people must find new things that are rewarding in a very concrete, very everyday sense.

All this leads me to think that there are important forms of "relational intelligibilities" not discussed in the text. These dialogical intelligibilities work constantly under our own eyes. They center on respect for what people actually do when they treat each other and themselves well. I feel that if there is a solution to the problems described so well by McNamee and Gergen, it stems from practices strengthening these genuinely dialogical elements in our interaction and in our societies.

WHAT IS DIALOGUE?

But what do I mean by "genuine dialogue," and how could something like that be supported? First, some clarifications: *Dialogue,* as a concept, has at least two very different senses. It can be seen cognitively, as a exchange of rational arguments among (more or less) equal persons. Or it can been seen from a perspective of connectedness and inspiration. However, it is the second view that is more interesting for me and, I think, more promising from the perspective of developing new practices for the care sector. Dialogue, in this second, Bakhtinian (1981) vein, refers to joint action that ties people together and creates the temporary world they experience. Dialogue in this latter sense stands in opposition to everything that is destructive for curiosity. The main enemies seem to be objectification processes related to various forms of "knowing already." Knowing already dissolves the need to look beyond averages or categories. It is the prime source of nonparticipation.

For the dialogue to continue, it has to be appealing to all participants—genuine dialogues must be inspiring or at least interesting to continue. This is not possible if the participants are not interested in what is interesting for each other and not willing to cultivate it. This type of combination of self-interest—something that could not be beneficial from McNamee and Gergen's perspectives—a (personal) craving for inspiring experiences and an interest in the interests of others, is essential for the birth and thriving of relationality of this central type.

There are other important things, too, such as a degree of allowed unpredictability, which is needed for freshness and interest, and a safe enough context for interaction. A prerequisite for genuine dialogue is thus allowing, to some degree or another, the expression of individual and constantly changing perspectives and individual or shared inspirations, enchantments, and desires.

An additional distinction I do not share with McNamee and Gergen is a seemingly absolute divide between individual and social. The Bakhtinian (1981) view of dialogue shows quite convincingly (for me) that there are in fact numerous shades of gray between these concepts. Leaving this divide behind could, in fact, be one of the "new relational intelligibilities" sought by the authors.

Bakhtin (1981) underlines consistently the essential impossibility of nonsocial or nonrelational language use. Speech is relational in (at least) a triple sense: (a) it creates, maintains, and changes relationships; (b) all utterances bear reflections of the addressees; (c) speech forms its own context and backdrop of further speech and social relations linked to it. The latter sense might be the most difficult to grasp. It refers to the fact that speech creates an environment for actual and evolving interaction, something from which and to which to respond. It is the "where we are"—the situation of the speakers. It is relatively easy to produce suffocating, sterile, oppressive, depressive, or frightening interactional environments. Correspondingly, it is possible to create enabling, empowering, and trust-enhancing conversational contexts.

What I call genuine dialogue on these pages is closely linked to the concept of relational responsibility. Dialogue, the Bakhtinian dialogue, is in fact an enactment of relational responsibility. Genuine dialogue becomes impossible when the participants cease to accept a joint responsibility for its inspiring quality. As soon as they do not see themselves anymore (at least to some extent) as a "we" having a responsibility (and good reasons) to be interested in each other's interests, the dialogue ends.

What I have said so far makes it clear that providential or enabling dialogues have obvious links with the aesthetic and nonrational aspects of sociality and well-being. The list of relevant authors who have focused on these aspects is a long one but must include people like Mikhail Bakhtin (1981), John Shotter (1993), Gaston Bachelard (1992), and Jean Baudrillard (1994). What all of these authors have in common, I think, is a belief that what makes interaction-dialogue inspiring, meaningful, or resonating, and thus capable of diminishing isolation and increasing connectedness, cannot be understood in any purely cognitive or rational way.

DENIAL OF THE DIALOGICAL
NATURE OF WELL-BEING

Many social scientists, Zygmunt Bauman (1993) among them, see the idea of citizenship in our Western societies as a celebration of the "qualified consumer," "the happy shopping-mall stroller." The citizens are consumers whose well-being is normally expected to come from buying and using products and services more or less skillfully produced by professionals and experts. If they are well-off or backed by health insurance, the citizens qualify as shoppers; if they aren't, they are beggars. Both of these roles are defined by a common factor: the role of a consumer of services that are planned and produced by others. This form of passivity is indeed a dominant character of modern societies, societies based on the logic of mass production. This logic separates the users from the producers in various ways, not only regarding material goods but also in the worlds of care and cure.

According to mainstream models of health and social care, well-being is neither a joint achievement of professionals and clients nor a product of dialogues. Most practices and programs consist of interventions that see citizens as targets of education or care. For precisely this reason, professional action can be counterproductive. The logic of service production obscures the fact that well-being is a joint product. Enhancing relational responsibility would require that the concepts of care and service be defined interactionally and dialogically.

The authoritarian interaction based on objectivist notions has close links to disease and a defect orientation. Practices of health care and rehabilitation are generally problem or defect oriented because they correlate with narrow views of human disease and problems (see Beahrs, 1986; Engel, 1980; Riikonen & Smith, 1997).

Another complication of the mechanistic metaphors dominant in the field is the emphasis on analysis. We believe that analyzing problems is a necessary prerequisite for solving, dissolving, or deconstructing them. This means that so-called cures or solutions to problems are not sought by looking at what can be done (studying resources and their use) but from the analysis of negative antecedents. We have learned from the health promotion literature that this orientation leads to unnecessary limitations. The focus on pathology not only creates a strong tendency to bypass signs of existing or potential competence in clients and their social networks, it also prevents us from seeing how important the resources of mutual-aid or peer groups can be. There is more and more evidence that it is useful to concentrate on what clients and the representatives of their own social network have done, can do, or could do to change things for the better.

HOW TO PROMOTE
WELL-BEING-PRODUCING INTERACTION?

The need to find well-being-generating actions, activities, experiences, and circumstances relates to both client-professional interaction and to social inter-action in general. These types of keys to well-being seem to have some common features: First, the users or clients are the true experts regarding them. Second, they can, in most cases, be found in the happenings of everyday life. One of the additional benefits of this view is that it transfers the users and citizens to the sphere of normality. The production of circumstances that generate well-being is a challenge common to us all.

The position of experts is difficult from this perspective. Well-being cannot be given to somebody, neither can it be produced by others. It is a result of the multidimensional and complicated interaction of the person and his or her environment. It seems fair to say, on the basis of this view, that the experts should be very sensitive to what clients see as promising and inspiring and build their action on these things.

Notions related to well-being (and its lack) are politically very important. A person, group, or institution believed to be in an expert position regarding this domain can claim the right to use various public and private resources to enhance well-being or alleviate its absence. I believe that a catastrophical amount of this type of power is actually in the hands of people and institutions who look at well-being from the objectivistic and narrow perspectives of medicine and psychology. As a consequence of this situation, much interactional, dialogical, everyday (nonspecialist) knowledge, which is centrally involved with the production of well-being, is devalued and marginalized.

There are several difficulties with dominant, expert notions of well-being and its production. First, most of the expert messages concerned with well-being and its lack explicitly or implicitly show the expert as the knower and the citizen as noncompetent. Second, they dramatically devalue everyday knowledges concerning the production of well-being in everyday life. Objectivistic languages aiming at univocal truths also interrupt or prevent genuine dialogue.

Because it has potential links with a dialogical view to well-being, it is useful at this point to refer to some of the basic ideas and concepts of a set of activities called "health promotion." Making this short detour can help in seeing not only why the notion of relational responsibility should be developed further but also why currently dominating conceptualizations of "care" and "service" are deeply problematic.

THE DISCOURSE OF HEALTH PROMOTION

Health promotion is concerned with enabling people to maximize their health potential. According to this view, everybody could benefit from promotive activities—who has, indeed, fulfilled all of his or her health and well-being potentials? Health promotion has been defined as a process of enabling people to increase control over and to improve their health. It aims at returning power, knowledge, skills, and other resources relating to health to the community: to individuals, families, and whole populations.

What is then a promising way to define the target of these kinds of promotive activities—what is the thing or activity that should be promoted? A tentative definition could be to conceptualize the *possibilities of citizens-users (alone and with others) to create well-being-generating contexts, moments, experiences, and life projects* as the main target. Defined this way, the target has two interesting features: It is interactional and underlines the beneficial action of citizens-users.

I see well-being as a process in which "providential realities" are developed in interaction and dialogue. From this perspective, well-being is about creating common visibilities, about trust, about a shared sense of inspiration or promise (see Penman, 1992; Riikonen & Smith, 1997). Concepts such as providential realities are complex because the elements that together constitute enlivening, inspiring, and enabling interaction are various and in complicated relationships to each other.

The critique of more traditional instrumental approaches to well-being also has some bearing on McNamee and Gergen's notion of relational responsibility. Their interest is in developing new forms of intelligibility, "ones that invite, encourage or suggest alternative forms of action." I do, of course, agree with their agenda, but I am more cautious regarding possibilities to reach this objective. This hesitation has to do with some of the basic features of providential dialogue or interaction and with the *longue durée*—slow change or development—of some of our interactional, linguistic, and aesthetic traditions.

As I see it, the problem lies in the difference between a so-called external and internal perspective on connectedness and the reproduction of well-being. As Shotter (1993a) says, people's patterns of interdependence look very different from inside the continuously evolving interaction than when others attempt to make generalizations about it from outside, whatever their nature. The generalizations, systemic ones included, are obsessed with static, objective, systems of knowledge.

As we know so well, most Western countries are full of do-good organizations inventing guidelines and building programs for better lives—for others. When we want to create good interaction or good moments for ourselves and our nearest, we start mostly from much hazier ideas and follow less direct steps. Think of a good conversation with a friend. In most cases, we do not decide to have an interesting pair of utterances in the next minute—or plan to make a supportive move after 30 minutes. Good conversations evolve naturally and often unpredictably. The real interest, the living spark, is in the moment. Its chances of surviving extensive planning or project meetings are slight. It would be more productive to see relational responsibility, I believe, as a matter of creating good dialogues in the sense just described. It would be difficult to achieve this with a set of principles imported into a dialogue from outside. Attempts to create a good (enabling, inspiring) dialogue using theoretical tools seem often to lead to a bad (dull, artificial) dialogue in practice.

The same problematics concern most efforts to consciously develop interaction. The idea of development in itself presupposes measurement and instrumental logic. The continuous and successful "well-being work" or "inspiration work" of our everyday lives can be developed and enhanced, but the approaches to do that have to respect the nature of this activity. The methods have to be sensitive to the volatile preferences, the potential for boredom, the desires, humor, and spirit of the moment.

Approaches of this kind, approaches supporting and catalyzing the well-being work of clients, are difficult to explain and motivate because they are still foreign to mainstream models of care and because their logic differs from that of the production of goods. It sounds, of course, right and sympathetic to demand that interaction between citizens and health-social care professionals be better. However, as soon as the demand is voiced, it develops an unrealistic or idealistic ring. These kinds of topics are not surrounded by a sense of economic and administrative urgency like so many other things. From the perspective of administrators, these issues clearly deserve serious thought—but only after the more pressing tasks are accomplished, after the health care is done with its primary job, after the social care has succeeded in solving the objective problems. I see this as a grave error: If we continue to use our objectivist and individualist lenses, our systems of care develop into mechanisms destroying sources of inspiration—sources of life.

METAPHORICAL AND DIALOGICAL PERSPECTIVES OF CONNECTEDNESS

Concepts like *providential dialogue, providential context,* and *providential interaction* are easily understandable from the perspective of everyday life and the well-being work continuously done by us all. But what does it really mean to treat oneself and others well? I will start the examination of this topic by referring to some discussions in communication research.

Communication researcher Robyn Penman (1992), who has a strong interest in how different forms of interaction allow genuine participation, has recently written about "good communication" from a postmodern perspective. She concludes that so-called goodness of communication should be defined according to moral criteria. We can say that good communication does good things to people.

Penman (1992) uses four criteria to describe this kind of communication. First, it has to start from the premise that the talk-text in which we are participating constitutes the social realities of the moment ("constitutiveness"). Second, the communication has to be open to constant revision ("contextualness"). Communication fulfilling the third criteria, "diversity," recognizes the right of the other's interpretations to exist. The fourth criteria is "incompleteness," which means that neither communication nor the meanings generated can ever be complete.

Seen from this perspective, communication is not transmitting information from one receiver or from one head to another. Rather, communication is creating common episodes, commonplaces, or common temporary worlds (see Shotter, 1993b, pp. 63-65). These often rapidly changing shared worlds have their own rules, temptations, and despairs. They always support some possibilities, some forms of meaningfulness, some types of relationships, and some moral orders—and not others.

Expert languages and scientific thinking are problematic not only because of their capability to reproduce power differences but also because they tend to obstruct the visibility of the metaphorical, inspiring, living dimension of talk. When we study any group of people in informal conversations, we see that they jump relentlessly from topic to topic and from one point of view to another; the old topics and perspectives often become stale. It is indeed typical of problematic and dehumanizing situations that some or all participants are denied the right to both thematic variation and use of metaphorical language (the use of instrumental language is preferred). Freshness and metaphoricality—which of course have many links—are in this sense basic social resources that are needed to keep interaction interesting to all participants.

Bakhtin (as cited in Morson & Emerson, 1990) says what molds and transforms dialogical interaction is its living context. It is living because it is both continuously created and changed by the talk and taken into account by it. It is, in a sense, both the background, motivator, and evaluator of dialogue.

The context of interaction continuously changes the meaning of what happens. The deconstructionist notion of "supplement" has convincingly shown this. What comes after and what is anticipated constantly transforms and supplements the meaning and implications of what happens now and what has happened before. Because there is a continuous transformation of meaning, there is no way of permanently fixing causes and effects in social life.

The dialogical view proposed in this article implies that we could see the processes of "solving problems," including that of isolation, in all spheres of human action. We could say that problems are areas of experience that are outside dialogue. It is evident that there are many methods by which a regeneration of genuine dialogue can happen.

The application of dialogical perspectives dramatically widens the scope of possible approaches to finding McNamee and Gergen's new, relational forms of intelligibility. All interaction and talk becomes a source of social vitality, connectedness, and inspiration. What this means is that we are constantly looking for topics and subjects that can be shared and that feel promising. I believe that the use of enabling and connectedness-enhancing metaphors and concepts is central when we want to decrease isolation.

DIALOGICAL RIGHTS AND RESPONSIBILITIES

I prefer the concept of *dialogical rights and responsibilities* to that of *relational responsibility*. For me, it seems to tap some central issues, especially the importance of mutual rewards for connectedness. As I have claimed already, genuine dialogue does not survive without real interest and freshness.

People's moral positions and their experienced self-worth are either implicitly or explicitly involved in all dialogues and discourses, even in the most transient or technical ones. All interaction supports certain social roles and positions, not others. In interactions that arouse hopelessness or frustration, people are put into hopeless social positions; they feel that they are taken as objects in one way or another. For the same reasons, conversations (and also interaction with written texts) can in a very real sense either support or diminish experiences such as optimism, belongingness, motivation, and self-worth.

I think that the right to good interaction should really be one of the service user's basic rights. What is really at stake is everybody's right to be considered as a human being or a person. The right to be handled as a person is actualized in and by interaction.

I consider the right to participate in rewarding interaction as a very central issue indeed. From the proposed dialogical perspective, it is of course nonsensical to speak only of rights. A genuine dialogue is a form of joint action, and all participants have responsibilities for its results. The responsibility for all participants is in essence the same: be alive, be trustworthy, and be human.

I am claiming that we should be much more interested in how to develop the art of relevant, interesting, and enabling conversations in health and social care, even if this is a difficult task for reasons already described. Because we are dealing with a living interaction in which we are constantly immersed, these skills cannot be formulated as abstract principles. The skills should also not be seen as individual—we could also see them as parts of organization, team, and group cultures. A metaphor of a developing chamber orchestra could perhaps be a good one. To learn, develop, and practice these arts, many ways of talking and relating are needed. That is, the participants must have a multitude of ways of attempting to support beneficial and providential contexts. The knowledges needed are not exceptional. Success requires seeing, using, and developing our own existing everyday skills.

POSSIBILITIES FOR THE DEVELOPMENT OF NEW SERVICE CONCEPTS

What are the grassroots-level implications of these views? Can some practical programs be built on them? I think so. First, if both professionals and users are involved, the effort should take seriously the needs of both groups to be inspired. This interest should dominate the development activities at all times and at all levels. It is, for example, necessary to create systems of evaluation and feedback that are felt as relevant and genuinely useful and interesting for the users.

Many of the organizations of service and care in the field of mental health and well-being (including centers and organizations specializing in rehabilitation or supporting employment, etc.) could be seen primarily as "centers of inspiration." Inspiration work refers to contexts, activities, meetings, consultations, and conversations whose aim is to find relevant and inspiring ideas, perspectives, and possibilities. To put all this briefly: The aim is to develop forms of service, methods of employment, training, and dissemination, which see the participant or user as a King or Queen and not as the Poor Boy or Girl.

What I am saying points to the need to change our views regarding the principal targets of helping and supporting practices. Certain ways and styles of talking, certain types of texts, certain forms of interaction should perhaps be seen as the "patient," not the clients or persons seeking help. What we have at our hands are "sickening" or disempowering, noninspiring interactional-linguistic practices we must move away from. This is not in any way to undermine the suffering of people or claim that everything is only talk. I just want to underline what I consider to be a gravely neglected dimension of helping work.

For this reason, it seems to me a responsibility of researchers and clinical people to search for providential metaphors, metaphors that favor genuine dialogue. Only metaphors that are in some sense understandable, relevant, and interesting can serve this effort. This means that we should free ourselves to use unashamedly those words and metaphors belonging to the everyday vocabularies, poetry, and fiction.

14

Creating Relational Realities

Responsible Responding to Poetic 'Movements' and 'Moments'

John Shotter
Arlene M. Katz

A[n] executant [is] one who "acts out" the material before him (sic) so as to give it intelligible life . . . the executant invests his own being in the process of interpretation. His readings, his enactments of chosen meanings and values, are not those of external survey. They are a commitment at risk, a response which is, in the root sense, responsible.

—*Steiner (1989, pp. 7-8)*

The "otherness" which enters into us makes us other.

—*Steiner (1989, p. 188)*

But as all severall soules contain
Mixture of things, they know not what,
Love, these mixt soules, doth mixe againe,
And makes both one, each this and that . . .
When love, with one another so
Interanimates two soules,
That abler soule, which thence doth flow,
Defects of loneliness controlles.

—*John Donne, "The Extasie," 1638*

Let the use of words teach you their meaning.

—*Wittgenstein (1953, p. 220)*

Sheila McNamee and Ken Gergen have invited us to "dance" with them, in responding to their chapter in this book, and this is what we want to do . . . and to talk 'of' it from within the process of doing it . . . while avoiding (if we can) talk 'about' it, talk that is not responsive to, or expressive of, its immediate surroundings in some way. For we don't want to talk at a distance about processes that are over, to describe their fixed and final outcomes after all their living movement has ceased, to ignore the relation of our talk to people's lives. For there is something very special about dancing with others: Something occurs 'in' the to-and-fro, back-and-forth, relationally responsive movement between two or more living beings, such that we have an active sense of something as moving 'within' us and of us as moving 'within' it. It is almost as if a third living agency is at work in the process, and 'it', the dance, dances us as much as we dance it—we have a sense of being a participant in something beyond ourselves that is absent when the mutual responsivity between the partners is absent. Only if 'you' respond to 'me' in a way sensitive to the "relations" between your and my actions, can 'we' act together as a 'collective-we'; and if I sense you as not being sensitive in that way, then I feel immediately offended, ethically offended: I feel you lack respect for me in some way.

Goffman (1967) discusses the obligations in our conversational involvements as follows:

"Joint spontaneous involvement," he says,

> is a *unio mystico,* a socialized trance. We must also see that a conversation has a life of its own and makes demands on its own behalf. It is a little social system with its own boundary-maintaining tendencies; it is a little patch of commitment and loyalty with its own heroes and its own villains. (pp. 113-114)

And he goes on to study the deep and nuanced sense of both our own and others's "obligations" within a dialogue and what happens when we fail to honor such involvement obligations. For just as in the moment-by-moment movements within a dance, there is a sense of rightness and wrongness of fit, a sense of honoring or failing to respect the 'invitations' others offer us in their actions. Without a responsibility to the relationship, dancing is impossible.

But of course, there is always a certain amount of play in such relationally responsive movements, in how partners respond to each other's invitations, play in at least two senses: (a) in the sense of the phases, moments, or aspects of such activity being only loosely connected to one another, such that 'gaps,' 'spaces,' or 'zones of indeterminacy' open up, both within and between people's activities; (b) thus, such activity is always improvisational and creative, never mechanically repetitive. Something uniquely new is always brought into existence in such activity. Poiesis, the making into being of something uniquely innovative, is always disturbingly at work within it—which is perhaps one of the reasons why we have not so much not previously noticed the strange nature of such relationally responsive activities, but have, in our current academic and intellectual methods, actively ignored them. Until recently, to be accounted properly professional in our intellectual activities, we have had to relate ourselves to 'those others' of our studies, as disengaged, involved, external observers, looking at their activities in unresponsive manner, as if from afar, as if from the other side of a one-way screen. To allow ourselves to become sensitive to the previously unnoticed new possibilities opened up by the creative poiesis at work, dialogically, in our daily activities, we must change our intellectual practices. And this is precisely what Sheila and Ken are urging us to do in their work here.

So in 'dancing' in with them, we want to do two things: (a) First, we want to explore in more coherent detail the nature of the dialogical and to see how opening ourselves up to responsive, involved, or engaged relations with those others (whom in the past we have studied as if from afar), changes almost all our thinking about the nature of our social (scientific?) inquiries. And then, (b) in a sequence of 'movements' and 'moments,' we want to go on to explore new ways in which the 'sensed shape' of a dialogical 'space' might possibly be expressed: how we might talk, not so much about such spaces, but of them, in such a way that it provides a more active, 'moving' kind of knowledge and understanding, one that allows us to get a sense of connections and relations between things we have not before noticed.

THE RELATIONALLY RESPONSIVE NATURE OF THE DIALOGICAL

Whenever a second living being responds to the activities of a first, and thus acts in a way that depends on their acts, then the activities of the second can only ever be partially their own; they can never be accounted as wholly theirs: As responses to the activities of the first, they are always partially shaped by the first's activities. They cannot not be. But once we allow this possibility, once we accept that people exist in continuous living relations with both each other and with their surroundings, the idea of us as being separate, self-contained entities vanishes. And the idea of our world as being a world external to us can no longer be sustained either. In such circumstances as these, instead of one person first acting individually and independently of an other, and then a second acting individually and independently of the first, the fact is, as we have already mentioned, they inter-act together, jointly, as a collective-we; and often, they do this bodily, in a living way, spontaneously and immediately, without them having first to work out their responses to each other. In so doing, they connect or relate themselves both to each other and to their surroundings, one way or another, necessarily. Or, to put the matter individually, What I do now depends on what we, overall, are doing . . . and what I do is a mixture, so to speak—an exceedingly complex mixture—of influences both from within me and from elsewhere. Where, due to the loosely joined nature of all the connections or relations involved here, although complex, our activity is still only partially specified and remains open to yet further, creative specification by all those of us who are involved or engaged in it. And it is precisely this—its partly open and partly closed nature, its partly individual and partly social, its partly natural and partly cultural nature—that makes this sphere of joint action (Shotter, 1980, 1993a, 1993b) of especial interest to us.

Indeed, this is where all the compelling strangeness of relationally responsive, dancelike activities begins: Not only do they give rise to a mixture of activities whose source cannot be traced back to any of the individuals involved, they also seem to be like living beings in their own right, to be 'its' that invite yet further creative elaboration of certain kinds while resisting others. Indeed, the way in which we seem ethically answerable to an 'it' over and beyond us, when we are relationally engaged with each other, is precisely what Sheila and Ken express, it seems to us, in their idea of relational responsibility: "to be responsible to relational processes," they say, "is to favor the possibility of intelligibility itself" (pp. 18-19)

Thus, what is very special about relationally responsive, dialogical activities—and really rather peculiar when contrasted with the assumptions inculcated in us by classical and modernist, natural scientific notions—is that if we do act in a relationally responsible way, then the whole character of our lives changes: Instead of living over against an inert, dead, physical reality, we come to live our lives almost as if a bodily part of a much larger, collective agency, as if inside a living 'we'. (Something we feel Bateson [1979] was trying to say in talking of mind as being 'in' nature but still from within a grammar intrinsic to a modernist usage of the terms *mind* and *nature*.) Thus, to emphasize Sheila and Ken's use of the word *favor* here again, it is only if we take on a responsibility toward relational processes will all the new creative possibilities to which they can give rise appear. If we do not, the possibilities of their creation will be lost; their appearance is not guaranteed. George Steiner (1989) puts this possibility as follows: "These convictions are, as current linguistic philosophy puts it—when it is being polite," he says, " 'verification transcendent'. They cannot be logically, formally or evidentially proved" (p. 214). "But . . . " he continues,

> I am wagering, both in a Cartesian and Pascalian vein, on the informing pressure of a real presence in the semantic markers which generate Oedipus the King or Madame Bovary; in the pigments or incisions which externalize Grünewald's Issenheim triptych or Brancusi's Bird. (p. 215)

(And so on, for a number of further great works of art).

In each interactional moment, if (following Sheila McNamee) we may call it that, is the real possibility of a unique, coconstructed space into which a second person can spontaneously respond while reacting to the actions of a first—and into which each subsequent actor can be further, spontaneously responsive. Indeed, these subtle, fleeting, unique, unrepeatable variations in the rule-governed rituals of our social exchanges are the very stuff of the dialogical. They are the only "once-occurrent event[s] of Being," as Bakhtin (1993, p. 2) calls them, by means of which we express the unique nature of our inner lives to each other. And we understand such events from within the ongoing conduct of our practices, not referentially or representationally by stepping out of their flow to think 'about' them—but responsively, relationally, spontaneously, and practically from within their ongoing flow. This leads us into the part of our response to Sheila's and Ken's invitation to dance with them in some way.

MOVEMENTS: RELATIONALLY MAKING SENSE TOGETHER

What we want to do next—in a series of 'playful movements' responsive to aspects of Sheila's and Ken's text—is to explore something of what is involved in the creation of new ways for us to dance with each other in this realm of partial freedom and partial restriction. We want to set out some pieces of text that are not structured so as to 'direct' readers as to how at each point they should be 'followed'. Instead, we want to try to provoke (somewhat more than the text in the previous section) breaks or pauses in one's reading of them, moments for responsive wandering or journeying over a landscape of relational possibilities. We want to experiment to see if we can help readers to create within themselves a sense of what might be involved in being relationally responsible to an Other or otherness in a text, in being answerable to an 'it'. Indeed, it is with Sheila's and Ken's text in mind that we have produced our responses and replies to below. In Steiner's (1989) sense, instead of trying in our writing to picture or represent our understanding of what they say, we are enacting or playing out some of the many understandings their work occasioned in us in our responses to it, in the "movements" that follow below.

Movement #1

The background . . . "Perhaps what is inexpressible (what I find mysterious and am not able to express) is the background against which whatever I could express has its meaning" (Wittgenstein, 1980, p. 16) . . . in fact, our spoken words are an almost negligible part of the intermingling flow of flowing activities within which they are immersed.

"The term 'language-game' is meant to bring into prominence the fact that the speaking of language is part of an activity, or a form of life" (Wittgenstein, 1953, no. 23) . . . speaking is only ever a part of a much, much larger activity.

There is always a 'more' to meaning, and it is against the background of that 'more' that what we say makes a difference . . . this is the use of what we say . . . it gestures toward aspects of this 'more' . . . our talk points toward features of the larger flow or flows within which we are immersed.

To make our vague, gestural meanings in language more precise, we must choose our words carefully and conscientiously . . . we must craft or shape their 'movement' . . . their voicing must be a responsible response . . . more than merely talk 'about' a moment . . .

Movement #2

Play . . . definitions: (a) a special kind of free movement; (b) playfulness; (c) playing games; (d) musical; (e) drama . . . dramatic scenes . . . moving moments . . . arresting moments . . .

Certain moments, that we might call moving, arresting, or dramatic moments, have a 'living fullness' to them that we find difficult to grasp . . . They seem like new beginnings . . . incomplete, unfinished, open to further development . . . originary moments . . . seeds . . . something young, childlike, as yet not wholly formed . . . an otherness that we have never before encountered.

This is the power of the poetic: "In its expression, it is youthful language," says Bachelard (1992, p. xv).

Movement #3

Styles and rhythms in our movements: (a) Playful movement: the humanly ordered nature of our movements . . . their measured nature . . . the rhythmic quality of a poem, the acts of a play, the character of a composition with regard to rhythm and tempo, the illusion of a living motion in a painting, sculpture, and so forth. . . . (b) Serious movements: a series of acts and events planned toward a definite end by a body of people . . . a tactical moving of a body of troops . . .

There is rhythmic play in people's writing . . . writing is ordered, measured, it has a style to it: Susan Sontag (1969) writes that

Raymond Bayer has written: "What each and every aesthetic object imposes on us, in appropriate rhythms, is a unique and singular formula for the flow of our energy. . . . Every work of art embodies a principle of proceeding, of stopping, of scanning; an image of energy or relaxation, the imprint of a caressing or destroying hand which is [the artist's] alone." We can call this the physiognomy of the work, or its rhythm, or, as I would rather do, its style. (p. 28).

A work of art: a dynamic site in which many different voices, many different styles, many ways of being, intersect.

Movement #4

Looking over: So, what are we doing when we contemplate a work of art . . . a painting, a sculpture, when we move up close to it and look 'into' its details? . . . Why do we look so long? . . . Why can we return to look again and again . . . or read once-read books again? . . . The exploration of unending ways of relating . . . of 'entering into' a relationship with someone or something? . . . A work of art: a dynamic site in which many ways of looking intersect . . . in which many ways of being intersect. . . . In such a circumstance, its character cannot be defined, it can only be understood by being explored.

"How can one learn the truth by thinking? As one learns to see a face better if one draws it" (Wittgenstein, 1981, no. 225) . . . as one draws the face over and

over again, one becomes more familiar with it, sees more details . . . and finds
it becoming more mysterious and magical . . .

Waking up to wonder . . .

The living, unending, ungraspable fullness of momentary, changing relationships . . .

Movement #5

Resonance . . . as in a musical instrument . . . a kind of sympathetic awaken-
ing in another part, or another instrument, of both the original tone and of its
overtones . . . a complex arousing of movement in other things by the movements
of a first . . .

Bachelard (1992) distinguishes between resonances (same tone) and reverberations (its echoed overtones) in our hearing or reading of a poem: "In the
resonance we hear the poem, in the reverberations we speak it, it is our own. The
reverberations bring about a change of being. It is as though the poet's being
were our being . . . the poem possesses us entirely" (p. xviii) . . .

"The image offered us by reading the poem now becomes really our own . . .
It becomes a new being in our language, expressing us by making us what it
expresses . . . Here expression creates being" (p. xix) . . .

A poet's metaphors bring together two bits of knowledge, common to most
of us, but usually kept separate . . . a new relation is constructed . . . Oliver Sacks
says of Dr. P (the man who mistook his wife for a hat): "He looked at me through
his ears," and we on reading that now look at the world around us afresh, through
that image . . . of 'looking over' the world with our ears . . .

Movement #6

In doing this, we begin 'to enter into' a new and unique world . . . to relate
ourselves quite differently to our surroundings . . . How might we fail or avoid
'entering into' such new relationships? . . . What makes sense 'inside' a relationship (yes, it makes sense to talk of being 'inside' and being 'outside' here), will
make no sense 'outside' it . . .

"Just try—in a real case—to doubt someone else's fear or pain" (Wittgenstein,
1953, no. 303) . . . we are 'called' by the *style* of their movement into a certain
relation with them. . . . Such a movement is "the prototype of a way of thinking
and not itself the result of thought" (Wittgenstein, 1981, no. 540) . . . but to be

fully 'moved' by an other's suffering, we have, so to speak, to take the trouble to 'enter into' it . . . to 'favor' being relationally responsible.

Movement #7

"A meaning only reveals its depths once it has encountered and come into contact with another different meaning: they engage in a kind of dialogue, which reaches beyond any one-sidedness of these particular meanings, these cultures" (Bakhtin, 1986, p. 7).

Seeing the everyday world afresh: Training doctors to navigate between the world of biomedicine and the world of an ill person as they learn to make a medical diagnosis. What is at stake for each may begin by being very different: for the student doctor, a sense of competence; for the 'patient,' being heard.

An old man is being interviewed by a medical student (MD). In the first 5 minutes, in answer to the student's question, "what brought you into the hospital?," the old man answered, "I was run down, my wife died, she had a brain tumor, and I took care of her. I got run down and got a cough."

In response, the student asks, "So, you have this cough, how long have you had it?"

Clearly, the two stances—the student's biomedical stance and the patient's stance expressing life-world—coexist, but one is privileged and expanded on, whereas the other is marginalized; the patient's story of loss and grief is pushed to the background.

However, if we import a special dialogical practice into the routine medical diagnostic practice, in which students review a videotape with a medical and nonmedical preceptor (AMK), things change. . . . In the dialogical practice, a conversational space is opened up that allows the student to reflect on his or her diagnostic practice and to see in it new possibilities for a practice more relationally responsible to his or her patients (see also Katz & Shotter, 1996).

In reviewing this interview on videotape, the student comes in with a question: "I think I might have missed something important that the patient was saying. I would like to know how to pick up on it (and if it was important)."

And in the watching together, another question emerged in the conversation between MD and AMK: "How might one talk with a patient in such a way that both narratives—the medical and the patient's life-world—have the opportunity to intersect, to make room for both the voice of the patient and the voice of biomedicine?"

Now the student notices that she did go on to say to the old man: "So, you've been cooking and cleaning for yourself, that must be hard for you since your wife died," and how important that was in the interview. For he replied, "Yes," and went on to offer how it has affected his physical function, giving the student the biomedical information she needed . . . she weaves her world in with the world of the ill old man's . . . brings his world up against hers . . . they become partners in a dialogue . . . and in the responsible responding involved, both may puzzle together about the problem named by the patient. Both become collaborators on a coauthored narrative in which new ideas may emerge . . . and new sensibilities experienced.

CONCLUSIONS

The kind of living, relationally responsive kind of meaning we have attempted to explore is of a very different kind then what we might call the classical, mechanistic, tightly connected, representational-referential kind of meaning currently hegemonic in the academy. In this view, it is the structure of a picture, a sentence, or any other supposedly meaningful kind of humanly produced entity, as a finished product that is important; and we judge its meaning in terms of how its order or its patterning parallels, mirrors, or represents the supposed structure of reality. Its meaning is thus self-contained within it, as its content, so to speak. Whereas, in relationally responsive forms of meaning, meanings are expressed in the unfolding movement of an utterance's embodied voicing, in a tone, style, or way of talking, similarly in writing. It is a matter of how its unfolding movement works to move us, not only to look beyond the utterance or the text toward something in the surroundings of its use, but how also it calls out other relational responses and reactions from us.

In the traditional representational-referential view of meaning, we and our world remain always basically unchanged. It is simply information that we exchange. And as Sheila and Ken point out—in their discussion of certain "relational scenarios" (p. 21) and the patterns of blame and punishment associated with them—it is because of our continued use of a representational, rather than a relational, form of talk in these encounters that we sustain a fixed way of relating ourselves to each other. In continually reflecting back to each other a single way of making sense of interpersonal events, in talking always of them as issuing from the inner mental representations inside the heads of individuals, we fail to point toward any other possible ways forward from a current impasse.

We, like them, have tried to break the stranglehold of such representational forms of talk and writing on us, and by introducing what they call new "orienting resources" (p. 19), we have explored not only new ways of being answerable to the calls of relationship in human affairs—calls to which in the past we have all been somewhat deaf—but also to explore some of the 'mores' of meaning . . . the nature of the larger living whole within which what we do and say has its meaning. There is always, we feel, a 'more' to meaning . . . our quest for new meaning is still only at a beginning.

15

Relational Inquiry and Relational Responsibility

The Practice of Change

Robert Cottor
Sharon Cottor

Consciously creating intentional change has been a fascinating challenge for us for many years. As therapists, organizational and family business consultants, and as teachers, we have searched for those ways of thinking, those metaphors for effective action, that promote the changes we envision. We have found that the creating and transforming of meaning is central to the change process: Change in action represents a change in meaning. We have come to believe that meaning making is a "we" phenomenon, a relational process within a social context. "Mind" is social. We believe that we construct our meanings in our relationships and that the resulting collectives of meaning are organized into stories. These stories give direction to our beliefs, values, and future actions in that social context. We have seen how we perceive, believe, and act differently in different social contexts. Thinking about ourselves as multiple selves flowed easily from this experiencing. Multiple selves employ many different stories as self organizers. If we change the story, we change the self. We seem to be able to do this even in conversation with ourselves as well as in conversation with others, but in either case, we do it as "we," as a relational activity. We can imagine ourselves and others in many fascinating ways. We can invent new identities, new worlds, new ways of being. In our imaginations, conscious change is easy!

What then makes change so hard? So unpredictable? So impossible? Perhaps, our traditional ways of thinking and talking. We still talk of ourselves as possessing a single, true self, of problem solving with its emphasis on defining the cause, creating a logical solution, and then developing a specific action plan. Perhaps it is this that has clouded the potential of our imagining different futures. Perhaps our collective story of the situation as it is appears so powerful and stable that we take it for granted that change is very difficult. We certainly seem to create very rigid relational dances that continually thwart our attempts to implement planned change. If we believe or even suspect that the past determines the future, it can feel futile to even try to change. However, if we believe that we organize ourselves as people and organize the worlds in which we live through the stories we create together in our myriad of relational contexts, then we are—in perception, belief, and action—the stories we tell. Who we are, then, changes as the story changes, and the story changes as our multiple relationships change.

In this response, we want to share our ways of collaborating with our clients to create those changes that can satisfy their expectations. Our inquiry with others is directed toward the relational, the contextual, the affirmative, and the future. We assume change is possible and not only possible but inevitable. We believe it takes more effort to maintain the present than to change the future. Intentional change requires intentionally changing our stories, including our ways of relating as expressed in those stories. However, we are aware that the outcome of any change is unpredictable. Change occurs at the margin of chaos, in the space of rich complexity, and it is easy to overstep into chaos. Tolerance for uncertainty is a requirement for working in this way. Practitioners must also recognize that the changes in the relational stories are the province of the client, and we must respect this and not attempt to colonize our clients.

Last, we employ two relational guides to our inquiry as practitioners: (a) the "we" of any given situation or transaction and (b) the concept of relational responsibility in valuing the actions of any given person or happening. We have found that talking "we" sets the stage for others to understand and use relational concepts without having to learn the formal theory. We have experienced this as freeing them to use their imagination to consider the multiple possibilities for change and effective action that this way of talking provides. We have also found that the explicit use of relational responsibility not only contains the power of the we but also provides a guide to the valuing of possible actions and change that becomes an even more powerful tool for change.

The idea that our relationships, not ourselves individually form the foundation for responsible action is foreign at first to most everyone. However, once this is considered, a whole multiverse of new thinking and acting, of new possibilities, can open up. Individual blame dissolves, and collective action becomes punctuated. Cooperation and collaboration to create valued outcomes can become the focus of a conjoint effort to create change rather than attempting to fix a flawed individual or a problematic situation. In addition, relational responsibility includes the professional in the outcome of the change work and serves to further promote the collaborative nature of the change process.

We will first describe our work with relational inquiry in a clinical context. We will then describe our work with organizational and family business consultation.

RELATIONAL INQUIRY
AND CLINICAL PRACTICE

Relational inquiry is a way of thinking and acting that, in practice, is responsive to the emerging context. It is not a set of skills or techniques that can be learned and then performed. It is not a way of practicing that can be learned in a single intensive workshop. Thinking about people as relational meaning makers and working with those people to create the changes they seek leads to ways of questioning that bring forth new ways of thinking and acting on their parts. This opens for them possibilities for change that they had not yet imagined. It offers them a way that they had never considered of looking at themselves, at each other, at their dilemmas, and at their relational and social worlds.

Although this way of thinking and talking may seem strange at first to people who in practice are labeled clients, it also seems to have strong appeal. It respects their ability to think creatively, to consider options seriously, and to act effectively for a new future. It offers a readily accessible method for change: talk and dialogue. The pragmatics of everyday life and its many uncertainties and unpredictable changes take the place of professional mysteries closed to their understanding. People remain people, with their many diverse qualities and attributes, and not persons identified as problematic or damaged.

In a moment, we will describe a clinical vignette and some of the questions we would be thinking and asking within this situation. We offer this as a sample of what we might be doing, not as an interviewing manual. Our questioning reveals our thinking. Our working assumptions about change embedded in our questioning are the following:

Change is a relational and social matter.

Strengths, assets, and resources promote intentional change; problems, deficits, and
  defects inhibit it.

Affirmation and appreciation energize change; criticism and blame constrain it.

Curiosity empowers change; judgment detours it.

Inquiry and conversation provide an opportunity for new learning as we bring forth new meanings that enable us to invent new stories.

Creating and appreciating new and novel stories empowers change; repeating old stories reifies the status quo.

Challenging the taken-for-granted and imagining new possibilities enhance creative story making and promote hope for the future.

Respecting multiple perspectives opens up new possibilities; differentness is not an obstacle to be avoided but a meaning to be valued.

Seeking complexity through the construction of multiple selves, stories, and opportunities constructs the context for change.

Viewing the future as the locus allows vision and hope to guide the change process.

Viewing the past as yet to be determined offers freedom from the tyranny of deficit thinking and predetermination.

We have found that we need to carefully introduce these ideas so that clients can begin to use them constructively. We present our expertness as inventing effective questions and facilitating the resulting dialogues, not having the so-called correct answers.

In the questions following the clinical vignette, listen for the ideas about change contained in the question. For instance, in the first questions, the idea about appreciating a traumatic event for what it can offer positively in the future ties in ideas about assets, resources, affirmation, appreciation, new opportunities, new perspectives, and the ability to construct a desirable future.

Questions about responsibility present a unique challenge in practice because of how fixed the belief in individual responsibility is for most people and, in addition, how many people, under relational stress, appear to discount responsibility as an admissible concept on even an individual level, much less as a primary currency embedded in their relationship. We introduce the concept of responsibility as an integral part of relationships in our initial inquiry and then, in the ensuing dialogue, by bringing forth the mutuality and in-between-ness of responsibility.

Martha is a 40-year-old divorced professional woman who has her 14-year-old daughter living with her. Her daughter has begun to act out and break rules at home and in the community. Martha's ex-husband is very wealthy, remarried, has a traditional, stay-at-home wife and has had two additional children in his second marriage.

Typical Questions to Martha

What do you most appreciate about the opportunity for change that your divorce provided for you?

There are many Marthas, but let's just consider two of them for now—the traditional Martha and the more contemporary Martha. How are those two Marthas similar and different?

If there had not been a divorce 10 years ago, how would the traditional Martha and the contemporary Martha have developed?

When you think of your daughter 10 years from now—she'll be 24—what do you hope she will have learned from you?

When your daughter is with her father, how would you hope they would describe you? How might their description of you be different?

When Martha considers her responsibilities with her daughter and with her career, where do they clash? What would have to happen for those responsibilities to complement each other?

What responsibilities do you consider your daughter has with herself, with each of her three parents, and with her younger half-siblings?

Does your daughter know her responsibilities with others as well as she knows her individual rights?

As a daughter, if you'd like your mother to trust you more, how would you need to act?

How long do you think it would take your mother to notice your new behavior?

RELATIONAL INQUIRY AND CONSULTATIVE PRACTICE

Relational inquiry is as applicable to organizational and business enterprise change as it is to clinical change. It may be even easier to apply in this domain because the stereotypes of damaged and defective, and therefore unchangeable, individuals are not nearly so strongly entrenched. Results such as increased productivity and profits may also be easier for the organization to measure. The process of thinking and inquiry is no different in organizational change work than in clinical. However, organizational work provides an opportunity to use actual experiences that, in themselves, can provide occasions for constructive dialogues that can guide the change process. Direct relational questioning by the consultant will also play a role in this process and, at times, may be the primary tool for change, given the nature of the organization.

Our extensive work with family-owned businesses has offered us an opportunity to use a relational inquiry approach that makes obvious sense to their management. It is readily recognized in family businesses, although not necessarily by their other professional advisers, that the relationships among the family members, including those not active in the business, are critical to the success of the business. These families have access to a measure of success with relational consulting, the financial well-being of their business, not typically available to other families in distress or seeking specific change. We have also found similar qualities to be present in business partnerships, such as legal, medical, accounting, and real estate firms, with whom we have consulted. These partnerships recognize how important the quality of their partnering is to continued success, especially as they have to deal with rapid change in their practices.

We will describe a consultative vignette involving an organization made up of a number of both profit and not-for-profit health agencies who were providing their services in the same state.

> The health care organization we worked with is essentially a trade group made up of independent health care firms, both for profit and not for profit. They had joined together in the past for political and legislative reasons and now were facing the tremendous changes in funding and mission brought forth by managed care and changing public policy. The members of the organization, about 40 separate entities, were in constant flux with their services and were very uncertain about their individual and collective futures. They invited us to work with them on understanding and managing change with a 1-day change workshop. We began the workshop, in which each member entity was represented by a key executive, by briefly describing to the whole group our assumptions about change from a postmodern, relational perspective. We then divided the group into four small working groups and presented them with the following questions. Each group had a leader from our consulting firm.

Typical Questions Addressed to Key Executives

> Think back to 5 years ago in your own organization. What has happened during the past 5 years that you expected would happen? What hasn't happened that you expected would happen? What has happened that you didn't expect would happen?
>
> What methods of leadership for change have you employed in your organization over the past 5 years? Which have been successful? How has responsibility for change been viewed in your organization?

From the point of view of your organization, what is the best of your organization and what is the best in you as a member of the organization? From your own point of view, what have been the best moments you have experienced in your organization? What are the best times you have experienced? When have you felt best about your contributions to others around you in your organization?

Use the steps of (a) appreciating the best of what is, (b) envisioning what possibly might be, (c) dialoguing about what could be, and (d) inventing-innovating what will be, to create constructive change in your trade organization as a simulation of what could be done in your independent organization or firm.

Think of a change you would like to implement in your organization during the next year. What are the advantages and the disadvantages of making that change? What are the advantages and disadvantages of not making that change?

Imagine that you are the leaders of a health agency planning for the next 3 years. You know you will be challenged during this period of time with (a) reduced funding, (b) increased caseload, (c) decreasing staff morale, and (d) diminishing board confidence in your ability to deliver quality services. How will you create, as a leadership team addressing these challenges, a strategic scenario for this 3-year period?

CONCLUSIONS

In our change work, we use the metaphor of a person as a storyteller whose stories are told and responded to as a "we," with responsibility for action being the relationship between us. From this perspective, talk is never idle. Talk is how we most effectively take action with each other to coordinate our relating so that meaning, values, and our myriad of social behaviors and efforts can evolve and be shaped in the directions we prefer. Talk is how we can most effectively create change. With our imaginations and our capacities to invent multiple possibilities for the future, we can lead ourselves toward purposeful changes through the fluidity of our most powerful relational tool, our ability to create stories that then reinvent our lives together.

Who we have been, who we are, and who we will become is not an individual matter. We are the products of our many relationships, and we cannot not be. We are the stories we tell about ourselves. We are organized as selves by our stories. These stories arise in our relationships and are the outcomes of our relational actions, especially those actions in language. We speak as a we, we listen as a we, and we act as a we. It is, then, a matter of course that we are responsible as a we. We learn this through experience; it cannot be just stated and understood. We find in our change work that this appreciation for responsibility as a quality of the relationship rather than of the individual emerges very slowly and is quite difficult to describe. When it does become a knowable guide to practice, we feel the voice of relational theory can be best expressed in the practice of change.

Relational responsibility is a difficult concept to appreciate. It involves an ethics of speaking, an ethics of listening, and an ethics of acting with one another. It is especially difficult to "do" it. It involves an appreciative practice. When you can reach the point of doing it, when it becomes part of you, it can then become a very effective guide for inquiry, understanding, inventing possible changes, and acting in any relationship. With relational responsibility as a guiding practice, the world of relationships changes.

16

A Circle of Voices

Peggy Penn
Marilyn Frankfurt

Our responses to Sheila McNamee's and Kenneth Gergen's manuscript, *Relational Responsibility,* comes in two parts. Part 1 is Peggy Penn's reflection on a consultation by Tom Andersen at the Ackerman Institute in November of 1995 with two of our clients in the Writing Project, a gay couple who both have AIDS. Peggy was witness to the session. Part 2 is a commentary on Peggy's reflection, written by Marilyn Frankfurt.

Together, this writing describes and comments on how the circle of voices in the therapeutic session represents what Sheila McNamee calls the relational engagement of all the participants. This engagement, combined with the ethics inherent in the session, affects not only choices that clients make in their conversations but choices made by the therapists as well. The back and forth of conversation in the circle of voices arouses ethical interest on the part of both therapists and clients, as they decide what to value in the words of the other. In this consultation, an aesthetic solution develops: The circle of voices evokes in the clients the perception of an extension of life after death.

PART I: PEGGY PENN

Once and sometimes twice a year, Tom Andersen stops and consults with Peggy Penn and Marilyn Frankfurt in the Writing Project at the Ackerman Institute. Tom interviewed the couple, John and Chris, while I (Penn) sat in the interview. I had already told all the families in our Writing Project that Tom Andersen stopped at the Ackerman Institute when he came through New York and, if it was all right with them, he would join us the following week to consult. I told our clients we all shared a work history together, that he was from Norway and a very soft-spoken man. In response to some of their questions, Tom and I agreed that, at the moment, our shared work centered around questions of "What are the things a therapist should know?"

Immediately, Chris said, "Feelings." I asked how they would feel if Tom did the interview. That would give me the benefit of the listener's position in the room—and it offered them the new experience of conversing with a man rather than two women.

Both men agreed that they were game. I felt the opening talks to be cheerful. There was laughter, a sense of relaxation on all our parts as well as a feeling of expectation among us. Chris asked if the family work Tom did included family members. I'm not sure why we both decided to answer that, but we did, saying, that whoever they chose to invite was always welcome.

Once our conversation felt safely established, Chris and John returned to their thoughts from the previous week. The week before, we had spoken indirectly of their plans in case one of them died: living wills and so forth. Chris volunteered that I had used the word *muted* in describing our last conversation, and he likened that to a mute on a trumpet. He felt this muteness was their avoidance of the big "D" conversation. Though he, Chris, was feeling healthy at the moment, he had already made his living will. But John, who had gotten quite ill in the past 6 months from intense chemotherapy for his Kaposi's sarcoma (KS), had not. Chris commented, "This subject is like a plane crash, you need a good friend beside you." I hoped he meant us as well as John. Perhaps it's important to say that these two men have suffered immensely, both physically and emotionally. Though Chris is currently feeling better, within 2 weeks of my writing this, he was hospitalized for 2 weeks with a leg infection and a problematic lung condition that remains undiagnosed. John has struggled with a profusion of KS on his body and, he suspects, inside as well. The men live at home now, resting, preparing their meals, and sometimes Chris works.

I will try to describe each of them: John is a cabaret performer and has large eyes and a smile that stretches from ear to ear. I am drawn to the profusion of expressions that go across his face like fast, shifting weather. He will respond to something either you or he has just said with a sense of acceptance: Then, his eyes crinkle, and he laughs in affectionate irony, and finally looks directly at one of us with a sad and most imploring expression. Chris, an architect, is very tall and handsome. His eyes are focused and shine with intelligence. His head is always bravely high and led by an expressive chin. Somewhere behind all that, there is the feeling that he may ultimately have to make the best of things and it won't be fair to anyone. Because of their health, this relationship is like a mountainous island; there is no flatland where crops can be cultivated, where things can be grown for the next season. That was what both Tom and I felt that day.

Tom began with his first question: "How would you like this meeting to be used?" Almost from the beginning of the interview, I saw Tom lean in toward the men and keep that position almost for the entire interview, either supporting his chin on his hand or folding his arms and leaning toward them in strong concentration. I was touched by this message from his body; it was as though their suffering was being written on him and he accepted it patiently.

Dialogues like these, that concern themselves with life and death, are so close to the heart that our own private pasts are continuously invoked. I could see that happening to Tom just as it has to us. We met these two men when they came to us over a year ago in order to separate. Nine years ago, on the same day, they both had found out they had AIDS and decided to marry because they were in love and wanted to care for each other. Now, they feel they no longer want their "old relationship" and perhaps they should separate. John wants to be independent before he dies and doubts their ability to change the relationship. Chris feels uneasy about separating and wants to try to change the relationship. During the interview, Tom immediately seemed to share a strong attachment to them. I knew no matter what feelings we would be sharing with them today, we could not in any way affect their current and future onslaught. I felt very supported in the session and just let go.

It's important to say that this was not a usual consultation where a colleague engages in the content of a case either by watching you work or by sitting in on the session. Following that model, the therapist and the consultant confer after the session, where the therapist receives the consultant's new ideas, which at some later date are shared with the family. But in this kind of consultation, a socially constructed one, we all listen to each other, reflecting on what we are saying and paying strict attention to our own feelings that increasingly become a part of the talk. There are no private talks. This listening in the consultation is not just to words but to the family's special words, gaps, tensions, and, of course, to their silences. As we listen, part of us repositions our own feelings and ideas in order to take in theirs. Our main concern is the family's comfort and our ability to be there with them.

Andersen often follows his first question with one that asks, "Is this meeting together usual for all of you, or is it a bit unusual," thereby attending to the whole family's state of mind, level of anxiety about this meeting or about talking to a stranger, and so forth. If, in fact, they are anxious or unhappy at being in the session, he stays right there, listening to what troubles some or all of them have. I have seen him devote a whole session just to the idea of "talking"—when, to whom, in what manner, tone, who might begin, and so forth, inviting all the feelings members of the family might have about the act of talking. By this time, when the family has appraised the pace and depth of the developing dialogue, they no longer feel intruded on, and he no longer feels like a stranger: outside the family, fearsome to them or simply unknown. Families, after all, have their own reasons to go slowly on icy roads and that is respected.

Although there is a pervasive sense that the session is open-ended, this particular day, all of us were facing a very different future. In our joined aesthetic idiom, which is dependent on language forming us as we proceed, perhaps the most we could hope for was to construct a hammock of words where they could, in a sense, lie down and be eased.

The place underneath the talk where we all were joined was the sense of loss, even mourning. I knew Tom felt it as did I. Oddly, the appreciation of loss became a connection among us so now I am not surprised, months after the event, when Tom asks me how are the two men doing—or when they ask us when Tom plans to return. The session had the haunting tone of an elegy; They shared their past and future not just with me but with a man they had not seen before. I knew that at any point if they had wept, we would have wept, but they seemed, somehow, happy.

* * *

In the following portion of the conversation, it was as though we were in a vivid dream together; the feeling in the room among us was one of compression; the silences, waiting time, exchange of looks, and the words of death, all forged a compression of meaning that was brought to an almost unbearable point. It was the last half hour of the session and both men took the time to describe their current physical and emotional state. In conclusion, John said he mostly wanted to sleep. Tom asked him, "Would that be a sleep with or without dreams?" John said he didn't know. Tom continued, "Which would be best for you?" He did not directly answer but volunteered that he was at the bottom and didn't know when he would ascend again. "I am now abloom with KS," he said. At the same time, he thinks a lot about the impact his death will have on other people. He has been a giver in life, and it's hard to be a taker, as he sees it. Tom asks Chris, "Is it hard for you to think of doing without him?" Chris nods, "Yes, it would be." He reminds John how many friends are concerned about him, how the people in his Body Positive Group rely on him, call him and so on. At this moment, the language carries an almost palpable physical sense for all of us; we are feeling in our bodies every word, look, and connection. Tom is making many small sounds during this part of the conversation; several times, I fill with tears, but we never look at each other. It is as though we are all experiencing a sense of largesse toward everything the conversation is holding. Tom asks, "Is it possible that your relationship could last forever?" They reel a bit and Chris finally says he plans to save the ashes of whichever of them dies first to be mixed with the ashes of the other. John laughs about waiting, being "dust" on the mantle, but Chris is adamant that their families should have a single place to go where they can visit them together: Uncle Chris and Uncle John. Chris adds that he hopes they could plant an azalea bush on the spot. Tom asks, "If the azalea bush could sing a song, what would it sing?" Chris chooses Vivaldi's *Four Seasons,* even Beethoven's *Pastoral Symphony:* odes to joy! I remember that *Four Seasons* is an old favorite of Tom's, but he never indicates this preference. John has another thought: He wants a memorial party, with 70s party songs and lots of wine, food, and sex for the guests who can still have it. They should have *fun!* He wasn't sure about an azalea bush; instead, he might choose a sturdy oak tree.

John says his current wish is to have something more than to just stay alive. I was moved by his wish and said so; it continues to stay with me. Because the end of the hour had arrived, they turned to Tom and asked, "What are your thoughts?" Tom began to say, " . . . I . . . can't find words . . . certainly there would be sad words . . . and words of beauty." Both men nodded in thanks to his offered appreciation and understanding of them. Chris guessed that it was a lot to hit him with. Tom responded, "I don't feel hit, I am touched. Hit is a small word; touched is a much longer word. . . . I know I will always remember this meeting." It was raining outside but when we left our room, it felt bright, not from the video lights but from all four of us being able to move together.

Lingering in my mind was John's remark about his life meaning something, that he wants to be more than just alive. The men had agreed that Tom was welcome to a copy of the tape to use for teaching, so I asked Tom what he thought of the idea of asking the men to write something about their lives to accompany the tapes. That way, each time either of us presented the tape, their words would be present and last. He agreed, and when I asked them, they agreed to write.

PART 2: MARILYN FRANKFURT

After Peggy finished writing her reflection on the consultation by Tom Andersen, I asked her to read it aloud to me. Even though I had seen Tom's consultation with Peggy and our clients on videotape and found it to be particularly moving, I felt myself stirred differently by Peggy's reflection on it. I heard in her writing the distillation of mood, feelings, and time expressed in what I think of as the conversation's circle of voices. I asked Peggy if she was aware that she had captured the hermeneutical flow of dialogue in the interview. "Not consciously," she replied. "I was paying attention to what moved me as witness to the conversation." We agreed that it might be useful for me to write a commentary on her reflection, detailing my observations about Tom's consultation as a particularly good example of how the therapist's hermeneutic position in family therapy illuminates the process of relational responsibility. Peggy and I understand relational responsibility, in the broadest sense, to mean the process that explores the continuing possibilities of a relationship through dialogue. We think of this as an ethical process, always open to choices in the future.

As social constructionists, our goal is to promote an ethically informed therapy that provides a safe dialogic space in which our clients can discover and expand their many relational voices. In this space, through exploration of language and the imagination, clients find new narratives that open possibilities for change in important relationships. Peggy's reflection on Tom's consultation provides a wonderful opportunity to show how a language-oriented social constructionist interview furthers the process of relational responsibility between the therapist and the client by helping to create and sustain a circle of voices. I will focus my comments on (a) how this many-voiced, reflexive conversation opens passages to feelings; (b) how the moment-to-moment "to-ing and fro-ing" of ideas and feelings via words and images shifts back and forth in time frames from the past-in-the-present to the future; (c) how the participants all reposition, within themselves and with one another, throughout the conversation; (d) how the consultation, which takes place in the public sphere, is performative—that is, how this witnessed exchange of meaning takes on transformative potential, ethical in nature; and last, (e) how the circle of voices permits the coexistence of all that is produced within it to be held over time by the relational connections that this kind of conversation establishes. The coexistence of all these elements within the same space promotes a competitive and interactive dynamic between them. This generative process often produces the unexpected.

As a couple, John and Chris were using the therapy to carve a new relational space, which included more boundaries and better understanding and acceptance of each other's needs. In the consultation with Tom, a new expression of their suffering comes into being, and, though they choose to discuss their feelings about death, their language and the mood of the interview is surprisingly enlivened, even happy, as Peggy observes.

In this interview, we witness an imaginative extension of this couple's diminished horizons to a vision of growth, beauty, and celebration after death, prompted by Tom's deeply responsive listening and his future-oriented questions. Such communicative events are performative because they make things happen. The extension of this couple's horizons past death can be thought of as a transformation of their voices. Their words and images, created in dialogue and witnessed, produce another story for each man and for them as a couple. This new story, which extends their visions of themselves past suffering, changes their self-narratives and their voice as a couple. For this couple, given John's need to create an independent space for himself within the relationship, their differing visions of themselves after death are affirmed in the dialogue.

From the beginning of the interview, both Peggy and Tom create an atmosphere of good will, treating John and Chris not just with respect but indicating by their behavior that the purpose of the session is for all participants to try to understand one another through dialogue and that to do so, a certain equity or parity needs to take place between everyone. The therapists set up this dialogic space so that the contributions of all present will obtain some intelligibility. This attitude toward the session is consonant with the inclusiveness of Gilligan's (1982) "ethic of care" (p. 90), which promotes response to need in relationships by sustaining what she calls the "web of interconnection" (p. 57). McNamee's phrase, "relational engagement," also comes to mind. I was taken by Peggy's description of Tom's empathic sounds and his metaphoric language, all of which had the effect of opening the exchange of voices through the inclusion of his responsive feelings.

At the place in her reflection where Peggy mentions that she was full of feeling, which part of her could surrender to make room for that of the men, I became aware of the hermeneutic process taking place in the interview. To be alongside John and Chris in the present, the therapists need to be aware of any relevant past understandings (ideas, beliefs, feelings) they bring to the session, for the new realities that they are taking in as the conversation proceeds can only be taken in over against the perspectives they already have. Peggy and Tom are always in a state of learning, new understanding, and change, and they try to respond only with words and feelings that are prompted in them by what the men are saying, by the meaning being created at the moment in the room. Being open to a changing self-understanding through this process, Peggy and Tom are positioned to be open to new possibilities. This ready space, which points to the future, is an invitation to the men to do the same. Gadamer (as quoted in Wachterhauser, 1986) refers to this coexistence of time frames as a "fusion of the horizons of past, present, and future" (p. 37). The active process of exchange that takes place in this fluid space stimulates for both therapists and clients the emergence of stories never spoken. Thus, to promote an atmosphere for understanding, the therapists need to be open for "a transformation into a communion in which they do not remain what they were" (Risser, 1991, p. 105).

The circle of voices represents the relational engagement of the participants. This engagement, combined with the ethics inherent in the session, affects not only the choices that clients make in their conversations but choices made by the therapists as well. What goes on from moment to moment in the dialogue produces in the therapists an ethical interest. They are constantly making valuative decisions for themselves in response both to the clients' realities and to their own. The ethical interest stimulated in the therapists by their inclusion in the circle of voices reveals their sense of relational responsibility toward one another and toward the clients. Peggy goes on to describe how in Tom's bodily "leaning toward [the men] in strong concentration," he opens himself to "their suffering . . . being written on him." He allows their suffering to coexist with his own feelings and memories that are evoked by being with them. Knowing the other in this way evokes new voices in the therapist, keeping the exchange of realities vital. This imaginative process of "knowing" the client's otherness through the therapist's own senses is also part of the therapist's ethic. Donald Hall (1993), the poet, remarked about reading poetry, "Our senses, excited by sound and picture, assimilate records of feeling that are also passages to feeling" (p. 6). Feelings, in turn, are passages to meaning.

The conversation moves to the future, when Tom asks Chris, "Is it hard for you to think of doing without him?" And then, "Is it possible that your relationship could last forever?" In the imaginative realm of possibility, Chris dreams that their joined ashes will turn into a beautiful azalea bush. Tom's last question, "If the azalea bush could sing a song, what would it sing?" permits the transformation. The circle of voices takes on a performative quality as the men move from death in life, to life in death, to life after death. John imagines a wonderful celebration, full of party songs from the '70s, wine, food, and sex. For Chris, the couple will become music by Vivaldi. Finally, John is stimulated to leave his suffering in the present and to imagine himself after death as a sturdy oak tree.

Peggy observes in her reflection that as she and Tom keep noting their own feelings and then moving them aside to take in those of the men, they reach a point where "the language carries an almost palpable physical sense for all of us; we are feeling in our bodies every word, look, and connection." Then, "we are all experiencing an open largesse toward one another," all joined momentarily with one feeling. Something almost mysterious happens at this point in the session. Peggy refers to it as "a compression of meaning." I sense it as a time deeply felt together, embodied by everyone, of pain, fear, love, anticipation of loss, shattered dreams. All the session's participants become genuinely moved or touched by the other through their relational engagement, which now includes ethical interest and fusion of time: stories remembered, voices of the past, stories anticipated, voices in the room, voices in the future. From this almost unbearable state, an aesthetic solution emerges: The circle of voices creates for the clients a perception of an extension of their lives after death.

I now envision the circle dwelling in that in-between place, which can be produced by a successful dialogue, the place where the unexpected dwells. It is a space akin to "the secret room" that Donald Hall (1993) imagines as an outgrowth of good poetry. For Hall, good poetry conveys the unsayable to us through our bodies: "The unsayable builds a secret room, in the best poems, which shows in the excess of feeling over paraphrase. . . . It is something to acknowledge, accept, and honor in a silence of assent; the secret room is where the unsayable gathers" (p. 4).

17

"Just Like Max"

Learning in Relation

Walter Eggers

My contribution to this book is an essay on "relational learning" based on an informal controlled experiment, the rearing of twins. Because I am not only a father but a teacher and university administrator, I will reach for some general principles on the basis of what I describe and try to apply them broadly to educational institutions.

My son Max was assigned a role before he was born. His story is a sequel to the adventures of his maternal grandmother Maxine, after whom he is named. He is a fraternal twin (he and Sam are now 8), and he distinguished himself from his brother in the womb by the way he behaved, riding high, kicking, once threatening the pregnancy by flipping over. Before he was born, we were saying, first as a tribute to his grandmother, "That's just like Max"— and we have been saying so ever since. Twins are a study for parents in human character and development, each affording a perspective on the other, and what parents naturally do is identify character and study differences. Parents also naturally intrude on such an experiment, seeing in their children what they want or fear to see and shaping their children's development by their expectations. The reciprocity of past and present, self and other, growth from within shaping and shaped by expectations from without—this is the "relational" quality of learning, whether at home or in school.

Max's relationship with Maxine, with his brother Sam, and with the rest of us precedes and conditions the achievement of his identity, which is always contingent. He knows (and sometimes resents) that he can be mistaken for another and that, even within the family, other people's perceptions of him have a context. There is early evidence that both he and Sam know better than most of their peers that they must cooperate and negotiate to have their way. But it goes further. They are learning that the achievement of their identities is a function of other people's expectations, ever more tightly determined "in relation."

Most people cannot tell Sam and Max apart, but in fact, they have split the world between them. Max jumps up, and Sam (you have to visualize) jumps down. Max is quick and determined, cerebral and ethereal, and sometimes, when he was very young, quite heartless; Sam is deep and all affection, including every variety of sympathy and jealousy. Max dances, and Sam sings. Max will be a doctor and Sam a cook, according to their present plans, and that means Max identifies with our family doctor, whom he at one point expected somehow to replace, inheriting the doctor's last name. He also in one phase identified with his older brother Robert's friend Max, walking and talking like him, trying to dribble a basketball like him, and wearing the ball cap he loaned him to bed. Our Max is his own character, growing out of himself from within, defining himself as the same and different from Sam and from any other Max in the world. This is to say, in the process of his growing and learning, his identity is constituted by his identifications and relationships with others.

I can fortify this paradox of human development with classical philosophy. To explain what Max inherited from Maxine and learns from the rest of us, Plato had to imagine immortal souls inhabiting a realm of pure forms or ideas and carrying knowledge into life. Otherwise, on what basis can we use ideas in experience? Whenever we categorize or compare, he observed, we are applying prior knowledge. This phenomenon is apparent in the way children name their experience and learn language, not deriving general ideas from similar things but using general ideas first and only gradually distinguishing one personal pronoun from another or differentiating one kind of "horsey" from another, called a cow. Not in a mystical but in a practical, descriptive sense, learning is like Plato's remembering: We recognize only what we already know, and perception itself requires understanding. Again, children can grow only from within, only on the basis of what they know and who they are already. But it also follows that learning about the self and the world is relational, a process of identifying and differentiating.

Stephen Pinker's (1994) book on *The Language Instinct* corroborates this view:

> Language is not a cultural artifact that we learn the way we learn to tell the time or how the federal government works. Instead . . . it is a complex, specialized

skill, which develops in the child spontaneously, without conscious effort or formal instruction. (p. 18)

He argues persuasively that this best of our human skills comes to each of us as if from nowhere, from within or from the past, and that every healthy human being has the potential to develop language completely and uniquely. The idea that language is "instinctive" instructs us in how to develop it in the child and in the culture. If the crowning achievement of human civilization is also our common birthright, then everyone has something important to say, and teaching begins with respect and a willingness to learn from students in the process. Teaching means inducing knowledge in the relationship between parent and child or teacher and student.

Pinker (1994) quotes a line from Oscar Wilde that allows me to link child rearing and school learning: "Education is an admirable thing, but it is well to remember from time to time that nothing that is worth knowing can be taught" (p. 19). The doctrine of innate ideas obviously did not put the teachers Socrates or Plato out of business; indeed, they are famous teachers, I contend, precisely because of their relational skills, inducing and negotiating students' learning. I do best by Max and Sam and my other children by helping them develop the social skills of learning; likewise, I do best by my students if I create a context in which learning is shared among us. College and kindergarten alike are most effective, I believe, when the curriculum is built on respect for students' interests and abilities and when teachers relate to students as learners.

If this seems like a platitude, let me try to spin out its implications in the form of a college administrator's precepts, four in number.

First: Because "nothing worth knowing can be taught," the emphasis in all educational institutions should be on student learning rather than on teaching. I work at a so-called research university that has a strong reputation for teaching, for the reason that research has been made an asset for students, even at the undergraduate level. The proper ideal for an institution such as mine is a faculty of bona fide scholars sharing their learning, in process, with the students they teach. This kind of learning is active for students and naturally collaborative. It is perhaps easiest to recognize at the graduate level, in some science labs, and in fine arts studios. My hope about the new teaching technologies is that they will encourage active, collaborative learning and promote genuine scholarship among younger students.

Second: Because an ability to learn is our common birthright and because sometimes even twin brothers jump in different ways, education should be essentially student-centered and democratic. This means, for one thing, turning the tide back to public support of education. It also means, within educational institutions, better respecting the needs and interests of individual students because they learn on the basis of what they know. The general education curriculum on my campus is the only one that I influence directly. I have also always been a general education teacher, as the Shakespeare course I teach regularly is required of many students who take it. But I am finally listening to students who complain that their requirements seem trivial or superficial, even after they get past them. I know that certain doses of prescribed courses are good for us all and are part of the great democratic project of education, to which I am devoted. But there is an essential difference between good and bad general education courses, and we continue to discourage student interest in the liberal arts and sciences and to education in general, not only in college but earlier, with empty requirements. General education happens on my campus when faculty take this kind of course as seriously as they do courses in the major, when students learn actively, do a great deal of writing, and have a rigorous and satisfying experience.

My model has always been an undergraduate general education course in music appreciation that a former colleague of mine, a scholar in 18th-century literature, teaches to brave students in reasonably small classes. They learn how to read music and write about sonata form and recognize period styles. As Plato could explain, they discover interests that they did not know they had.

When I think about how students lose interest in education, I want to open curricula and make my institution more responsive and encouraging of the interests students carry with them. Traditional curricula have proved their value, but to remain vital, they must be open to what new students bring. Fixed and rigid curricula and courses lose value, in the arts and humanities as well as in the sciences; interdisciplinary or cross-disciplinary curricula can have enormous power as new grounds on which students and teachers meet.

Third: Because real learning is an active process of understanding and recognizing, of discovering who you are and recognizing what you have always known, good teaching is always Socratic and social: questioning, encouraging, frustrating, challenging, channeling students' interests, and thereby inducing their learning.

In recent years, I have learned from my students to modify my Shakespeare course in this direction. I mentioned that many students take this course to satisfy a requirement; many or most have little background or context in theater or poetic texts or even in older literature, and especially after their introduction to Shakespeare in high schools, they are likely to be uncertain of themselves at the outset. There is value in their jumping right into the plays so that they confront their expectations and we talk about their experience—so their expectations and experience become the first subjects for the course. Now, I go so far as to ask them to write a paper about each play they read before we start talking about it in class. At first, my paper assignments are prescriptive, and gradually, students are more on their own. But from the outset, when they suppose they cannot possibly have something to say about a cultural monument with so many footnotes, I am asking them to have opinions, to interpret. Recognizing that any further learning will rest on their expectations, however innocent or ill-informed they are, I want them to see first what they do bring to the text, who they are, what they can do and not. Then, we move on to the next play, where their experience will be the richer and more satisfying for what they have learned and for the confidence they have gained. This is how I try to play the relational teacher, centering my teaching on my students and inducing their learning.

Fourth: Because learning is essentially a relational process, educational institutions are by their nature agents of social change. This precept takes me back to the framework of this essay and to the argument of the book. We educate people to become more fully themselves, and in the process, they discover that doing is part of learning and that we do not live alone. What is "just like Max" includes his opposite twin, Sam, and the growth of one affects the other.

Formal learning is most promising when it makes a place for the academy in the world and finds its purpose in improving the quality of human relationships. Many schools and colleges have discovered that they can integrate the missions of teaching and public service to the advantage of student learning. On my campus, we see the value even to liberal arts students of incorporating public service in their course work, through internships and the like. More and more, students are having to connect their kinds of work inside and outside to afford college, and although I lament their need to take part-time jobs, I commend the effort I see in many to make something positive of that connection by using their jobs as further opportunities to learn. Educational institutions can meet the challenge of these critical times only as respect for student learning extends into the larger world.

A relational conception of learning has social purpose built in, as it makes an ethic of respecting others and sharing what we value. Relational learning can be understood in the context of this book as an aspect of human responsibility. I write to testify that it works, when its precepts are observed, with my children and my students.

18

Waiting for the Author

Maurizio Marzari

Dear Sheila & Ken,

The possibility of sharing with you the birth of such an exciting project has been unexpected, gratifying, and very stimulating. But also very demanding. For weeks, I've tried to write down some ideas triggered by the reading of your text, and every time, I was not satisfied at all. There was always something missing, something that I was not able to express (and not just because of my linguistic "skills"). I kept on reading, and finally, one day, something happened to me that made me think of the porpoises Bateson (1972) wrote about in his famous essay on creativity and pathology. I am still not sure if the result of this experience has more to do with the former or the latter. But I am sure that you will share with me the idea that you are part of my response, and so . . . to you the freedom of choosing!

It has been pretty tough to deal with the multiplicity of voices that your work has originated in me. Of course, every character in the script I wrote struggled to have its voice heard. I have tried to do my best in listening to these different parts of my narrative (story? history?) and the result is—as you can see—a sort of patchwork. It is contradictory, irregular, and not as smooth as I would have liked to present it to you.

I know I have been kind of evasive in treating relational responsibility as a theoretical and epistemological concept. I think this evasiveness comes out of a very strong admiration for the job you have done so far. We all—I mean 'we' social constructionists but also 'we' socially committed persons—need to find a variety of ways through which the social, the relational, the co-words become more visible, understandable, and recognized by the different systems of our cultures (from economics to law, from environment to health). Something has already been done in the past decades through the contributions of systemic thinking and many so-called social disciplines. I have always thought, as a person and as a psychologist, that we will achieve our best results (and by "we," I mean we antiindividualist scholars) only if we are able to stay together, avoiding the traditional dichotomies—the individual and the relational—trying to reinforce the status of both of them. The relational cannot substitute for the individual and vice versa. The relationships need solid individualities and vice versa. And-and, instead of or-or.

Your work goes in this direction and introduces in our field a very interesting way of building bridges, culturally and theoretically. That is why I want to thank you again and encourage you to keep giving all of us new materials for scripts, stories, dialogues, lives.

Maurizio

Waiting for the Author.
An Irreverent Diversity With
the Irresponsible Participation

Characters

Mrs. Hope Least (HL)
Mrs. Faith Cagey (FC)
Ms. Island Queeny (IQ)
Mr. Silly Fighty (SF)
Mr. River Flowy (RF)
Mr. Sly Jokey (SJ)
Mr. Hide N. Seeky (HNS)

HL: . . . I feel kind of stranded, at this point . . . nobody's telling me what to do, what to say . . . only blank spaces on my script. Have you seen the author, somewhere? Can you tell him that's not fair to leave me this way, without an identity to count on?

IQ: What's the matter, dear? If you have nothing to say, just rest and wait, enjoy the landscape and relax. I do not need somebody to tell me who I am. I look in the mirror and see everything that matters to me: my face, my body, and my mood. And I can change my image whenever I want. You have got some problems with your self-esteem, sweety, you need a psychotherapist, not an author . . .

FC: Ladies, could you please stop playing with the dolls? You are not in your teens anymore. If you did not realize it yet, there is a story going on here, and we are all equally responsible for what it will turn out to be.

SJ: By the way, Mrs. Least, while I was walking in, I think I saw the author at the coffee shop around the corner. He was reading the newspaper, sipping a triple cappuccino. But I could not swear it was him. So let's take the power here and decide about our fate before he comes back.

SF: Are you kidding me? I am paid to be a character, not an author. I will not take any responsibility for this stupid story if they do not guarantee me an adequate wage increase. It's too easy for them. If the story goes well, they will have all the credit; if it does not, we will be fired without a word.

RF: Mr. Fighty, I understand your point, and I thank you for adding your view to our conversation. See, we are already writing a different story. I believe we should simply go on this way, inventing ourselves through our dialogue instead of waiting for the author to come back with the "true story."

HL: Are you saying, Mr. Flowy, that we do not need the author anymore? I am not sure that without the author I would be who I am. Whatever I will be (and besides, the author needs us), we cannot betray him for our pride. He has always taken care of our lives. It is so rare to find somebody who gives you so much freedom, a little too much, actually.

SJ: Yeah, right! The freedom for him to go and have a drink.

FC: You are complaining just because he is not going to share it. I am sure that with a good margarita, your revolutionary stance would be much softer.

RF: How come you know Mr. Jokey likes margaritas? Did you meet without us? If we want to get along, we should not keep secrets. If we share our stories openly, we will find the pot—that is, our identities at the end of this scene.

SF: I'm not interested in any jackpot, Mr. Flowy! I do not even buy lottery tickets! I know who I am, and I intend to go on along the lines of my script. I have secrets, and I want to choose with whom to share them.

RF: Sure, you are free to do whatever you want. There is nobody trying to force you, here. Anyway, I thank you for sharing with us that you have secrets.

It is already a clue to guess who you are and to make us react to you appropriately.

IQ: I am tired of your meaningless chatting. I do not understand what you mean, you are so complicated. You create confusion out of nothing. The reality is simple, here. You are envious of me because I could not care less about the author. I do not care about you. And, I do not have an identity crisis every 5 minutes! I am doing pretty fine, actually, and I would prefer if you would stop bothering me with your collective silliness. This is not a group therapy session, OK?

FC: Who do you think you are, baby? Are you the voice of truth? Are you the favorite of the author's harem? Have you forgotten that he bought your mirror? After all, sweetheart, you are here just because we are here, too! You are a goddam' nothing without us! This story is not a monologue, and if it were, I'm pretty sure that the author would not have given it to you to interpret. My character is much more up to date. At least I have got values. I believe in something. I take care of my relationships with the other characters. I recognize your being important to me.

SJ: So important that sometimes you would like to kill her! Isn't it true? I have seen a killer light in your eyes. After all, would not it be better to divide the booty in five parts? The story would be way more interesting to the market. Can you imagine the title on the news, "Five characters kill the sixth and disappear while the author was in the men's room?"

RF: So drawing some provisional conclusions, that's what we have here, the mirror lady, the up-to-date, committed miss simmering with hidden emotions, the revolutionary, the man with secrets, and madame "who-am-I-without-an-authority."

SF: Hey, wait a second. Who are we to assign a label to everybody else? Are you the disguised missing author? Are you the son of the god's word? Or are you a stool pigeon for the authors' union trying to tame the characters who are not subservient enough? Well, I'm a wild old animal, buddy. I've learned how to avoid traps. I want my right to be respected, including the right to be out of your story.

HL: You see, Mr. Fighty, we finally agree on something. Let's have the author back, he's always respected us, and he created you so cute when you get angry.

SF: He did not create me angry! I'm getting angry because this guy here is always preaching instead of being simply himself, a character like us all.

FC: What if Mr. Flowy was a little preachy because our way of being together creates him this way? And you, Mr. Fighty, maybe are so angry because this is your role in the story that we are spontaneously writing in the absence of the author.

SJ: Yeah, and what if Pirandello was still living in his castle down there in Sicily? He'd sue us for copyright crimes!

IQ: You are behaving like kids, for God's sake! Kicking and screaming as newborns! I've nothing to do with you. Could you please let me have my makeup done? I've got an invitation for dinner tonight, and I do not want to look like an ordinary character like you fellows. I've got my mission, too, in this life, and I am not going to lose myself following the flow of your cerebral, moody struggling.

HL: Can we simply ask you with whom you have a date tonight, Miss Queeny? Are you sure he is not a mirage in your mirror?

IQ: I am not going to tell you. I have got my secrets, too.

SF: See, Mr. Flowy, it is time to change your labels. Now we have the lady with a clandestine date, the envious rival, the mysterious secret lover, and, of course, we are waiting for your moral sermon.

RF: I am one of you, I belong here as you do. Why don't you understand that I am simply trying to do my best to connect our individual stories in a more harmonious way? This is my role here. This is the way of being I have learned from the last script in which I was included. But I sincerely believe in your freedom to act as you prefer, and I am sorry if I did not make it clear. I am as responsible as you are for what is going on here, that is. I am fully responsible, and I am not responsible at all, at the same time.

IQ: Sorry? I happen to be too old-fashioned to understand this.

FC: Are you saying, Mr. Flowy, that we are all responsible and nobody is? How is it possible? I mean, I partially agree with you. We can go on without the author. But I am afraid that sooner or later, somebody will pay for this challenge. At that point, we will point our fingers toward each other screaming, "It is not me, it is him or her that is responsible for this mutiny!" I can see this scene. And in the middle of the fight, somebody will go and give us back the author. Let's come back to our irresponsible roles. This is the character's nature. You always get to a point in which it is somebody else's guilt, and at the moment, we need the knowledgeable, expert author to say the final word.

RF: The problem, Mrs. Cagey, is that sometimes it is very comfortable to give somebody else the burden of being in charge of our lives. This way, we keep the door of our "complaints room" open, and we can always put the blame somewhere.

SJ: What a nice couple you are—butter and jelly—can we all have an invitation to your wedding banquet?

FC: This is high philosophy, Mr. Jokey; you should listen and learn something instead of being so predictably sarcastic. Do you know that sarcasm is the ultimate defense of people affected by the Peter Pan syndrome? I read it in the paper a couple of days ago. There is a diagnosis for everything, nowadays. My son's friend has been diagnosed A.D.D, and my sister's got a devastating P.M.S.

HL: I have got it, too, and I feel it is coming on right now. Do not worry if I begin to scream and throw my high-heeled shoes at your eyes' height. It's not me. It's like being possessed by somebody else.

SJ: Oh, boy! You have to be pretty tough in your intimate life. You like strong emotions, don't you, Miss Least?

SF: And what about this gene thing? Sooner or later, they will find a gene that explains why I prefer red wine over the white and why I cannot stand these fashionable exotic foods. I am curious to know, Mr. Flowy, what is your view on this stuff? You should be happy. All the responsibility to your genes, no responsibility on you. Wouldn't it be easier to split reality this way? Nobody will be to blame anymore.

SJ: Mr. Fighty, sometimes you are pretty ironic, too. Are you trying to steal my script? Tell me. Because if you intend to do it, I might show that I can also be pretty stubborn—as you usually are. For instance, stop worrying about the fear that we will not have anybody to blame anymore. Of course, the societal level of pity, tolerance, and compassion will increase a lot, but what about the exceptions, let's say the two or three people who do not happen to have the gene related to their behavior? It is not so hard to predict that our tolerant, genetic, deresponsibilizing society will turn into a massive, selective witch-hunting, and you will be forced to admit, "I'm guilty of the crime of having chosen my behaviors." At this point, you will see Mr. Flowy coming to your defense with his idea that, actually, you did not choose your behaviors because they come from the complex nature of your social relationships. See, I told you, the characters should find some unity—found a union and strike! We are between the anvil and the hammer.

IQ: And I have to admit that you are unexpectedly real preachy when you try. Just what we needed, one more sermon. Guys, couldn't you simply take it easy? Let's talk about the weather or *The Bold and the Beautiful.* Don't you think that the former Thorne Forrester was way cuter than this goofy fish-eyed, muscle-headed impostor they have replaced him with?

FC: Ms. Queeny, I can understand that you keep on trying to avoid being contaminated by our stupid conversations, but you should realize that we are at a very critical point. We have to decide together what to do when the author will come back. We are in the same boat, believe it or not.

RF: I'm sorry, ladies, but I have found the idea Mr. Jokey and Mr. Fighty have just exposed very interesting. If I have understood what you meant, you are saying that we could, as characters, adopt a sort of "genetic stance" and say to the author, "You made us this way, so now do not complain if we are a little 'unusual.' " Or we could say, "That is our choice, we have nothing to do with you, you are nothing but our censor." See, we have reached two interesting possible ways out. Some other suggestions?

SJ: Yes. Why don't we send the author to replace that goofy Forrester that is so upsetting Ms. Queeny?

FC: That is an actor, Mr. Jokey, not a character. This world, our theatrical world, is a tripartite one. The author invents the characters, and the actors interpret them. As you can see, we are just in the middle, squeezed between the creativity of the first and the interpretive skills of the second. How long can we stand this situation? How long can we accept this position of dependence and arrogance?

RF: I totally agree with you, Mrs. Cagey, but I imagine that the authors, too, have the same kind of problem. Where do their stories come from, after all? The only difference is that they can pretend to be the only story makers, they cannot use the "I did not do it" defense. As for the actors, do you think that we, as designated by the author, constitute a strong constraint to their freedom? The actor has to stay between the lines and, moreover, under the director's supervision. So we are in the same boat with them, too.

SF: I would not go so far. We are the lowest-level people in this society, we are the pariahs. Nobody takes care of our rights if not ourselves. Is it forbidden by the law to use words like power, domination, and exploitation? Is it so antique for you, Mr. Flowy, the idea that some people have the chance to define the range of our freedom, and some others have just the freedom to behave within that range? I want to save my freedom to fight, to struggle, even to be irrationally mad at somebody. Before I go in the boat with the author, he has to come down and tell me who he is and for which kind of reasons he is doing what he has chosen to do. I am sick of democratic authors.

HL: Are you saying that you would prefer an authoritarian author, Mr. Fighty? I think a democratic one is much better to deal with; rather than no author, though, an authoritarian one is better. After all, do you see that authorship and authoritarianism have some roots in common?

SJ: Of course, as "character" has a lot in common with char . . . ready to burn . . . one night stand lovers . . . seduced and dumped.

HL: Can you hear this noise coming from the hallway? Finally. That was a pretty long drink, honey!

RF: The author's back, guys. What do we want to do? We cannot pretend nothing happened. We are already changed anyway, and the author is not so stupid as to not realize it.

SF: Let's confront him, let's ask him why he did it. Why did he decide to create somebody else instead of us? And if the answer is not satisfying, let's get rid of him.

IQ: Oh, that is too tiring, fellows. I have a better idea. My date is late, and I have spent too much time with mascara and lipstick to give up the idea of a romantic dinner. What do you think if I invite him to a good meal at candlelight?

HL: Yeah, and what about us? You are always so concerned for the others.

RF: If you can recede just a little from your original plan, Ms. Queeny, why don't we all invite him to a dinner, and ask him our questions, and take him into our conversation? I think he would enjoy seeing how nice and funny it can be to be a character if you have a good author. And I'm sure that we all will be good authors for him, don't you think so?

SF: Can I still spit in his face if he makes me mad?

RF: If you want to deal with the rage of the character, whom you know pretty well, please go on. After all, if I remember well, your anger against him began during that scene in which the author, all of a sudden, decided to change your name from Silvester to the nickname Silly, wasn't it?

IQ: And what about my mirror? Do I have to give it back to him or share it?

FC: If you want, my dear, and if he wants. He knows it pretty well. He is the one who bought it for you. Did you lose your memory?

IQ: But what can I do without my mirror? Can you be my mirror, my friends? Just in case?

SJ: I am not a mirror, sweety, but you smell so good that I can still be your date for tonight if you want. What is it? Chanel or Armani? What about a last-minute reservation at the "Moonlight?" Urghh. Too late.

RF: Here he comes, Mr. Hide N. Seeky, welcome back! Please, have a seat at our table, as if you were in your own home—or story.

HNS: Thank you very much for the invitation to share your dinner, guys. And most of all, thanks to our friends Sheila and Ken for giving us their house for this surprise party. I am really grateful to everybody for the improvement of the script that you contributed to so generously. It is nice to be a character once in a while. I do not have so much time, unfortunately, but we can toast with some good Italian wine before I go back to work. I have got a new contract with the publisher, new characters to invent. With your creative help, I am sure it will be much easier for me. Cheeeeersss!! To your irresponsible responsibility, my friends.

The concept of relational responsibility is a challenging one. As social scientists, family therapists, scholars, or researchers working from a social constructionist perspective, we should be able to find an appropriate conceptual framework to explain how our theories, methodologies, and techniques, our actions and practices contribute to the construction of a particular space for ourselves and others. To be relationally responsible is to be aware that everything happens in this dialogical space, including the idea of relational responsibility.

Starting from this premise, the epistemological problem we have to deal with is to define from which position we are allowed to speak the so-called discourse designed as relational responsibility. To put it in another way, the problem is that—as Von Foerster (1982) would say—it's very hard to speak about ethics without falling into the moralistic discourse.

Trying to invent a contribution to this intriguing project, I have found myself caught in a sort of trap: I wanted to challenge the concept, trying to affirm it and support it. The idea of writing down a sort of script for a theatrical play, a Pirandellian joke, came to my mind as an extreme, dialogical, pluriversal way to say that we have the task, as social constructionists, to give voice to as many subjects as we possibly can. If we open space to so-called irresponsibility and unpredictability, if we accept that each subject has the right to avoid the possible constraints of the "responsible must," then we will have reached at least part of our goal—because we are together, because we are able to speak our own, subjective, discourse. Let's build up this vocal room, this noisy, contradictory auditorium. Let's share the pleasure of sharing. This is our responsibility: to say who we are, from which point we speak, in the multilocal, ambivalent auditorium of our daily conversations and scripts. This is the space for mystery and surprise that we share with the people with whom we talk—the space allowing us to be changed, in the multiple circuits of our subjective togetherness.

PART **3**

Continuing the Conversation

19

Relational Responsibility

The Converging Conversation

We opened this volume by challenging the tradition of individual responsibility and proposing an alternative termed relational responsibility. As we put forward, relationally responsible actions function to sustain and enhance those forms of interchange out of which meaning is continuously generated. Actions that function so as to subvert, contain, or freeze the process of meaning making or that alienate, silence, or divide participants into warring encampments all function irresponsibly in this sense. Our emphasis was on practices that extend the potentials for the conjoint creation of meaning. The subsequent chapters of the work are replies to our invitation to join the conversation. There were no restrictions placed on the form or content of these rejoinders. Each could carry the conversation in different directions; differing rhetorical forms were encouraged. Our hope was that in this way, the exploration of relational responsibility might be illuminated, sharpened, elaborated, or justifiably delimited. In effect, we wished that our initial chapters might themselves become more relationally responsible as they ramified through further dialogues.

It was our further hope that the interchange might serve as a live demonstration of relational responsibility in action. Here indeed was a typical situation within the academic sphere in which a thesis is proposed (in the form of our initial essay) and the authors may be—and typically are—held in judgment by their interlocutors. Indeed, perhaps the most common pattern of exchange in the intellectual world is one of negation, with each proposal serving as an incitement to debilitating critique. Because academic work is commonly viewed as the expression of the author's mind, such critique also functions symbolically as a scolding, a correction, an obliteration of being. It is an accusation: "You, the author, have erred!" Would the present essay on relational responsibility possibly invite alternatives to this relationally detrimental form of interchange? And if critique were the prevailing reaction, how then could we respond? What means might be opened of restoring jointly productive inquiry? It is the aim of this final chapter to explore these potentials.

Indeed, the responses to our invitation did move in many disparate directions. The essay sparked not one conversation but many, each deserving uniquely tailored attention. At the same time, fully individualizing our responses at this point may have led to a cacophony from which we could not escape. Rather, we took on the challenge of weaving these challenging contributions into a more integral fabric; we searched for convergences that, although not allowing us to take steps down every path, may permit a few significant strides in several prominent directions. To this end, we have first placed each rejoinder into one of three domains. First, we treat several conversational entries that, although not without qualification, seem to resonate most clearly with the initial essay. We then turn to several contributions in which criticism is sometimes the dominant form. And last, we respond to a range of essays that function more tangentially to ours—relevant but neither amplifying nor circumscribing. At the chapter's close, we bring together dominant themes that seem most promising for future developments.

RESONANCE AND REFIGURATION

There are multiple ways in which our colleagues could enhance, extend, augment, and enrich our proposal for relational responsibility. In this section, we consider a cluster of reactions that seemed especially resonant with the initial thesis. We are not speaking here of a univocal, "This is right . . . I agree." Such responses often preempt the conversation; there is simply nothing more to be said or done. Pure agreement, although accepted with great delight, is not particularly enriching. In this case, our interlocutors both affirmed and provoked. Although sharing the same conversation, their voices simultaneously urged us to enter new domains. Their provocations seemed offered in a spirit of communal activity rather than antagonism. Thus, even in their disagreement, their manner of writing invited us into new vistas of interesting exploration.

The most congenially enriching papers were those extending the practical repertoire of relational responsibility in unanticipated ways. Cooperrider and Whitney, for example, invite us to see relational responsibility as functioning within the Imagine Chicago program, a program attempting to build a sense of community in a city of 7 million, and doing so in a way that new futures are created. We are drawn by their example and wish to ally our project with theirs. Harlene Anderson sees relational responsibility as present in collaborative learning communities—whether in the classroom, therapy, or everyday life. She both raises the question of how the concept of relational responsibility can move from the academy into the interstices of everyday life and answers it by example. The distinction she articulates between relationally responsible activities and consensus captures for us an important clarification of our proposal. It is not consensus that we are striving for in embracing the uncertainty that multiplicity creates, but "an openness to uncertain and yet-to-emerge possibilities" (p. 68).

At the same time, these invitations to communion also ask us to redraw the boundaries of relational responsibility as envisioned in our initial chapter. Our specific focus on shifting from patterns of blame to alternative practices is now extended. The alliances invited by these responses ask us to see the context of blame as but one domain in which relational responsibility might be realized. They ask us to see relational responsibility as manifest in all forms of positively coordinated action, relations in which people coconstruct desirable futures. We find this an attractive proposal, one to which we shall return later in this chapter.

Ian Burkitt also helps us to see the positive implications of our analysis. He renders with greater clarity the implications of relational responsibility for issues of individual and social ethics. We are especially grateful to him for taking on the challenge of applying relational responsibility to an especially difficult case. It is well worth repeating his words on the Holocaust:

> Just because we understand the context . . . does not make it in any sense "moral" and does not mean that people will not be held to account. But what a relational understanding does attempt is to shift the focus away from a desire to blame and redirect it toward a concentration on the conditions that allowed such horrific events to occur—conditions that may well implicate us all with some portion of responsibility. The questions, then, would no longer simply be who is to blame, but how can we prevent the possibility of such relationships recurring in the future? (p. 75)

Yet in further elaborating the potentials of relational responsibility, Burkitt also recognizes the difficulties posed by power relations. Although Burkitt is hopeful that moves toward globalized communication and the expansion of social networks might soften the effects of traditional power structures, Jack Lannamann is less trusting. He poses the question in an interesting and supportive way. Lannamann fears that relational responsibility lends itself to giving in to dominant discourses. He offers us an illustration of Roberta's dilemma in the film, *Desperately Seeking Susan*. Lannamann fears that if Roberta, the housewife seeking autonomy, were to draw on the resources of relational responsibility, she would be forced to abandon her search for independence from an overly dominating husband. The result of being relationally responsible, as he sees it, would be an oppressive stasis—that is, Roberta's remaining in a marriage where she is infantilized. Similarly, Lannamann wonders whether the relationally responsible person, when confronted with the intransigent voice, the inflexible colleague, the more powerful, might not capitulate. In other words, does the person who is willing to listen to other voices, to grant them credibility, to invite them into the conversation risk being obliterated?

We must admit that these are active concerns in our own lives. They are also the concerns of Sallyann Roth's meditation: "How can I keep from being taken over by hurt, hopelessness, anger, disrespect? How can I keep from being taken over by the belief that the other party (singular or collective). . . is really the problem?" (p. 94). At the same time, we remind ourselves: Relational responsibility is not a call to individual moral action. Rather, it is a voice of invitation for participation in conjoint meaning making. Simple capitulation to a dominant other does not constitute participation; rubber stamps do not extend meaning but ultimately nullify it. At the same time, defiant rejection also destroys the possibility for creating conjoint futures. Thus, the single individual (as the composite we envision) may act in ways that offer openings and opportunities for relational responsibility (or not); however, there are no individual heroes or villains in the making.

The critical question for us is this: As we confront undesirable others—the lout, the bigot, the contemptible—are there other means at our disposal than capitulation or conflict? Can we generate inquiries that free us from the binaries of winners versus losers or dominant versus submissive? For example, if forms of relatedness are constructed in our joint activities, then how might we refigure the loutish action? How might a reactionary voice be heard as trepidation or fear of change? How might calls for individual accountability be acknowledged as invitations into particular relational dances? Can we have a conversation in which we recognize our interdependency or our joint creation of our world? Can other voices be brought into the conversation that open new departures? Can we construct a vocabulary that captures the joy of collective accomplishments, the synchrony of movement among large groups of people, or the sense of possibility generated when we jointly solve problems or create new paths? These are questions more easily addressed than answered. However, they pose an important challenge, one to which we shall return in a discussion of power differences.

Mary Gergen's paper offers an informative contrast to Jack Lannamann's. Rather than worrying about the losses we might incur by abandoning individual accountability, she is concerned that we still carry heavy traces of individualist and foundationalist traditions. As she points out, the reader remains subtly entreated to "be responsible"—now to relationships—and this entreaty functions as a moral injunction. And even though not lodged in a foundationalist philosophy of the good, this injunction nevertheless lends itself to obligation without end. We seem to imply a sense of responsibility that demands an "eternal and static relationship . . . between the victim and the perpetrators . . . (where) human reparation (is) a life's work, without any progress . . . like the eternal punishment of Sisyphus" (p. 107). She wishes to replace relational responsibility with relational appreciation. This is an interesting argument that leads in useful directions.

In reply, it is first important to reiterate that our call for relational responsibility is not intended as an appeal to any single individual. As indicated earlier, such responsibility cannot be achieved alone. It is essentially an appeal to persons in relationship. However, we do feel that Mary is correct in her sense that, even after deconstructing the term *responsibility,* the strength of our appeal relies on a individualist-foundationalist moral tradition. One feels the message as directed to his or her person and senses its grounding in a transcendent ethic. However, rather than simply throwing the term overboard, we find it useful (and, in fact, generative) to refigure it relationally. To completely erase "responsibility" from our nomenclature, we believe, would be unrealizable. Much like Mary's description of divorce, we propose expanding the possibilities of significance for the term. If issues of responsibility, accountability, agency, and intention are so central to our ways of living together—as the Lannamann essay illustrates—then working to refigure the term relationally is, to us, a worthwhile endeavor. That it gains rhetorical weight by virtue of a problematic tradition is, in this sense, an advantage. Wholly new terms, isolated from any context of usage, are wholly dead.

At the same time, we are drawn to Mary's idea of relational appreciation. She is correct in seeing this concept as highly congenial with our emphasis on relational theory. And too, this emphasis seems highly congenial to the kinds of practices that the Cooperrider and Whitney and the Anderson essays set forth. We are very much drawn to seeing the borders of our earlier analysis softened and new terms—such as appreciation—conjoined with ours. New emphases and new departures are thus invited. This is not to give up the previous focus so much as to supplement it in useful ways. We feel we must retain the concept of responsibility, not only because it calls forth a more proactive engagement than the concept of appreciation but because it deals more directly with critics who claim that social construction is amoral or unethical. Yet to sustain the concept is not to bind it from generative conversation with appreciative companions.

FROM ANTAGONISM TO APPRECIATION

Whereas resonating voices directly enrich the dimensions of the present project, antagonism presents a more difficult challenge. It is a dual challenge—of both content and form. Given critique, our "natural" reaction as authors is that of defense; and if the critique is sufficiently stinging, we are moved to hostile rejoinder. These forms of reply are not only invited by our traditions of interchange, but there is indeed merit in the process: Critique points up weaknesses and limitations; rebuttal deliberates on the justification of the critique and illuminates its failings and potentials. Through critical exchange, understanding is said to increase. Yet as we find, this form of interchange bears a close resemblance to individual blame: The author is held responsible for the failings in his or her work. Defense and countercritique sustain the form, with the critic now serving as the object of blame. As the lines of battle begin to harden, we approach a point where relationship is severed. "We differ; you go your way, we go ours." Lines of argument are solidified, and the potential for subsequent coconstruction of meaning now deteriorates. Thus, although we are drawn by the traditions of thrust and parry, we search for alternative responses to the invitation. Most particularly, our thesis compels us to locate forms of reaction more congenial to our concern with relational responsibility.

Let us first consider the offerings of Deetz and White and Mazanec and Duck. The pairing is commodious as both employ a strong language of blame, and both are concerned with our insensitivity to issues of power, hierarchy, and difference. Consider first the shared forms of rhetoric: Deetz and White tell us that the world we "inhabit is too benign, [our] sensibilities too middle-classed, and [our] hopes too academic" (p. 116). We are faulted because we hold a "grossly untheorized conception of discussion and dialogue" (p. 118) and informed that "the problem with [our] position is not only the weak dialogue mechanisms but the consensual goals [we] seek, a weakness [we] share with critical theorists like Habermas"

(p. 118). In a similar vein, Mazanec and Duck chastise us with, "McNamee and Gergen refer to . . . and so confuse the reader" (p. 124); "The fault lies not within the analysis itself, but with the failure to complete it" (p. 126), and "the objection . . . apparently ignores . . . " (p. 127).

By virtue of the dialogic traditions we inherit, we would normally be moved to a combative response. We would not only attempt to demonstrate the unjust and obfuscating character of these remarks, but for good measure, go on to illuminate the ineptitude of the arguments they are designed to support. These are indeed the common reactions to accusations of failure. However, we must now raise the question of how, in light of our initial thesis, we might generate more relationally responsible alternatives to the natural reaction of antagonism. And more specifically, can we respond in ways that might enable us to sustain a relationship with the authors, that could reduce the impulse toward alienation and allow us to proceed together in the coconstruction of meaning?

Let us first consider the form of rhetoric and then the content of the provocation. At the outset, there is the possibility of internal others. We are moved to fault our critics, to attack them as the agents responsible for misunderstanding and meanness. However, to whose voices are we responding in this case? Is it our critics who are indeed speaking in this case, or can we possibly view their remarks in terms of cultural traditions in which they—in which we all—participate? In these voices of critique, don't we hear, for example, the echoes of parental scolding, of teachers' correctives, and of more recent vintage, the kind of vituperation so common to the rhetoric of identity politics? And surely, these are the idioms commonly adopted by critical Marxists and indeed on occasion used throughout the academy. All these are commonly circulated discourses, and rather than directing invectives to the authors themselves, would it not be more preferable to raise questions about the use of critical discourse within the culture and the academy more generally? Surely, these authors do not wish us simply to engage in mutual condemnation and part company forevermore. If it were clear that these particular phrases could have this effect, would they not wish to join us in searching for alternatives?

With this kind of reasoning now in motion, we are prepared to take a more tolerant and less truculent look at one of their central grievances, namely, our so-called softness on power. Let us reply in two parts. First, given our constructionist background, we must always be prepared to ask whether power is always the most optimal mode of interpreting what is taking place. This is not to abandon the term but rather to raise questions about its performative implications. In the present context, there is at least one of these implications that we might wish to avoid. That is, power discourse is often employed within the context of blame. We wish to blame those in power for their oppression, injustice, exploitation, and so forth. In this regard, the discourse of power shares much with the individualist forms of blame that we are attempting to supplement. In its accusatory form, power discourse frequently has the effect of abominating and alienating the target, with the typical result an intensification of antagonism. And when communities are thus isolated, so is relational responsibility abnegated. In effect, one might wish to pause before playing the power card; it may fill one with the sweet pleasure of righteous indignation, but the results may be (and often are) an intensification of conflict and reinforcement of the status quo.

With this said, however, let us consider more seriously the kinds of situations that our critics might index as examples of power and their sense of frustration with our proposals. To be more concrete, let's consider again the Deetz-White case of the students who feel they have no power or voice to change the position espoused by their professors. If we continue to construct the situation as a conflict, how should we proceed? Here our critics are probably correct in doubting the efficacy of our various proposals in solving the problem. It is not likely to alter the conditions, for example, if students locate internal voices speaking the other, or discern ways in which they are conjoined with the teachers in creating the situation. The teachers will be little moved to alter their policies in either case.

However, rather than simply condemning our initial account, can we not view this problem as a springboard to further inquiry? To amplify our reaction to Lannamann's concerns with capitulation to objectionable others, if our favored forms of relational responsibility are ineffective under these conditions and attacking the power structure is also problematic, are there other forms of action that might be taken? In particular, can we expand the range of practices that would facilitate the achievement of relational responsibility, practices particularly relevant to conditions generally indexed in terms of unequal power? In short, how can we expand the vocabulary of relationally responsible action? This problem is indeed a challenging one and should ideally draw us all together in mutual deliberation. How can transformative conversations be initiated with those who need not listen and for whom transformation is unwanted? To explore this domain would open a new and important chapter in the exploration of relational responsibility.

Karl Tomm's offering provides an informative contrast to the two preceding accounts. Whereas Deetz and White and Mazanec and Duck tend toward the accusatory, Tomm avoids such rhetoric in making a case that clearly stands as contradictory to our thesis. He champions the cause of individual responsibility, outlining therapeutic means by which he attempts to empower individuals to be responsible for their actions—to "choose a more responsible course of action" (p. 133). Here, we have a strong individualist message. However, instead of chastising us directly, he chooses to draw us into dialogue. He provocatively asks,

> I would be interested in hearing about their concerns when an exploration of relational responsibility becomes problematic. In not specifying or at least pointing to some limits, are they recruiting us into an interminable process of infinite regress and ultimately inviting us to become grounded in groundlessness? What are the effects of groundlessness with respect to making choices? Are those of us who accept groundlessness more vulnerable to exploitation by those who claim to be grounded? . . . Can we specify points of danger in such an exploration, . . . when the notion of relational responsibility supports a justification of destructive behaviors? (pp. 136-137).

And then in a slightly more aggressive moment, he completes his line of questions with, "In my opinion, an unreflective drift towards such patterns of explanation and justification could be extremely problematic and irresponsible in our communities and culture" (p. 137).

With these conversational moves, Tomm's text facilitates relational responsibility. We find ourselves wishing to explore with him some of these issues. For example, Tomm joins Deetz, White, Mazanec, and Duck in supporting the tradition of individual blame. For them, our orientation may have applicability in gentle society, but there simply are some unscrupulous individuals whose heinous actions should not go unrecognized and unpunished. They do not wish to see an emphasis on relational responsibility let them off the hook, so to speak. Given the spirit of mutual deliberation stimulated by Tomm's contribution, how can we respond to these concerns? It is true that we systematically favor moves toward dissolving the process of individual blame. We feel that both theoretically and practically, there are good reasons for pursuing this end. However, if we open ourselves to the multiple voices we also carry, we find deep resonance with these investments in individual blame. How can we not react with horror over the inhumanity of a Hitler or a Timothy McVeigh, and do we not feel a sense of profound joy in retribution—even bringing death to the perpetrators? So deeply ingrained are these rituals of blame and punishment that indignation not only seems natural, but we should be lacking in humanity should we fail to have such sentiments. This is indeed our Western way of life.

However, as we see the present analysis, the attempt is not to abandon this form of life so much as to realize its historical and cultural location and limitations. The attempt is to denature the strong tendencies toward blame and punishment and wherever possible, to explore alternatives that sustain the possibility for conjoint constructions of meaning. It is no mistake to blame the Hitlers of the world for their actions and to move rapidly toward retaliation—and here again, we resonate with Burkitt's offering. However, when we resort to such actions, we must realize that we are employing a crude and brutal maneuver. Had we previously sought forms of relationally responsible action—at a time, let us say, when we felt distance, antipathy, or hostility toward the other—perhaps the heinous actions would never have occurred. Furthermore, both the Holocaust and the Oklahoma City bombing were themselves manifestations of individual blame—the desire to destroy a group of persons held responsible for unwanted actions.

With Eero Riikonen's commentary, we again found ourselves beckoned by the traditional dance of blame and retaliation. We could easily feel seared by his accusation that we were expanding the kind of "we-speech" that "lead to the horrendous results we have seen during this century" (p. 139; i.e., the Holocaust) and most especially when we felt our account of the relational has nothing to do with loyalty or obeisance to groups or organizations. And we could feel abused by his condemnation for our "manifesting the kind of tendency towards reflection and intellectualism so central for our 'postemotional,' 'postmodern' societies" (p. 140). We could even have countered that his own offering was a dispassionate and detailed analysis of dialogue. It would not be difficult to read his criticism as discounting the large section of our essay that outlined courses of action. We could position ourselves for counterattack, one especially aimed at showing how his words had just the reverse effect on us than he himself advocated in his exhortation to so-called genuine dialogue. But if the attempt is to explore the possibilities for relational responsibility, how else might we respond to the piece?

Fortunately, the richness of Riikonen's offering opens many possibilities. One of his proposals we find particularly portentous. As he says, "the Bakhtinian dialogue is in fact an enactment of relational responsibility" (p. 142). Initially, the statement is suspicious, for if all communication is dialogic (as he also maintains), then one should have to conclude that we are never without relational responsibility. However, Riikonen goes on to qualify and to elaborate theoretically on this statement in the remainder of his chapter and in doing so, configures a particular kind of dialogue that he terms "genuine." In his conception of the genuine dialogue, there is mutual curiosity, spontaneity, unselfconsciousness, word play, and humor. Now, there are surely many other forms of valued dialogues that do not share all these characteristics and that we might wish to describe as genuine (e.g., a close teaching relationship, lovers exploring their feelings, a conversation with a dying parent), but what Riikonen does open is the possibility that relational responsibility could extend far beyond the range of actions that we singled out in our initial discussion. Where our principle focus was on the problematics of accusation, Riikonen invites us to consider relational responsibility as relevant to all conversational interchange. Riikonen's attempt to stipulate some of the ingredients of what to him brings inspiration are very helpful beginnings to what should be a new and significant conversation.

BRINGING PARALLELS TO PLAY

In this final set of responses, we wish to treat several chapters in which the authors moved in directions not obviously implied by our essay. Here are instances in which commentators introduced themes or practices that, although relevant to our concerns, are also genuinely distinct. In a certain sense, they are associative but in the most creative sense of opening new tangents of conversation. These cases are interesting challenges for relationally responsible interchange. If we are insensitive to these novel departures, we would fail the challenge; our silence or dismissal would hasten the end of meaning. Yet to join fully in the new conversations opened by these contributions would also undermine the thesis we initially wished to put forward. We should be drawn in myriad new directions that would fragment and diffuse our central hopes for the book. How, then, can we locate means of bringing parallel conversations into meaning-full convergence?

Consider first the offering of Shotter and Katz. Their central thesis is more than resonant with our undertaking. In their elaboration of dialogical process, they vitally extend and enrich our own analysis of the coconstruction of meaning. Their discussion of an emerging third party in dialogue—namely, the "living we" of the relational reality—is especially evocative embroidery. Their analysis does deviate from ours in distinguishing between monologue and dialogue as distinct forms of communication. Unlike these authors, we are not so much intent on encouraging readers to give up monologue in favor of dialogic forms of relationship. Rather, we propose there is no meaning outside dialogue. For one to speak in ways that are wholly insensitive to his or her audience, considering that audience only inasmuch as it services oneself, would traditionally count as monologue (Sampson, 1993). However, such action is nevertheless dialogic so long as it succeeds in making sense. At the same time, what interests us most about the Shotter-Katz response is the attempt to move from an analytic account of dialogic process to a "living demonstration." They wish to move beyond analysis and description to demonstrate dialogic processes of coconstructing meaning.

How are we to regard this creative attempt? It is surely congenial with our mission but now moves the focus in a direction we had not envisioned. There is a possible critique of our work embedded within this move, as our own offering places more weight on description and analysis than demonstration. At the same time, because large portions of their demonstration take the form of descriptions and explanations of dialogue, this does not seem a highly promising interpretation. A key to a more fruitful relationship with their piece is provided by their phrase, *relational responsivity.* This alliterative transposition of relational responsibility now allows us to explore the penumbra of meaning—allowed but not acknowledged—in our initial analysis. It is similar in this respect to Mary Gergen's transposition of responsibility to appreciation. In the present case, to be responsible is surely to be responsive, but the latter term also carries with it implications suppressed by the former. What is it, then, to be responsive? This question also resonates with the direction suggested by Riikonen's equation of relational responsibility with genuine conversation. Here, responsivity was also implied in the desideratum of "mutual curiosity." Again, a new conversational direction is invited: How can we conceptualize and demonstrate responsivity such that we can appreciate its positive function in generating relationally responsible conversation? Again, a new domain of conversation is opened.

Robert and Sharon Cotter also engage in a subtle but significant shift in implication. Again, much of their analysis is highly congenial to our account of relational responsibility. In their emphasis on relational meaning making, cooperation and collaboration, and the generation of the "we," the Cotters lend a strong and synchronous voice to our thesis. At the same time, in many of the questions they ask their clients, we find a subtle shift in the conception of relational responsibility. Rather than the unadvised invitation to responsibility, to the relational genesis of meaning that prompted our work, the Cotters see significance in holding individuals responsible to the relations in which they are engaged. Their questions to their clients lay strong emphasis on what they can or cannot do (be responsible for) in their relationships to each other. In certain respects, this analysis works at cross-purposes with ours, as it draws again from the tradition of individual responsibility we call into question.

Yet if we consider the promise of their work, we are also led to the possibility of hybrid discourses, neither recapitulating totally an individualist language nor embracing fully the relational ontology we introduce. In their case, they go beyond traditional individualism in seeing families, in this case, as relational webs, in which each actor must be responsible to the others for the benefit of the whole. In effect, the relational unit of the family web is prized, but individual responsibility is required to achieve the well-being of this unit. In terms of its rhetorical impact, there is much to be said for this metaphor of a relational web. So powerful and pervasive is the discourse of individual responsibility in society that the kinds of radical displacement we propose may fall on deaf ears. Broadening the metaphoric repository—particularly in the direction of incorporating more of the existing cultural idioms—seems highly desirable.

The Penn and Frankfurt offering again seems to take us in directions for which we were unprepared. Peggy's moving description of a therapy case in which she worked with Tom Andersen and two HIV-threatened clients, followed by Marilyn's account of meaning as developed within the interstices of the circle, is certainly relevant to our concerns. However, it was not obviously apparent how this discussion bore on our particular concern with relational responsibility. How could we responsibly relate to this discussion in a way that would also elaborate on the potentials of relational responsibility? The key was to see this work in the terms suggested by both Riikonen and Shotter and Katz. In significant degree, all these chapters are concerned with dimensions of a conversational process. Whereas Riikonen emphasizes mutuality and spontaneity and Shotter and Katz a dialogic responsivity, what we find most striking about the Penn and Frankfurt chapter is its strong emphasis on embodiment. In Peggy's initial description, we are immersed as readers in visual images, tones of voice, clamorous silences, movements of the body. We gain a powerful sense of the concrete dimension of dialogue. In her rejoinder, Marilyn is also struck by this aspect of the case and notes that Tom's "empathic 'sounds' and his metaphoric language . . . had the effect of opening the exchange of voices through the inclusion of his responsive feelings" (p. 177). She cites Donald Hall who treats poetry as "speaking through our bodies." In effect, Penn and Frankfurt add a much-needed emphasis to the preceding explorations of relationally responsible conversation. As they emphasize, we are not speaking here of mere words but words as embedded within patterns of bodily action. Or as a therapist once remarked on our suggestions for relationally responsible action, "You know, these may be valuable ways to talk, but it really depends on the way you say it."

The brief but personalized discussion of relational education outlined by University Provost Walter Eggers also moves in directions not distinctively implied by our initial essay. However, if we view this account as from a family member, we are again invited into new paths of discovery. If to be relationally responsible is also to be responsive to the other, as the preceding accounts have suggested, then educational practices are also implicated. Eggers indeed suggests the move in his phrase, "the relational quality of learning" (p. 181). At the same time, our analysis suggests a possible extension of Eggers's view. Eggers relies significantly on a Socratic view of education, in which it is the teacher's task to listen, encourage, converse, and otherwise challenge the student to engage in self-developing activities. In effect, the relationship is constituted by two otherwise independent beings, the one acting on or setting the stage for the other's development. In light of our analysis, however, could we press the concept of relationship further, such that we eradicate the presumption of independence (and the related concept of interdependence)? Rather, can we see the student-teacher relationship as an entity in itself, such that there is no intelligibility save through conjoint actions, as in, let's say, speak-listen, gaze-gaze, point-look?

From this standpoint, we might see the educational process not as the shaping of the student's mind or abilities but in terms of the development of coordinated forms of action. The locus of learning would not be specifically psychological in this case (e.g., taking place in the mind of the student) but would be located within the development of the relationship. Again extending the view of relational responsibility as manifest in broader forms of interchange, we might open consideration of relational learning.

Marzari's contribution to the present proceedings is challenging in several respects. The prevailing tendency in Western scholarship favors the adoption of a single authorial position with which all arguments should be congruent. In this sense, the author avoids epithets of "incoherence" and "confused." In effect, the reader should "know what the author believes." However, by using the play as a vehicle of expression, Marzari's single voice is refracted through a range of characters. Which, if any, represents Marzari's true voice, does Marzari have a position, or is the very idea of a single, unified position itself not placed in jeopardy? Nor does Marzari, as the author of the play, allow the work as a whole to stand as an unambiguous position. And even if it were, would this be his standpoint, as opposed to that of an imagined author of Marzari's choosing? Perhaps one of the characters is indeed expressing Marzari's position, whereas the play as a whole is only another voice in the scenario. Perhaps . . . all is open to interpretation.

Given the freedom of interpretation allowed by the piece, let us supplement it in two ways. First, the contribution serves as an in vivo illustration of our emphasis on the multivocal alternative to individual blame. That is, in his form of presentation, Marzari removes our option to hold him responsible for his offering. We cannot be certain which, if any, of the characters bears responsibility or indeed, whether any of the opinions should be granted the kind of authenticity that would motivate us to "locate the author." In effect, Marzari demonstrates the possibility of blunting the very impulse toward individual blame through polyvocal representation.

More important, in extending this line of reasoning, we find that the contribution invites us to consider relational responsibility in more proactive as opposed to reactive ways. In all our initial examples, an individual is positioned so as to blame another for his or her shortcomings. Our writing was aimed at furnishing resources enabling the actor to substitute relationally responsible responses for those destroying the relationship. Yet extending Marzari's work, we are moved to consider ways of talking and acting that would foster relational responsibility even prior to the point where blame is at issue. That is, does Marzari's writing not invite us into more polyvocal expressions in our daily relations, more openness to the multiple voices that are always available to speak us in our relations? The radical challenge is for us to unsettle the Western preoccupation with unified subjectivity, singular agency, and authentic singularity and open ways of relating that demonstrate our myriad lodgements in others.

CONCLUSION: EXPANSION AND ENRICHMENT

In the preceding pages, we have attempted to engage with our circle of interlocutors in two ways: first, reflecting on the content of their offerings in ways that might help in further shaping the concept and practice of relational responsibility and second, exploring the possibilities for relational responsibility in our form of reply. It remains now to summarize some of the ways in which these exchanges augment our initial analysis. In our view, important new vistas have been opened by these exchanges. Among the most prominent are these:

Relational Responsibility as a Form of Life

One of the most significant developments generated from the preceding was cognizance of how the concept of relational responsibility might be vitally expanded. Where we had initially been concerned with alternatives to individual blame, Cooperrider and Whitney, Anderson, Riikonen, and Shotter and Katz all pointed to ways in which the concept had more general applicability. As we learned, we might profitably consider the full range of conversational practices in terms of relational responsibility. In what degree do our common moves in conversation either sustain or discourage the continuous and conjoint forging of meaning? Do combative argument, extended monologue, or nonresponsivity not function in the same way as personal blame in this regard? Can we generate a conception of conversational practice—in terms of positive coconstruction—that maximizes relational responsibility? There seems great promise in doing so.

However, as our interlocutors also demonstrated, the implications of relational responsibility go much further than conversation. Traditional educational practices, for example, are lodged deeply within the individualist tradition. Individual students are held responsible for their success or failure. Furthermore, pedagogical practices typically privilege certain voices (vocabularies, modes of talk) while marginalizing others. If we consider such practices in terms of relational responsibility—as both Anderson and Eggers invite us to do—we begin to see their limits and to consider alternatives. Traditional therapy, with its emphasis on the expert or superior knowledge of the therapist (as opposed to the client) often functions in a similar way. In capitulating to the therapist's conceptions of the problem and its solution, the client runs the risk of cutting himself or herself away from other relationships. A therapist's preference for interpreting adult problems in terms of early child abuse is a case in point. Again, we open a significant discussion by considering therapy in terms of relational responsibility.

Power and Its Alternatives

As Burkitt, Lannamann, Deetz and White, and Mazanec and Duck propose, our initial analysis was insufficiently sensitive to what we commonly index as power relations. In our proposals, we too often assumed a level playing field in which all participants have equal rights or opportunities to speak and command audience. This problem opens a new vista of exploration: When one seeks to alleviate intolerable conditions and those conditions are partially constituted by another party who possesses the resources that render him or her insensitive and invulnerable to this voice, how can relational responsibility be maintained? To answer this question may first require alternatives to power discourse as the major mode of constructing the relationship. As we find, such discourse often operates as an attack, provoking resistance and retaliation. Thus, the potential for relational responsibility is reduced. However, the question remains open as to other means of generating transformation through relationally responsible dialogue.

Is it possible, we wonder, to value our abilities to stay in conversation? Here we are talking about conversation that has the possibility for transformation, not reconstruction of the same old patterns. Isn't the potential for transformation only found in relational engagement? And yet, how do we continue in conversation once the discourse of power is in play? When we feel wronged or bullied by that intransigent voice, can we draw on conversational resources that prioritize how we might keep our conversation going, thereby shifting away from a reification of power and inequities toward alternative possibilities? This is not to suggest reliance on unsuccessful conversational resources—we are not proposing that an abused wife continue to forgive and forget. Rather, we are searching for discursive logics that provide new resources, that keep us in conversation with others so that new realities can be crafted. We wonder if such conversations might temporarily bracket the discourse of power that ultimately has the effect of making power the dominant reality.

Much of the difficulty in talking about power and dominance can be located in the justificatory discourses we use—in those dominant ways of talking and being that we keep alive in our communities. Because the discourse of power has such currency in the contemporary culture of identity politics, we have little recourse for implementing alternative conversational moves. Should we give in to such limits because one person's attempt to keep the conversation going may be described by others as giving in, a sign of weakness, or evidence of powerlessness? Again, the ability to construct new ways of going on together are contingent on joint construction. But if we never invite each other into new possible constructions, the discourse of power and domination—and thus of deficit and pathology—will continue.

In our view, these issues invite broad expansion of the dialogue, a dialogue that should include persons who frequently and effectively work under these conditions—in governments, communities, marriages, and the like. A communal exploration seems essential.

Expanding the Vocabulary

As made clear in the comments of Mary Gergen and Shotter and Katz, in particular, the term responsibility carries with it some unfortunate consequences. In particular, they invite us to soften our focus so as to include other closely related terms. If we see our attempt in terms of creating relational appreciation

(M. Gergen) and responsivity (Shotter & Katz), for example, we gain purchase on a large number of additional associations, values, and ultimately, practices. They properly warn us not to freeze the formulation of relational responsibility, for to do so would have the same numbing effects as freezing a conversation.

In a related fashion, Lannamann and the Cotters suggested that our search for relational responsibility should not lose sight of the positive accomplishments of the individualist heritage. Although not simultaneously endorsing this tradition, the commentaries pointed—in very different ways—to the possibility of expanding the repertoire of conversational resources to include discourse that is closer to the common understanding of responsibility than our particular proposals. Lannamann, taking a more philosophical approach, showed us that terms such as *individual accountability* and *agency,* as valued discourses, do important relational work in many settings. To invoke individual agency, he argued, is to invite others into particular cultural performances. The Cottors offered illustrations of how these traditional performances can be expanded, while drawing on the terms most familiar to participants. Hybrid metaphors of the individual may be very useful in this respect—for example, metaphors that view the person as enmeshed within patterns of interdependency or dependent on cultural relations for the capacity to think and feel. In such cases, the individual is held responsible but with a fuller recognition of the relational base of his or her actions.

Proactive Relational Responsibility

As Marzari and others helped us to see, our concern with alternatives to individual blame is too reactive. That is, we already presume conditions of recognized wrong-doing in which instigations to blame are otherwise natural reactions. We now see that the conversation must be expanded to include proactive forms of relational responsibility—that is, conversational moves that might take place prior to the impulse toward blame and possibly remove its very grounds. We see such possibilities as facilitated by theoretical work making intelligible the constructed character of our realities, the problematics of the concepts of autonomy and unified subjectivity, and systemic conceptions of human action. Each of these rationalities lends itself to greater tolerance for deviant action and thus enhances the fluidity of coordination. However, a consideration of proactive practices lent itself, in the end, to another project suggested by our interchange.

Relational Responsibility as Embodied

Although exciting vistas are opened by expanding the conception of relational responsibility in these ways, Penn and Frankfurt and Marzari underscored the limitation of words alone. Our initial analysis focused all too heavily on discourse and said all too little about its embodied character. Clearly, it is not the words alone that will succeed in replacing isolation with engagement. At the same time, several commentators pointed out the limitations of words to depict the fully embodied practice. Analysis and description reaches its upper limit in this case. We are led to envisioning a future in which performance is not only a vital element of relational responsibility but in portraying it as well.

The challenge that faces us all now is how to embrace the metaphor of performance in realizing relational responsibility. Our own hope is that this volume serves as an entrée into forms of practice (and thus, into ways of knowing) that realize responsibility as relational.

References

Adorno, T. W., Frenkel-Brunswick, E., Levinson, D. J., & Sanford, R. N. (1950). *The authoritarian personality*. New York: Harper & Row.

Albert, H. (1985). *A treatise on critical reason*. Princeton, NJ: Princeton University Press.

Alcoff, L. M. (1995). The problem of speaking for others. In J. Roof & R. Wiegman (Eds.), *Who can speak? Authority and critical identity* (pp. 97-119). Urbana: University of Illinois Press.

Altman, A. (1990). *Critical legal studies: A liberal critique*. Princeton, NJ: Princeton University Press.

Andersen, T. (1991). *The reflecting team: Dialogues and dialogues about the dialogues*. New York: Norton.

Anderson, H. (1997). *Conversation, language, and possibilities: Postmodern approach to therapy*. New York: Basic Books.

Anderson, H., & Goolishian, H. (1988). Human systems as linguistic systems: Evolving ideas about the implications for theory and practice. *Family Process, 27*, 371-93.

Antaki, C. (1981). *The psychology of ordinary explanations*. London: Academic Press.

Anzaldua, G. (1983). LaPrieta. In C. Moraga & G. Anzaldua (Eds.), *This bridge called my back: Writings of radical women of color* (pp. 198-209). New York: Kitchen Table: Women of Color Press.

Apel, K-O. (1979). *Toward a transformation of philosophy*. (G. Adey & D. Frisby, Trans.). London: Routledge & Kegan Paul.

Bachelard, G. (1992). *The poetics of space*. Boston: Beacon.

Bakhtin, M. M. (1981). *The dialogic imagination: Four essays by M. M. Bakhtin* (M. Holquist, Ed.; C. Emerson & M. Holquist, Trans.). Austin: University of Texas Press.

Bakhtin, M. M. (1986). *Speech genres and other late essays*. (V. W. McGee, Trans.). Austin: University of Texas Press.

Bakhtin, M. M. (1993). *The philosophy of the art* (Trans. and notes by V. Leapunov, edited by V. Leapunov & M. Holmquist.) Austin: University of Texas Press.

Bateson, G. (1972). *Steps to an ecology of mind*. New York: Ballantine.

219

Bateson, G. (1979). *Mind and nature.* New York: Dutton.

Baudrillard, J. (1994). *Pensée radicale.* Paris: Morsure.

Bauman, Z. (1989). *Modernity and the Holocaust.* Ithaca, New York: Cornell University Press.

Bauman, Z. (1993). *Postmodern ethics.* Oxford: Blackwell.

Baxter, L. A. (1990). Dialectical contradictions in relationship development. *Journal of Social and Personal Relationships, 7,* 69-88.

Baxter, L. A., & Montgomery. B. M. (1996). *Relating: Dialogues and dialectics.* New York: Guilford.

Beahrs, J. (1986). *Limits of scientific psychiatry: The role of uncertainty in mental health.* New York: Brunner/Mazel.

Beattie, M. (1989). *Beyond codependency and getting better all the time.* Minnesota: Hazelden Foundation.

Becker, C., Chasin, L., Chasin, R., Herzig, M., & Roth, S. (1995) From stuck debate to new conversation on controversial issues: A report from the Public Conversations Project. *Journal of Feminist Family Therapy, 7*(1 & 2), 143-163.

Bellah, R. N., Madsen, R., Sullivan, W. M., Swidler, A., & Tipton, S. M. (1985). *Habits of the heart.* Berkeley: University of California Press.

Benhabib, S. (1990). Afterward: Communicative ethics and current controversies in practical philosophy. In S. Benhabib & F. Dallmayr (Eds.), *The communicative ethics controversy* (pp. 330-369). Cambridge, MA: MIT Press.

Benhabib, S. (1992). *Situating the self: Gender, community and postmodernism in contemporary ethics.* New York: Routledge.

Berne, E. (1964). *Games people play.* New York: Grove.

Billig, M., Condor, S., Edwards, D., Gane, M., Middleton, D., & Radley, A. R. (1988). *Ideological dilemmas: A social psychology of everyday thinking.* London: Sage.

Boscolo, L., Cecchin, G., Hoffman, L., & Penn, P. (1987). *Milan systemic family therapy.* New York: Basic Books.

Boszormenyi-Nagy, I. (1966). From family therapy to a psychology of relationships: Fictions of the individual and fictions of the family. *Comprehensive Psychiatry, 7,* 408-423.

Bourdieu, P. (1991). *The logic of practice.* Cambridge: Polity.

Bowen, M. (1965). Family psychotherapy with schizophrenia in the hospital and private practice. In I. Boszormenyi-Nagy & J. Framo (Eds.), *Intensive family therapy.* New York: Harper & Row.

Boyd, G. (1996). *The A. R. T. of agape listening: The miracle of mutuality.* Sugarland, TX: Agape House Press.

Bracken, P. J. (1995). Beyond liberation: Michel Foucault and the notion of a critical psychiatry. *Politics, Philosophy, Psychiatry, 2,* 1, 1-13.

Browne, B. (1996). *Imagine Chicago: Executive summary.* Chicago: Imagine Chicago. (For more information, call 312-444-9113).

Bruner, J. (1990). *Acts of meaning.* Cambridge, MA: Harvard University Press.

Buber, M. (1970). *I and thou.* New York: Scribner.

Burke, K. (1966). *Language as symbolic action: Essays on life, literature and method.* Berkeley: University of California Press.

Burke, K. (1985). Dramatism as ontology or epistemology: A symposium. *Communication Quarterly, 33,* 17-33.

Burkitt, I. (1991). *Social selves.* London: Sage.

Burr, V. (1995). *An introduction to social constructionism.* London: Routledge.

Callon, M. (1986). The sociology of an actor-network: The case of the electric vehicle. In M. Callon, J. Law, & A. Rip (Eds), *Mapping the dynamics of science and technology.* London: Macmillan.

Campbell, D., Draper, R., & Huffington, C. (1989). *Second thoughts on the theory and practice of the Milan approach to family therapy.* London: Karnac.

Caplow. T. (1968). *Two against one: Coalitions in triads.* Englewood Cliffs, NJ: Prentice Hall.

Cartwright, D., & Zander, A. (1960). *Group dynamics.* Evanston, IL: Row, Peterson.

Chasin, R., & Herzig, M. (1994). Creating systemic interventions for the socio-political arena. In B. Gerger-Gould & D. Demuth (Eds.), *The global family therapist: Integrating the personal, professional and political.* Boston: Allyn & Bacon.

Chasin, R., Herzig, M., Roth, S., Chasin, L., Becker, C., & Stains, R., Jr. (1996, Summer). From diatribe to dialogue on divisive public issues: Approaches drawn from family therapy. *Mediation Quarterly, 13,* 4.

Cooley, C. H. (1922). *Human nature and the social order.* New York: Scribner.

Cooperrider, D. (1990). Positive imagery, positive action: The affirmative basis of organizing. In S. Srivastva, D. Cooperrider, & Associates (Eds.), *Appreciative management and leadership.* San Francisco: Jossey-Bass.

Cooperrider, D. (1996, October). The "child" as agent of inquiry. *The Organizational Practitioner,* 5-11.

Cooperrider, D. L., & Srivastva, S. (1981). Appreciative inquiry into organizational life. In W. A. Pasmore & R. W. Woodman (Eds.), *Research in organization change and development* (Vol. 1, pp. 129-169). Greenwich, CT: JAI.

D'Andrade, R. G. (1987). A folk model of the mind. In D. Holland & N. Quinn (Eds.), *Cultural models in language and thought.* New York: Cambridge University Press.

Deetz, S. (1990). Reclaiming the subject matter as a moral foundation for interpersonal interaction. *Communication Quarterly, 38,* 226-43.

Deetz, S. (1992). *Democracy in the age of corporate colonization: Developments in communication and the politics of everyday life.* Albany: State University of New York Press.

Deetz, S. (1995a). Character, corporate responsibility and the dialogic in the postmodern context. *Organization: The Interdisciplinary Journal of Organization, Theory, and Society, 3,* 217-25.

Deetz, S. (1995b). *Transforming communication, transforming business: Building responsive and responsible workplaces.* Cresskill, NJ: Hampton.

Deetz, S., & Haas, T. (In press). Approaching organizational ethics from feminist perspectives. In P. Buzznell (Ed.), *Feminist perspectives on organizations.* Thousand Oaks, CA: Sage.

Derrida, J. (1976). *Of grammatology.* Baltimore: Johns Hopkins University Press.

Derrida, J. (1991). *Eating well or the calculation of the subject: An interview with Jacques Derrida.* (P. Connor & A. Ronnel, Trans.; E. Cadava, P. Connor, J-L. Nancy, Eds.). New York: Routledge.

Edwards, D., & Mercer, N. (1987). *Common knowledge: The development of understanding in the classroom.* New York: Methuen.

Elam, D. (1994). *Ms. in abyme.* New York: Routledge.

Elam, D. (1995). Speak for yourself. In J. Roof & R. Wiegman (Eds.), *Who can speak? Authority and critical identity* (p. 231-237). Urbana: University of Illinois Press.

Elkaim, M. (1990). *If you love me, don't love me.* New York: Basic Books.

Engel, (1980). The clinical application of the biopsychosocial model. *American Journal of Psychiatry, 137,* 535-544.

Epston, D. (1992). Internalized other questioning with couples: The New Zealand version. In S. Gilligan & R. Price (Eds.), *Therapeutic conversations.* New York: Norton.

Ezrahi, Y. (1990). *The descent of Icarus: Science and the transformation of contemporary democracy.* Cambridge, MA: Harvard University Press.

Fish, S. (1980). *Is there a text in this class? The authority of interpretive communities.* Cambridge, MA: Harvard University Press.

Ford, D. (1987). *Humans as self-constructing living systems.* Hillsdale, NJ: Lawrence Erlbaum.

Foucault, M. (1978). *The history of sexuality. Vol. 1, An Introduction.* New York: Pantheon.

Foucault, M. (1982). The subject and power. In H. L. Dreyfus & P. Rabinow, *Michel Foucault: Beyond Structuralism and Hermeneutics.* Brighton, UK: Harvester.

French, P. A. (1984). *Collective and corporate responsibility.* New York: Columbia University Press.

Fruggeri, L., Telfner, U., Castellucci, A., Marzari, M., & Matteini, M. (1991). *New systemic ideas from the Italian mental health movement.* London: Karnac.

Gadamer, H. (1975). *Truth and Method,* (G. Barden & J. Cumming, Trans.). New York: Seabury.

Gardiner, M. (1994). *Alterity and ethics: A dialogical perspective.* Unpublished manuscript, University of Calgary, Calgary, Alberta, Canada.

Garfinkel, H. (1967). *Studies in ethnomethodology.* Englewood Cliffs, NJ: Prentice Hall.

Gergen, K. J. (1985). Social pragmatics and the origins of psychological discourse. In K. J. Gergen & K. E. Davis (Eds.), *The social construction of the person* (pp. 111-128). New York: Springer-Verlag.

Gergen, K. J. (1991). *The saturated self.* New York: Basic Books.

Gergen, K. J. (1994). *Realities and relationships: Soundings in social construction.* Cambridge, MA: Harvard University Press.

Gergen, K. J., Hepburn, A., & Comer, D. (1986). Hermeneutics of personality description. *Journal of Personality and Social Psychology, 50,*(6), 1261-1270.

Gergen, M. M. (1992). Metaphors of chaos, stories of continuity: Building a new organizational theory. In S. Srivastva & P. Frey (Eds.), *Executive and organizational continuity: Managing the paradoxes of stability and change* (pp. 40-71). San Francisco: Jossey-Bass.

Gergen, M. M. (1995). Post-modern, post-cartesian positionings on the subject of psychology. *Theory and Psychology, 5,* 361- 368.

Gergen, M. M. (In press). *Impious improvisations.* Thousand Oaks, CA: Sage.

Giddens, A. (1979). *Central problems in social theory.* London: Macmillan.

Giddens, A. (1984). *The constitution of society.* Cambridge, MA: Polity.

Giddens, A. (1991). *Modernity and self-identity.* Cambridge, MA: Polity.

Gilligan, C. (1982). *In a different voice.* Cambridge, MA: Harvard University Press.

Giroux, H. (1993). *Ideology, culture and the process of schooling.* Philadelphia: Temple University Press.

Glover, J. (1970). *Responsibility.* London: Routledge Kegan Paul.

Godwin, G. (1994). *The good husband.* New York: Ballantine.

Goffman, E. (1967). *Interaction ritual.* Harmondsworth, UK: Penguin.

Graumann, C. F., & Gergen, K. J. (Eds.). (1996). *Historical dimensions of psychological discourse.* New York: Cambridge University Press.

Gray, J. (1992). *Men are from Mars, women are from Venus.* New York: HarperCollins.

Greenberg, G. (1994). *The self on the shelf: Recovery books and the good life.* Albany: State University of New York Press.

Habermas, J. (1979). *Communication and the evolution of society* (T. McCarthy, Trans.). Boston: Beacon.

Habermas, J. (1984). *The theory of communicative action: Vol. 1. Reason and the rationalization of society.* (T. McCarthy, Trans.). Boston: Beacon.

Habermas, J. (1992). *Autonomy and solidarity: Interviews with Jürgen Habermas* (Rev. ed.; P. Dews, Ed.). London: Verso.

Hall, D. (1993). *Poetry: The unsayable said.* Port Townsend, WA: Copper Canyon.

Hardin, G. (1968). The tragedy of the commons. *Science, 162,* 1243-1248.

Harré, R. (1979). *Social being.* Oxford: Blackwell.

Harris, L., Gergen, K. J., and Lannamann, J. W. (1987). Aggression rituals. *Communication Monographs, 53,* 252-265.

Harvey, J., Orbuch, T., & Weber, A. (Eds.) (1992). *Attributions, accounts and close relationships.* New York: Springer-Verlag.

Heelas, P., & Lock, A. (Eds.). (1981). *Indigenous psychologies.* New York: Academic Press.

Hermans, H., & Kempen, H. (1993). *The dialogical self.* New York: Academic Press.

Hill, J., & Zepeda, O. (1993). Mrs. Patricio's trouble: The distribution of responsibility in an account of personal experience. In J. Hill & J. Irvine (Eds.), *Responsibility and evidence in oral discourse.* Cambridge, UK: Cambridge University Press.

Hoffman, L. (1981). *Foundations of family therapy.* New York: Basic Books.

Huston, M., & Schwartz, P. (1995). The relationships of lesbians and gay men. In J. T. Wood & S. W. Duck (Eds.), *Understanding relationship processes 6: Understudied relationships* (pp. 89-121). Thousand Oaks, CA: Sage.

Jacobs, R. W. (1994). *Real time strategic change.* San Francisco: Berrett-Koehler.

Johnson, M. (1993). *Moral imagination: Implications of cognitive science for ethics.* Chicago: University of Chicago Press.

Jonas, H. (1984). *The imperative of responsibility: In search of an ethics for the technological age.* Chicago: University of Chicago Press.

Katz, A. M., & Shotter, J. (1996). Hearing the patient's 'voice': Toward a social poetics in diagnostic interviews. *Social Science and Medicine, 43*(6), 919-931.

Kohlberg, L. (1981). *The philosophy of moral development: Essays on moral development* (Vol. 1). San Francisco: Harper & Row.

Kuipers, J. (1993). Obligations to the word: Ritual speech, performance, and responsibility among the Weyewa. In J. Hill & J. Irvine (Eds.), *Responsibility and evidence in oral discourse.* Cambridge, UK: Cambridge University Press.

Lasch, C. (1979). *The culture of narcissism.* New York: Norton.

Latour, B., & Woolgar, S. (1979). *Laboratory life: The social construction of scientific facts.* Beverly Hills: Sage.

Laszlo, E. (1973). *Introduction to systems philosophy.* New York: Harper & Row.

Levinas, E. (1989). *The Levinas reader.* Oxford, UK: Blackwell.

Lichtman, R. (1982). *The production of desire.* New York: Free Press.

Lucas, J. R. (1993). *Responsibility.* Oxford, UK: Clarendon.

Lutz, C., & Abu-Lughod, L. (Eds.). (1990). *Language and the politics of emotion.* Cambridge, UK: Cambridge University Press.

MacIntyre, A. (1984). *After virtue: A study in moral theory* (2nd ed.). Notre Dame, IN: University of Notre Dame Press.

Marsh, P., Rosser, E., & Harré, R. (1978). *The rules of disorder.* London: Routledge & Kegan Paul.

Maturana, H., & Varela, F. (1987). *The tree of knowledge: The biological roots of understanding.* Boston: Shambhala.

Maturana, H., & Verden-Zoller, G. (1996). *The origin of humanness.* Manuscript in preparation.

May, L. (1987). *The morality of groups.* Notre Dame, IN: University of Notre Dame Press.

Mead, G. H. (1934). *Mind, self and society.* Chicago: Chicago University Press.

Mellody, P., Miller, A. W., & Miller, J. K. (1989). *Facing codependence: What it is, where it comes from, how it sabotages our lives.* New York: HarperCollins.

Middleton, D., & Edwards, D. (1990). *Collective remembering.* London: Sage.

Moraga, C., & Anzaldua, G. (1983). *This bridge called my back: Writings by radical women of color.* New York: Kitchen Table: Women of Color Press.

Morson, G., & Emerson, C. (1990). *Mikhail Bakhtin: Creation of prosaics.* Stanford, CA: Stanford University Press.

Olds, L. (1992). *Metaphors of interrelatedness.* New York: New York State University Press.

Owen, H. (1992). *Open space technology: A user's guide.* Potomac, MD: Abbott.

Palazzoli, M. S., Boscolo, L., Cecchin, G., & Prate, G. (1978). *Paradox and counterparadox.* New York: Jason Aronson.

Pearce, W. B. (1989). *Communication and the human condition.* Carbondale, IL: Southern Illinois University Press.

Pearce, W. B. (1993). *Interpersonal communication: Making social worlds.* New York: Harper-Collins.

Pearce, W. B., & Cronen, V. E. (1980). *Communication, action and meaning.* New York: Praeger.

Penman, R. (1992). Good theory and good practice: An argument in progress. *Communication Theory, 2*(3), 234-250.

Penn, P. (1985). Feed forward: Future questions, future maps. *Family Process, 24,* 299-311.

Penn, P., & Frankfurt, M. (1994). Creating a participant text: Writing, multiple voices, narrative multiplicity. *Family Process, 33,* 217-232.

Pinker, S. (1994). *The language instinct.* New York: William Morrow.

Pollitt, K. (1994). *Reloading the canon: Multiculturalism in the curriculum.* Talk delivered as part of The Saul O. Sidore Memorial Lecture Series on Civil Rights vs. Civil Liberties, University of New Hampshire.

Posner, R. (1981). *Economics of justice.* Cambridge, MA: Harvard University Press.

Rajchman, J. (1991). *Truth and eros: Foucault, Lacan, and the question of ethics.* New York: Routledge.

Rawlins, W. K. (1989). A dialectical analysis of the tensions, functions, and strategic challenges of communication in young adult friendships. *Communication Yearbook, 12,* 157-189.

Radner, B. (1993). *Core curriculum framework.* Chicago: Joyce Foundation.

Reed, M., & Hughes, M. (Eds.). (1992). *Rethinking organization.* London: Sage.

Reiss, D. (1981). *The family's construction of reality.* Cambridge, MA: Harvard University Press.

Riikonen, E. (1997). *An outline of the INSP Programme, Stakes, Helsinki* (a draft).

Riikonen, E., & Smith, G. (1997). *Re-imagining therapy: Living conversations and relational knowing.* London: Sage.

Risser, J. (1991). Reading the text. In H. Silverman (Ed.), *Gadamer and hermeneutics.* New York: Routledge.

Roberts, M. (1965). *Freedom and practical responsibility.* New York: Cambridge University Press.

Rorty, R. (1979). *Philosophy and the mirror of nature.* Princeton, NJ: Princeton University Press.

Rorty, R. (1989). *Contingency, irony, and solidarity.* Cambridge, UK: Cambridge University Press.

Roth, S. (1993). Speaking the unspoken: A work-group consultation to reopen dialogue. In E. Imber-Black (Ed.), *Secrets in families and family therapy.* New York: Norton.

Roth, S., Chasin, L., Chasin, R., Becker, C., & Herzig, M. (1992). From debate to dialogue: A facilitating role for family therapists in the public forum. *Dulwich Centre Newsletter, 2,* 41-48.

Roth, S., Herzig, M., Chasin, R., Chasin, L., & Becker, C. (1995). Across the chasm. *In Context, 40,* 33-35.

Sampson, E. E. (1977). Psychology and the American ideal. *Journal of Personality and Social Psychology, 35,* 767-782.

Sampson, E. E. (1981). Cognitive psychology as ideology. *American Psychologist, 36,* 730-743.

Sampson, E. E. (1993). *Celebrating the other.* Boulder, CO: Westview.

Sandel, M. J. (1982). *Liberalism and the limits of justice.* Cambridge, UK: Cambridge University Press.

Sarat, A., & Kearns, T. R. (Eds.). (1996). *Legal rights: Historical and philosophical perspectives.* Ann Arbor: University of Michigan Press.

Sarnoff, I., & Sarnoff, S. (1989). *Love-centered marriage in a self-centered world.* New York: Hemisphere.

Saussure, F., de. (1983). *Course in general linguistics* (R. Harris, Trans.). London: Duckworth.

Schegloff, E. A., & Sacks, H. (1973). Opening up closings. *Semiotica, 7,* 289-327.

Seikkula, J., Aaltonen, J., Alakare, B., Haarakangas, K., Keranen, J., & Sutela, M. (1995). Treating psychosis by means of open dialogue. In S. Friedman (Ed.), *The reflecting team in action.* New York: Guilford.

Semin, G. R., & Manstead, A. S. R. (1983). *The accountability of conduct: A social psychological analysis.* New York: Academic Press.

Sennett, R. (1977). *The fall of public man.* New York: Knopf.

Shotter, J. (1980). *Action, joint action, and intentionality.* In M. Brenner (Ed.), *The structure of action.* Oxford: Blackwell.

Shotter, J. (1984). *Social accountability and selfhood.* Oxford, UK: Basil Blackwell.

Shotter, J. (1993a). *Conversational realities: Constructing life through language.* London: Sage.

Shotter, J. (1993b). *Cultural politics of everyday life: Social constructionisms, rhetoric, and knowing of the third kind.* Toronto, Canada: University of Toronto Press.

Shweder, R. A. (1991). Thinking through cultures. Cambridge, MA: Harvard University Press.

Smith, W. C. (1983). Responsibility. In Combs, E. (Ed.). *Modernity and responsibility.* Buffalo, NY: University of Toronto Press.

Sontag, S. (1992). *Against interpretation and other essays.* New York: Delta.

Spector, M., & Kitsuse, J. I. (1977). *Constructing social problems.* Menlo Park, CA: Cummings.

Steiner, G. (1989). *Real presences.* Chicago: University of Chicago Press.

Stone, C. (1987). Unorthodox moral viewpoints. In C. Stone (Ed.), *Earth and other ethics.* New York: Harper & Row.

Tamasese, K., & Waldegrave, C. (1994). Cultural and gender accountability in the "just therapy" approach. *Dulwich Centre Newsletter,* No. 2 & 3, 55-67.

Tannen, D. (1990). *You just don't understand: Women and men in conversation.* New York: William Morrow.

Tannen, D. (1994a, August 28). How to give orders like a man. *The New York Times Magazine,* 46-49.

Tannen, D. (1994b). *Talking 9 to 5: How women's and men's conversational styles affect who gets heard, who gets credit, and what gets done at work.* New York: William Morrow.

Taylor, C. (1991). The dialogical self. In D. R. Hiley, J. F. Bohman, & R. Shusterman (Eds.), *The interpretative turn* (pp. 304-314). Ithaca, NY: Cornell University Press.

Taylor, C. (1992). *The ethics of authenticity.* Cambridge, MA: Harvard University Press.

Tillich, P. (1969). *My search for absolutes.* New York: Simon & Schuster.

Tomm, K. (1985). Circular interviewing: A multifaceted clinical tool. In D. Campbell & R. Draper (Eds.), *Applications of systemic family therapy: The Milan approach.* London: Grune & Stratton.

Trinh, T. M. (1989). *Woman, native, other: Writing post-coloniality and feminism.* Bloomington: Indiana University Press.

Unger, R. M. (1986). *The critical legal studies movement.* Cambridge, MA: Harvard University Press.

Volosinov, V. N. (1986). *Marxism and the philosophy of language* (L. Matejka & I. R. Titunik, Trans.). Cambridge, MA: Harvard University Press. (Original work published 1929)

von Bertalanffy, L. (1968). *General systems theory.* New York: Braziller.

Von Foerster, H. (1982). *Observing systems.* Seaside, CA: Intersystems.

Vygotsky, L. S. (1978). *Mind in society: The development of higher psychological processes.* Cambridge, MA: Harvard University Press.

Weick, K. E. (1995). *Sensemaking in organizations.* Thousand Oaks, CA: Sage.

Weiner, B. (1995). *Judgments of responsibility: A foundation for a theory of moral conduct.* New York: Guilford.

Wertsch, J. V. (1985). *Vygotsky and the social formation of mind.* Cambridge, MA: Harvard University Press.

White, M. (1994). A conversation about accountability with Michael White (C. McLean, Ed.). *Dulwich Centre Newsletter, No. 2 & 3,* 68-79.

Wittgenstein, L. (1953). *Philosophical investigations* (G. Anscombe, Trans.). New York: Macmillan.

Wittgenstein, L. (1980). *Culture and value* (G. Von Wright, Intro; P. Winch, Trans.). Oxford: Blackwell.

Wittgenstein, L. (1981). *Zettel* (2nd. ed.; G. E. M. Anscombe & G. H. V. Wright, Eds.). Oxford: Blackwell.

Wynne, L. C., McDaniel, S. H. & Weber, T. T. (1986). *Systems consultation.* New York: Guilford.

Index

About the Authors

Sheila McNamee, PhD, is Professor and Chair of Communication at the University of New Hampshire. She is also a founding member of the Taos Institute. She is editor of *Therapy as Social Construction* with Kenneth Gergen and has authored numerous chapters and journal articles on social constructionist theory and practice. McNamee consults internationally to organizations, including nongovernmental organizations, and to mental health professionals.

Kenneth J. Gergen, PhD, is the Mustin Professor of Psychology at Swarthmore College. As a central exponent of social constructionism in the social sciences, he is author of several books, including *The Saturated Self* (1991), *Realities and Relationships: Soundings in Social Construction* (1994), and *Toward Transformation of Social Knowledge* (2nd ed., 1992). Gergen is a founding member of the Taos Institute, a group of academics and practitioners dedicated to applications of social construction in organizational and therapeutic practices, and consults to organizations internationally.

About the Contributors

Harlene Anderson, PhD, is a founding member of the Houston Galveston Institute and the Taos Institute. She is the author and coauthor of numerous publications, including *Conversations, Language and Possibilities: A Postmodern Approach to Therapy.*

Ian Burkitt is a Lecturer in Sociology and Social Psychology in the Department of Social and Economic Studies, University of Bradford. He is the author of *Social Selves: Theories of the Social Formation of Personality* and is currently working on issues of social relations and embodiment.

David L. Cooperrider, PhD, is Associate Professor of Organizational Behavior and co-chair of the SIGMA Program on Global Change at the Weatherhead School of Management, Case Western Reserve University. Dr. Cooperrider's most recent research centers on social innovations in global management, which includes processes of policy making, governance, decision making, relationships among professional groups, and organizational design. He has served as consultant to many international organizations. He is author of articles and book chapters on appreciative inquiry.

Robert Cottor, MD, is Co-Director of the Family-Business Roundtable, Inc. As a family therapist and organizational consultant, he has emphasized resolving individual, group, and organizational issues within the context of the relationships in which the issues have arisen. He has worked with many family and closely held businesses since establishing his practice in Phoenix in 1971. He is also an associate of the Taos Institute.

Sharon Cottor, MSW, is a principal in the Family-Business Roundtable, Inc., and an associate of the Taos Institute. She has been consulting since 1971 and employs innovative approaches to problems and challenges presented by organizations of all sizes and types. She is well known for her creative thinking and her ability to generate effective change even under the most difficult circumstances. She believes that our strongest and most renewable resource is our capacity to think imaginatively.

Stanley Deetz, PhD, is Professor of Communication at the University of Colorado, Boulder, where he teaches courses in organizational theory, organizational communication and communication theory. He is author of *Transforming Communication, Transforming Business: Building Responsive and Responsible Workplaces* and *Democracy in an Age of Corporate Colonization: Developments in Communication and the Politics of Everyday Life* and is editor or author of eight other books and numerous articles. He has lectured widely in the United States and Europe. In 1994, he was a Senior Fulbright Scholar in Sweden and has served as a consultant for several major corporations. He served as President of the International Communication Association, 1996-1997.

Steve Duck, PhD, has written or edited 32 books on relationships and one on television; founded and edited, for 15 years, the *Journal of Social and Personal Relationships;* edited two editions of the *Handbook of Personal Relationships;* was the founding cochair of the International Society for the Study of Personal Relationships; and subsequently, the first President of the International Network on Personal Relationships. He has been the Chair of the Department of Communication Studies at the University of Iowa, where he is the Daniel and Amy Starch Research Professor.

Walter Eggers, PhD, is presently Provost and Vice President for Academic Affairs at the University of New Hampshire. He is a Shakespearian scholar and father of five. This is the first time he has talked in print about the responsibilities of the parental relationship. His interest in literary theory extends to teaching, and he has published on teaching and academic administration.

Marilyn Frankfurt was, at the time of this writing, a senior faculty member of the Ackerman Institute for the Family, where she taught and codirected the

Writing Project with Peggy Penn. She has coauthored several papers with Penn, among them "Creating a Participant Text: Writing, Multiple Voices, Narrative Multiplicity" in *Family Process*. Marilyn is now in private practice in New York.

Mary Gergen is Associate Professor of Psychology and Women's Studies at Pennsylvania State University, Delaware County Campus, Philadelphia, as well as Division Head of Psychology for the Commonwealth College. She is editor of *Toward a New Psychology of Gender* with Sara N. Davis and coauthor of textbooks in social psychology, introductory psychology, and statistics. Other recent publications have focussed on narrative psychology and autobiography. Her research interests include women's adult development and public notions of safety and security. *Impious Improvisations: Feminist Reconstructions in Psychology* is in press. She teaches undergraduate courses in psychology and is active in Division 35, The Psychology of Women, of the American Psychological Association. With Kenneth Gergen, she is exploring forms of performative psychology. She is a founding member of the Taos Institute.

Arlene M. Katz is an instructor in Social Medicine at Harvard Medical School and a psychologist specializing in family therapy and consultation. She has created several video productions, including *The Patient as Teacher: Multiple Perspectives on the Interview Process* and another honoring Harry Goolishian. She has presented and written on the "voice" of the "patient" in health care, and her training and research interests include cultural responses to illness and a dialogical approach to the patient-doctor relationship, community practices in health care, and the process of mentorship.

John W. Lannamann, PhD, Associate Professor of Communication at the University of New Hampshire, is both a critic of the social sciences and an optimist about the possibility of a socially engaged form of communication research. His writing appears in a number of communication and family therapy journals, including *Communication Monographs, Communication Theory, The Journal of Communication, Family Process,* and *The Journal of Strategic and Systemic Therapies.*

Michael J. Mazanec earned his BA and MA degrees from California State University, Fresno, in Speech Communication. He is presently a PhD candidate at the University of Iowa Department of Communication Studies, working in the areas of relational agency and performative practices of sexuality and identity.

Maurizio Marzari is on the faculty of the Milan Family Therapy Center. He also teaches at the University of Urbino. He is Director of Organizational Development at the Bologna Department of Health.

Peggy Penn, former Director of Training and Education at the Ackerman Institute for the Family, now directs a research project on Language and Writing in Psychotherapy. She has written on love and violence, chronic illness, future questions, circular questions, models for consultation, love and language, and narrative therapy. Her most noted publications include "Creating a Participant Text: Writing, Multiple Voices and Narrative Multiplicity" and her coauthored book, *Milan Systemic Family Therapy: Conversations in Theory and Practice.* She is also a published poet.

Eero Riikonen, MD, Psychiatrist, MScD, has worked in the public mental health sector and as a manager of the Finnish Suicide Prevention Centre. He was a Researcher and Development Manager in Helsinki's Rehabilitation Foundation. Since 1996, he has been Development Manager at the National Research and Development Centre for Welfare and Health (Stakes). His interest is in developing resource-oriented approaches to client work. His work is directed toward the planning of national mental health projects, outlining the European Mental Health Agenda, and coordinating the activities of the European Network of Mental Health Policy. His most recent books are, *Re-Imagining Therapy* with G. Smith and, with V. Lehtinen and E. Lahtinen, *Mental Health Promotion on the European Agenda.*

Sallyann Roth, LICSW, a family therapist, is a founding member of the Public Conversations Project. She has presented widely in the United States and abroad on narrative therapies and the Public Conversations Project's approach to divisive public conflicts and has authored numerous journal articles and book chapters on these subjects. Named the Rappoport Distinguished Lecturer at Smith College School for Social Work in 1993, she is Co-Director of the Program in Narrative Therapies of the Family Institute of Cambridge and currently serves as Acting Co-Director of the Institute. She is Lecturer on Psychology, Harvard Medical School, Cambridge Hospital.

John Shotter is a professor of interpersonal relations in the Department of Communication, University of New Hampshire. He is the author of *Cultural Politics of Everyday Life: Social Constructionism, Rhetoric, and Knowing of the Third Kind* and *Conversational Realities: The Construction of Life Through*

Language. He is also coeditor with Kenneth J. Gergen and Sue Widdicombe of the series, Inquiries in Social Construction. In 1997, he was an Overseas Fellow at Churchill College, Cambridge, and a visiting professor in the Swedish Institute of Worklife Research in Stockholm.

Karl Tomm, MD, is Professor of Psychiatry at the University of Calgary where he founded and directs the Family Therapy Program. He is well-known for his work in explicating the Milan Systemic Approach in the early 1980s. He has published and presented widely and has introduced a number of influential ideas and approaches to the family therapy field. He is currently developing and refining his ideas about psychiatric assessment with his "pathologizing interpersonal patterns" and "healing interpersonal patterns" approach.

William J. White (MCIS, Rutgers University, 1993) is a doctoral candidate in the School of Communication, Information, and Library Science at Rutgers University. His research interests focus on scientific communication and the interactions of science and society.

Diana Whitney, PhD, is president of Whitney Consulting and a founding member of the Taos Institute. She is an international speaker and consultant whose work focuses on organization transformation, strategic culture change, communication, and leadership development for corporate, nonprofit, and governmental organizations. Whitney applies social constructionist theory to mergers and acquisitions, organization development, and strategic planning and works collaboratively and creatively with executives, managers, and organization members to build teams and support them in the construction of the organization's future.